DIARY
OF A
MAN

DIARY
OF A
MAN

DERMOD MOORE
a.k.a. Bootboy

HOT
PRESS
BOOKS

First published in 2005 by Hot Press Books, 13 Trinity Street, Dublin 2.

Copyright © Dermod Moore 2005

The right of Dermod Moore to be identified as the author of this work has been asserted by him in accordance with the Copyright, Design and Patent Act 1988

British Library Cataloguing in Publication Data is available for this book

ISBN NO: 0-9545516-8-0

Edited by Niall Stokes

Editorial co-ordination by Lisa Coen

Design by Fiachra McCarthy, Andrew Duffy, Graham Keogh

Printed by Colour Books, Dublin

To my family

ACKNOWLEDGMENTS AND THANKS

Thanks to the following for kindnesses, large and small, in the years I've been writing Bootboy:

The Amazing Alborettis, Jayne Baird, Jonathan Burston, Antony Brand, Annalisa Caldon, Cathy Casey, Darby Costello, Jaqi Clayton, Dominic Davies, Marlyn Donovan, Carole Ellison, Hilary Fannin, Angie Fee, Judith Firman (for the joke), Michael Fontenelle, all in Group 22, Simon Harrison, Deborah Hegan, Dave Hegarty, Liz Greene, David Hirsch, Kally Kent, Marilyn Kernoff, Anne Larsson, Maud Larsson, Shaun Levin, Philippa Lubbock, Máire Lynch, Bríd McCarthy, Jackie McCarthy, Fiona Miles, Harry Moore, Jeanne Moore, Phil Moore, Giles Newington, Pascal O'Loughlin, John O'Reilly, Melanie Reinhart, Keith Ridgway, Juliet Sharman-Burke, Mark Simpson, Celia Snow, Marthannah Stevens, Niall Stokes, John Syer, Siobhán Tinker, Diana Whitmore (for the Trust), Tim Williams, the guy who sent me snowdrops and poetry, and all my clients, for all that they have taught me.

ABOUT THE AUTHOR

Dermod Moore was born in Dublin in 1963. At the age of 17, he co-founded the first Irish gay youth group and soon afterwards appeared on RTÉ's *Youngline*, and spoke about being gay, becoming the first gay teenager on Irish TV. A psychotherapist, writer, astrologer and erstwhile actor, he has lived in London since the early '90s. Since then, he has written a personal column every fortnight for *Hot Press* under the byline Bootboy, which has gone on to become one of the most widely read and popular columns in the magazine. *Diary Of A Man* is his first book. He is currently working on his first novel.

www.dermod.moore.name

CONTENTS

INTRODUCTION
BY NIALL STOKES

We are all looking for answers. But first – well, first we have to figure out what the questions are. Or even, perhaps, what they most pertinently should be.

Sometimes that's the hardest part. Love, sex, politics, spirituality, religion, art, money, possessions – they all make claims on our desire to understand things, to get ourselves sorted, to find fulfilment. They all make claims on our need to believe in something, anything. But no matter how hard we work at it, if we take a tough look at our lives and our experience, how many of us can say with conviction that we really know much of anything at all? How many of us can say that we are satisfied with what we have, or what we have done?

Part of the pleasure, I know, is in the search itself – the search, that is, for truth and meaning in our lives and for a glimpse even of enduring love. But no one wants to have to take on the burden of discovery all on his or her own. To be adrift and without bearings is the loneliest place on earth. And so it helps – helps immeasurably – to find that there are others out there who have confronted the issues that perplex us, who have been through the same dilemmas, or similar ones, and who have, where necessary, wrestled with the demons that come to haunt us in the dead of night. It helps to find that there are others who have asked the questions that form obscurely somewhere in the darkness of our unconscious and who have exposed them to the light of experience, intelligence, thought, empathy and genuine, heartfelt human concern.

This is what Dermod Moore has done in *Diary Of A Man* and he has done it with rare courage. As the title suggests, it is a book about men, and their emotional lives, experiences and feelings. But while it is a book about men, without even a shade of the kind of doubt that is essential to it, it is a book for everyone, men and women – for never has there been a greater need for us all to listen to what men have to say about themselves, their lives, their fears and their apprehensions. Never has there been a greater need, what's more, for thinking men – real thinking men, I mean – to find the voice with which to express themselves in the way that Dermod has so eloquently here.

Throughout *Diary Of A Man*, those experiences and feelings – of a single man alive and gloriously hungry for experience in a world that has unquestionably gone woefully out of joint – are explored in a way that is fresh, challenging and always, always powerfully and movingly honest. They are explored, also, in these thought-provoking diary entries-cum-essays in a way that gives readers a sense of how they might deal with similar experiences and feelings in their own lives.

Diary Of A Man is far from being a manual for anyone's life. But it does have the potential to illuminate things, to give us the shock of recognition that comes from knowing that we too have been that soldier – and to inspire us in relation to the way that we look at ourselves and how we can best get on with things, armed at least with whatever new fragment of elusive insight we have been made privy to.

Dermod Moore is gay, and so at its heart this is a book about being gay, and the particular challenges and pressures – as well as the manifold pleasures and endearments – which that involves in these early, possibly formative, years of the new millennium. For gay men and women, there is much nourishing eating and drinking in this, and a lot more besides – including plenty of horny shagging. For those who are not gay, the turf will be somewhat less familiar, but all the more fascinating for that, as Dermod reveals the machinations and seductions of the gay scene, and the quest for the ultimate in love, sex and sexuality that is such an integral part of it.

No subject is too tough, too raw to deal with: from paedophilia, through depression and suicide to so-called bug-chasing; from orgies, through S&M and internet sex to the mysteries of falling in love; from childhood needs through teenage alienation and drug use to adult independence and the need for human warmth, the search for truth in *Diary Of A Man* is unflinching.

There is anger here at what men, and women too, do to one another, and where it is in their power inflict on the wider world. But, even more fundamental is the philosophical and emotional sensitivity that I sense is the hallmark of a morally informed, anti-dogmatic, politically engaged and ultimately liberal view of the world at its most nuanced.

And have we worked out the questions that we need to ask ourselves by the end? Are we even one step closer to knowing if our answers are correct, even partially so? I will leave that up to you to decide. But there is, I think, immense reassurance in the warmth, compassion and wisdom that are evident, and in such abundance, throughout the book.

And for that matter in the lust. Even men who love women should know all about that...

*Niall Stokes is the editor of *Hot Press* and the author of *In The Name Of Love: The Stories Behind The Songs Of U2*. For more information on *Hot Press* go to www.hotpress.com

FOREWORD
BY MARK SIMPSON

Self-hatred is good for you. No, honestly, please don't look at me that way. Okay, so it's had a bit of a bad press lately – and if you want to dismiss someone nowadays the most effective way is to accuse them of hating themselves. Apparently this completely invalidates anything they have to say and in fact their whole existence. As if self-hatred were such a strange and freakish phenomenon that the rest of us are completely untouched by it.

But actually there is a lot to said for a spot of self-loathing. For starters, it's terribly economical: you don't have to splash out on romantic dinners or even have to leave the house to indulge in it. More to the point, hatred is far too precious a thing to waste on other people.

I'd like to add that self-hatred makes a refreshing change from self-loving, which is rather too common these days. Except that self-loving and self-loathing are usually merely flip-sides of each other. Even narcissists have to have standards.

You still think self-loathing is always bad and sad. Well, perhaps you'll at least agree that there's a good argument for not hiding self-loathing in the closet. Much healthier to have it out in the open. I wouldn't quite go so far as to advocate self-hatred marches, or a self-hatred disco (what would the playlist be like?), but it is something that we should be willing to talk about rather more freely than we currently do. Self-hatred, love it or loathe it, is after all, at the ambiguous heart of the human condition: it's the essential contradiction and eternal emotional short-circuit of consciousness. We all hate ourselves because our idea of ourselves can never quite match the reality – or because reality can never quite match our idea. More specifically, we hate ourselves because we can. That's the perverse joy of being human. Certainly self-hatred is at the heart of the writer's condition, whose job description reads: Strangle yourself with your self-consciousness until your eyes pop out – daily.

Mr. Moore, who isn't as cheap as me, doesn't tend to use the term 'self-hatred'. Instead he writes powerfully and personally about the dichotomies of "pride and shame, lust and love, hope and fear" that rule his life and, I suspect, the lives of more than a few of you post-everything people out there. In *Diary Of A Man*, he grapples with these creative conflicts manfully, honestly, inspiringly. So inspiringly that I might even take up therapy myself one day. And perhaps his acceptance that they are not resolvable, and probably shouldn't be anyway, is the most manly thing about him. More manly even than his well-licked DMs.

Moore oscillates Wildly between loving the delicious, promiscuous sexual freedom of a leathered-up homosexualist in the city and, well, if not exactly loathing it, certainly finding it a tad... disappointing. Is that all there is to endless fucking hot sex? Friction burns, a stained duvet and a mobile number that you've been given on the understanding that you won't ever call it? Mr. Moore is man enough to admit that he often feels lonely –but also to admit that his horniness is part of the reason why. He knows that the Utopian dream of masculine freedom made (pumped, waxed) flesh is its own form of punishment.

Or as he memorably puts it himself, lamenting the alienating culture of instant sexual (dis)connection: "We're raising perpetually horny creatures with the bodies of Gods and with hearts of stone. We're raising monsters."

True. Horribly true. But if Mr. Moore can tell me where I can I find one after 11pm on a wet Wednesday that's willing to travel rather than accom, I'd be very grateful.

*Mark Simpson is the author of *Sex Terror: Erotic Misadventures in Pop Culture* and *Saint Morrissey* among other books. His website is www.marksimpson.com

1: I'VE HAD ENOUGH OF ROMANTIC LOVE

STILL SEARCHING FOR MR RIGHT
14TH MAY 1994

Oops. Single again. Not much to say that hasn't been said before on the subject, by many others more talented than yours truly. But I'm going to say it anyway. It's the early hours of the morning as I write this, *A Taste of Honey* is playing comfortlessly on TV, and I am aware of how much surrounds me in apparent conspiracy to confirm that a homosexual's life is destined to be a lonely one. In the 1957 Tony Richardson film, Rita Tushingham plays the schoolgirl Joanne, Dora Bryan her mother, and Murray Melvyn plays Jeffrey, the camp student of textile design that she befriends. There's something bold, brash and appealingly pimply about this film, even now. The charming, tender sexuality of the black sailor who impregnates her: "I dreamt about you last night/I fell out of bed twice," he says, and we believe it. The impotence and fussiness of Jeffrey, the homosexual character. "I don't care much for women, sometimes," he retorts viciously, when pressed by Joanne to give details on what he actually does in bed. It's a cold, cold hatred we glimpse.

He has his moment when he turns on the mother and exposes her for the monster she is. But, ultimately, he leaves, to wander the streets alone with his drawings, after the mother, herself desperate, pushes him out of the cosy, sexless domesticity that he had created with the pregnant Joanne. ("You're like my big sister, Jeffrey," she mocks). It's a loveless, manipulative world, we learn; hard enough for the sensitive young daughter, but impossible for the touchy, delicate young man. He has no place to go. At one stage he makes a hamfisted proposal to Joanne to make a decent woman of her, to be the child's father; he even says he wants to make a go of it sexually, as he fumbles to kiss her. But she is not that desperate. She has a feisty pride; utterly individualistic, and yet doomed to the same life her mother led, a teenage single parent, constantly looking for someone to meet her needs. Always being disappointed, but hiding the pain through a cocky bravado. All through the film, hordes of young children wander around singing in ironic counterpoint to the cruelty of post-pubescent life.

You can tell I'm in a cheerful mood. I am not about to kiss and tell, and give you the gory details of the breakup. Suffice to say that we're still friends, and what we have in common will, I hope, outlast what was irreconcilable.

But each time I find myself single again, I get into this mood. Haunted by a vision of myself in thirty years time, propping up a bar, still on the lookout for *Mr Right*. See him there, his boyish charm long gone, shaved head concealing natural baldness, tired eyes telling many stories of betrayal and despair. Dressed to kill in leather, still sexy after all those years, DMs well-licked and shiny. Having explored every sexual avenue known to man, he is overwhelmed with a jaded sense of *déjà vu*, as youths approach him with what they believe is original charm. Every night he goes home to his dogs and cats and hard-core porn, and wanks himself to sleep, talking breathlessly on a videophone to a complete stranger, obscenities into the fibre-optic void. For no one can match his image of Mr Right, and he has given up trying. But old habits die hard, and his once hormonally-driven compulsion for endless sex has been replaced with a fear of missing out on something if he should fail to go out one night.

Occasionally someone with an eagerness to please or amuse will catch his attention, and he will oblige by taking them home; but there is something so uneasily cold about him, distant and reserved, that the sensitive ones are not interested in seeing him again. The ones who believe that they only deserve heartless bastards throw themselves at him, offering their bodies in total subservience, begging to be treated like dirt. He plays along, to please them; but it is not in his nature to hurt anyone, so it remains a theatrical charade, with the masks cracking after they have come, and come, and come again. He is, after all, a thorough lover, diligent, and considerate. He asks for nothing but perfection, but to his sorrow meets with murk all the time: jealousy, insecurity, unhappiness and pain. He is appalled, and is racked with guilt and shame; the murk mirrors his own self-loathing.

I don't believe I am going to end up like him, but I know I could. I know that the urge to seek redemption through sexual extravagance is a strong one in me, and in many other gay men of my acquaintance — the line between sexual celebration and compulsion is a thin one. Quite often I change my mind, countless times in one day, about sex, crossing the whole gamut from mortified guilt to sensuous contentment to orgiastic celebration. Sex, so easily available to gay men, offers us a way of learning about ourselves and our fantasy lives that is vivid and intense; the sexual playgrounds of the saunas, pubs, clubs and parks offer us stages on which to perform, with willing cast members only too eager to join in on cue.

But it is far too easy to confuse a sexual quest with a quest for companionship and love, that mystical union that we all believe is out there for us, somewhere. It is too easy for men to believe that horniness is the *sine qua non* of a prospective partner. Inner qualities of sensitivity and generosity are not immediately visible in most men, except the tenderest of flowers; the gay scene, despite what we as individuals could have learnt, continues to discourage those who express their feelings. Look around you. Gay male sexuality can be a hardnosed performance arena, far removed from the world of feelings. The knack, I suppose, is to try to mix the two. Which leads us back to Mr Right again. Is he a figment of my/our imagination, or is he waiting out there? Or has he been there inside me/us all along?

A *Taste of Honey* is vivid and truthful about Northern England in 1957. I am waiting for a film of its calibre to come out of Britain or Ireland telling the story of a post-Stonewall Jeffrey: a Jeffrey still as plain and spiky and whiny and uncomfortably camp. I wonder would he still be as lonely? Is there a place for him in our society, nearly forty years on?

TIME TO GET MOVING
10TH JULY 1996

I'm sorry, but I don't want to do this. I don't want to spend another minute waffling on about myself and my life. I'm in a crabby, stop-the-world-I-want-to-get-off mood. If you've nothing good to say, then don't say it. I'm moving flats this week. I've been in denial about it for months, and I'm paying for it now. I told you so, I tell myself. Which I did.

So far, all I have managed is to place five books into a cardboard box. This extraordinary feat I accomplished one evening last week. Overcome by the symbolism of it, I gave up, exhausted.

"So what's that all about?" prompts my inhouse therapist. (The one that has taken up a bijou basement residence inside my head; a sardonic presence at the best of times.)

"Well, golly, I guess it must mean that, unconsciously, I don't want to move, right?"

"Right."

For the first time in over eight years, I'm going to live on my own. Readers of a more protective persuasion will no doubt be alarmed by this news, as I've revealed enough navel-gazing tendencies while living with other human beings to make a move to increased solitude seem a surefire recipe for disaster. Now there'll be no stopping me sliding into total self-obsession. Like a sun-baked hippo sinking gleefully into the mud, nothing will get me out of my wallow. With just my eyes, ears and nostrils peeking into the air, I'll be invisible to the world. Mud, mud, glorious mud. Nothing quite like it for cleaning the blood. A childhood song. My little sister tried to play it as a request for me on the radio on the morning of my seventh or eighth birthday, before I went to school. But we weren't the sort of family that got requests played for them, or who won competitions on the backs of cornflake packets. Don't know why, we just didn't. Perhaps we didn't try often enough. Or perhaps we didn't have a good enough angle. The stupid song just didn't cut the mustard.

"You'd like to be invisible, then, would you?" (Predictable as ever, this shrink.)

"Yes, I'd like to be invisible. Who wouldn't? It's safer. But if you live on your own, you are invisible. You can watch TV naked. Cut your toenails in the bath. Sing Sondheim torch songs with mournful gusto, day or night. Have sex in the kitchen..."

"So you're invisible when you have sex?"At this, the wheels in the one-armed bandit in my head all click into place: Insight! – Insight! – Insight! The sirens go off, the lights flash, and the shrink whoops jubilantly as rivers of gold coins pour out, straight into his cardigan pocket. Paydirt.

"Right, we'd better leave it there..." I say, insistently. That's telling him. The advantage of inhouse therapists is that you get to decide when the session is over, not them.

I suppose another way of looking at it is that I'm this mad after living with people for the past eight years. I need a rest. The last time I lived alone, in a flat in Ranelagh in Dublin, I was happy enough. I spent half the time answering the phone for the woman who lived upstairs, with the euphonious name of Mary Shine. While there, I spent an entire frozen February digging up a wilderness, and transforming it into a garden. I seem to remember I was on caffeine cold turkey, coming down after a daily fix of a pot of strong black coffee. I used to get up early with my shovel every morning that month and hack away at the frosted earth. Perhaps I've always been weird, but never noticed it.

The worst thing about moving is that you end up playing your old singles before you pack them away. And then you start reminiscing, and then, worst of all, you begin evaluating where you've got to, on the road to wherever you're going.

Maybe that's what I've been avoiding. Not the box-hauling, the fridge-defrosting, the window-cleaning and the floor-washing. But the evaluation.

Who's to fail or pass me but myself?

Pass the J-cloth. I'm doing alright.

SOMEBODY, HOLD ME TOO CLOSE
15TH MAY 1996

Restless this weekend. Too much manic energy floating around. I went for a four hour walk on Sunday, right across North London. Instinctively, my body was telling me to get to the mountains and the fresh air and a pint at the Blue Light, but this was London not Dublin, and you could walk for days and still be stuck in bland, urban wasteland. So I did the next best thing, and ended up walking through the woods in Hampstead Heath. For those not in the know, Hampstead Heath is a large park, with wild woods, cultivated gardens and ponds. It is also the most notorious cruising ground in London, with apparently, all sorts of Dionysian orgies happening after dark. I say "apparently" not in mock coyness (perish the thought!) but because I have never been to the Heath after dark. This will no doubt ruin my street cred for any Londoner, but there you go. Too far to walk home afterwards; too dark, too unfamiliar. But the Heath at Sunday lunchtime, although full of the family-walking-dog brigade, has enough bedenimed single men strolling around to remind you of the sexual undertow of the gay scene. Which is what I really wanted to get away from.

So I walked for a while through the woods, listening to the birds and marvelling, still, at the tameness of English squirrels. And, for a while, it seemed that one could imagine oneself in the country – that is, until the next empty "Rubberstuffers" pack distracted the eye. They're the condom and lube packs that are distributed free in gay pubs and clubs. Although admirable evidence that safe sex is practiced, I couldn't help wondering about the nests of all the birds and squirrels in the woods: are they all lined with scraps of orange and navy cardboard, intermingled with stringy bits of sticky latex?

I wandered around for a bit, but I never quite felt that I had got away from it all. Too many people around. It's one of the ways that London can get to you.

I went for a pint, in the local gay hostelry. It's pleasant enough, as local pubs go, full of couples reading the Sunday papers over a drink and a quiche. In the corner, behind me, was a big, stocky man sitting at a desk. In drag. This was no subtle Soho outfit; it was a shocking pink and black taffeta monstrosity complete with befeathered hat and boa. He was sitting on his own, staring into the middle distance. He was waiting, bored. Behind him there was a sign: Palm Reader. Someone came over to him, sat down, and held out his hand. I couldn't hear the words, but the palmist was in earnest, which was all I needed to see.

As I was watching, I felt myself being taken in by the regulars beside me at the bar. They weren't subtle; I was a new face. They spoke to each other loudly, so I could hear; one of them asked the other what he was going to do that afternoon, anything special? The other one replied that no, he had nothing special planned: he was just going to go down to the Heath and have sex.

I realised by the silence afterwards that it was a performance, for my benefit; they had hoped I would react; either by blushing, or by giggling nervously; they didn't expect me to studiously ignore them. They would have been shocked if they knew how much I despised them for proving, once again, how tacky gay men can be.

When the palmist was free, I went over, and sat down. "It's a pound," he said, blinking his inch-long false eyelashes at me, unsmilingly. I fished out a pound coin and dropped it in the jar. "What's your name?" he asked. I told him. "What's yours?" I asked. "Madam...er...Ollie," he replied. "Give us your hand, love". I held out my left hand, and was surprised to find it held by the hands of a docker: big, calloused, hard-worked, with dirty nails. He told me about my long life line, my wobbly health when I was younger (of which I was unaware) and my love line. He told me that my love line and my health line didn't meet; he thought this was very good. The obvious implication was reassuring – but I wonder did he say that to all gay men. He told me that I had been a very naughty boy, up to now, but that there was someone significant coming up in my life, a partner, a soulmate, who would be with me for a very long time. He pointed this out by showing where my love line takes a distinctive swoop upwards, and also, by a line on the side of my right hand. As he was poring over my hands, the big pink ostrich feather from his hat was tapping me on my forehead.

It was over in a couple of minutes. I thanked him warmly; he had been kind. He pressed into my hand a three-pack of condoms, and asked me if I did the lottery. I said, yes. He looked at both my hands, and pronounced the number 13 to by my lucky number this week.

I left the pub and walked the three miles back to the flat. The word soulmate had struck home. I have built up so many defences against such a relationship happening that it's no wonder I'm lonely.

The previous day, I had spent an afternoon in a café reading a book, the first time I had done that in London. I used to do that all the time. It's a wonderful pastime, for one is in contact with two worlds at the same time; the world of the author, and the real bustling world of café society, which in Dublin is vibrant and always has the potential to surprise with the possibility of meeting old friends and making new. In London, there is nowhere like Bewley's Café, nowhere with that heady mix of people, open to life.

But during that afternoon, I had caught the eye of a handsome man. He sat down at a table, not too far from me, and we occasionally caught each other stealing glances. It didn't seem prurient or salacious, just curious, friendly. When he got up to leave, he turned around, and smiled at me; and I smiled right back. When he left, I felt sad; not because he had left, but because I didn't have the guts to go after him and invite him back in for a coffee.

On my long walk home, with *Madam* Ollie's words in my head, I realised that it wasn't fear of being rejected that prevented me running out to talk to this man, it was fear of being accepted. Fear that I might allow anyone to get close enough to me to be a soulmate.

There's a show on in town, called *Company*, by Stephen Sondheim. It's about a single man in his thirties, and his loneliness. It's achingly good. There's a song called 'Being Alive' which is kind of to the point; the hero, Bobby, sings about the relationship he wants, but has avoided thus far:

Somebody hold me too close;
Somebody hurt me too deep;
Somebody sit in my chair
And ruin my sleep
And make me aware of
Being alive

A LIFE OF QUIET DESPERATION
10TH NOVEMBER 1999

A recent, poignant report from the Samaritans has left me feeling sad, deeply sad. Entitled *Young Men Speak Out*, it paints a sobering picture of what they describe as the "Lads' Culture" and how it has such a damaging effect on young men, so many of whom take their own lives. Every week, at least twelve young men kill themselves in the UK; that's 17 per 100,000. In Ireland, the figures are much, much worse: 27 per 100,000 is the melancholy number. What is particularly disturbing is that the rate has increased by 60% in the past ten years.

The facts and figures are stark: 67% of suicidal young men say they have nowhere to turn for emotional help. More than one in three young men who are suicidal would "smash something up" instead of talking about their feelings. Less than one in five young men ask their father for emotional support. 78% of depressed and suicidal young men have experienced bullying.

"Boys are expected to be big and butch," said a 19-year-old who participated in the research. A 16-year-old lad added another twist:

"There is no point in telling anyone about it, you've got to take it 'cos they say you've got to be a man and grow up."

Adrienne Katz, co-author of the research, observed that it was striking "how many said 'Nobody ever asks me how I really feel'. We have to let lads know that it is safe to talk and that they won't be judged by society for being open about their feelings."

The research asked these young men about gender roles. Two thirds of those boys who have seriously considered, or have attempted suicide, agree with the statement that "It was easier when roles were clearly separate". These boys develop a front, or outer shell, hiding an inner turmoil. One subject described what it was like for boys like him: "They have to stop this shell from breaking down, keep this mentality – they might be incredibly scared people. On a very large scale, a lot of boys who appear totally OK, inside are falling apart". Another spoke of lads "dying inside but tough – scared to admit to themselves they need help."

Suicidal lads were more likely to have a father who "insists you fight your own battles", if one is around; but 41% of suicidal boys did not have a father living with them, compared to 18% of the group who were not described as suicidal.

A few myths about maleness were identified: 59% of the suicidal group said that "boys are expected to cope with problems themselves," compared with 33% of the others. The influence of peer group pressure is described thus, by one of the 16-year olds surveyed: "A boy can't let his feelings show, boys don't do this, men don't do this. You'll get picked on, they'll see you as weak. They won't want to know you." A 14-year-old says: "11-year-olds are changing to fit in and be real men. With the change to secondary school they get the impression from other boys – you're with older people, they don't do this so you shouldn't. There is a view that they should cop it – deal with it themselves. It's a feeling you get and you do what other people do."

Another teenager says: " I won't talk about a lot of things close to my heart with friends. I don't tend to talk about it – most boys wouldn't. Boys tend to want to be in a strong position."

There's the link, the real bone-crunching, soul-corroding core of the male curse, that's so hard to break: talking about feelings is a sign of weakness, and men want to feel strong. To be self-contained is to be a man. It starts from a young age and it doesn't go away. I still have it, and sometimes it's a real struggle when I realise that I'm doing it again – not talking about how I'm really feeling. To admit, yet again, that I'm depressed, seems so hard to do; to explain quite how lonely I feel sometimes is next to impossible. Writing, I will usually describe my feelings in the past tense; admitting to all sorts of things, but in the comfort zone of not-now, to reassure you, dear reader, that I'm not in little fragments over the keyboard. As often I am. And, indeed, today is another struggle to cope with the mismatch between how life was supposed to be and how it actually is. Nobody told me it could be this shit sometimes.

One important piece of information from the research offers a glimmer of hope, to those of us who would like there to be less such despair. At least two-thirds of suicidal boys would have liked more education on "relationships and emotional feelings," as opposed to mere sex education. In other words, they'd like, despite the inevitable bollocking that would greet the first poor sod to dare to be vulnerable in class, to learn more about feelings, and to practise talking about them. It would help, of course, if Dads and teachers were there to show a good example, to talk about their emotions, and ask how their kids are feeling every now and again; even if met with a gruff "OK" in response, at least the door is open.

But is it going to get any better? According to a recent report, a forecast has been made by the University of Kent that doesn't paint a rosy picture. Men, in the future, are more likely to be single (in 2010, 40% of households will be composed of a single person) and "to spend their leisure time lounging around their home, washing their take-away curry down with a beer while watching videos or playing computer games" on their own, while single women will enjoy "a full social life, with trips to theatre, cinema, gym, friends and evening classes and – in many cases – reaping the benefits of psychotherapy."

When are we men going to get our act together? Or are we going to stay stuck on the sofa and slouch idly by, as generation after generation of the most sensitive among us decide that a life of quiet desperation is not for them, and choose death instead?

THE SPIRIT OF LONELINESS HAS TAKEN OVER
12TH MARCH 2001

Just as I begin to write this, with the sort of grim synchronicity that I've begun to get suspicious of recently, I hear a thunderous slam, across the courtyard from me. It sounds like someone's trying to kick a door in. I hear a man shouting "Get out!" Within a few seconds, a forlorn figure of a woman, carrying a load of things in her arms, walks slowly out of the passageway opposite, with her head down and long hair in her eyes; and within a moment she allows herself to fall onto one of the seats in the courtyard, and she cries. It's the cry of despair, that wail when it's all over, when the defeat is final. I can't watch her, but can't not.

She surveys the jumble of things that have spilled on the table in front of her, and begins to put some of them – toiletries, brushes, and things like that – into her handbag. She's trembling, and her cries have become like hiccoughs. When she's done, she puts her hands to her face for a couple of minutes, and then stands up and leaves, hugging her bags.

I had considered going out to her, to somehow show a gesture of solidarity with the broken-hearted, but decided that the last thing she needs is to cope with a strange man, however well-intentioned, saying he knows how she feels. How could anyone else know how she feels, in that moment?

Romantic love, when it is over, is about one thing: the realisation that you are utterly alone in the world. In the throes of heartbreak, it is impossible to accept that there is anyone else in the world that hurts like you, that feels like you.

After Romance is the time when you most clearly see yourself, like that cruel moment at 3am in a nightclub when the flourescent lights come on, and you catch sight of your drunken face in a mirror. It's when all your illusions and pretences about yourself have been stripped away, when the fantasy that you are an evolved 21st Century human being, above such Neanderthal forces as rage and revenge and hate, collapses around your ears. It's when you realise the myth that you have for yourself has to change, for although you thought you were being nice and pleasant and accommodating, you were hiding such a desperate need for intimacy that it affected every move you made.

You become aware of how readily you were willing to sacrifice your pride in favour of relationship. And you didn't see it. You can't see it. Romantic love is about dreams, longings, wishes; not about really seeing someone as they are. Everything switches into a state of potential, of imminence – what is reflected back in each other's eyes is the essence of hope, of optimism, of expansiveness, a future yet unlived. It's an act of faith, that trust is possible, that someone is interested in you, that someone cares. That someone is ready to catch you should you fall. It's a blissful state. Some people manage to keep it going for years.

The deeper you fall in romantic love, the more you are willing, on some level, to neglect yourself. Perhaps it's a sign of how much you have been neglecting yourself, not loving yourself, not enjoying life. As Charity Hope Valentine says in the film *Sweet Charity,* when her fiancé jilts her with the words "I'd destroy you": "Well, that's OK, I'm not doing much anyway".

James Hillman, in his marvellous book, *The Soul's Code,* writes about the "pool of loneliness" after relationships have ended. "We feel ourselves curiously depersonalised, very far away. Exiled. No connection anywhere. The spirit of loneliness has taken over."

Far from seeing loneliness as pathological, Hillman sees the way we have defended ourselves against it as being highly suspect. We can blame society, and see it in political terms: if society were different, then people wouldn't feel this pain of loneliness. That's one way I've worked with it; if gay men were more open about their feelings, and not ashamed of them, then the next generation would be spared the loneliness that I have endured. It's illogical, but it's what has driven me anyway.

We can look to therapy to cure us of it; if I understand myself and how I relate better, then I will become more lovable. Build up a circle of friends, join groups of like-minded people, think positively, meditate, hug trees. After nine fucking years of therapy, I'm still single. There's always Prozac.

We can see it in theological terms, loneliness as a sign that we have been cut off from God, the wages of sin for living a life corrupted by materialism and sexuality. Loneliness, in so many ways, is a sin, proof that you are a non-believer. *Mea culpa.*

The existential way seems most attractive to me now: "Build the project of your life with your own heroic hands," as Hillman so eloquently puts it, when you forge a life out of the deepest feelings of meaninglessness. The challenge is to turn loneliness into individual strength. But fear cannot be permitted in the rigorous wasteland of existentialism. Fear is weakness. And who isn't afraid? To live life truly existentially is to disallow interdependence and relationship, for each moment must be lived to the full without reference to any other being, for trust is impossible.

Hillman says that to be alive is to feel lonely. Desperation grows worse when we seek ways out of despair. The archetypal quality of loneliness is not necessarily a painful experience; it has flavours of nostalgia, sadness, and a yearning imagination for "something else" – not here, not now.

Each of us finds ways of coping with this sense of loneliness as best we can. Some take more numbing routes, such as drink, mindless sex, and other drugs. Some take the religious route: seeking redemption for the original sin of self-consciousness, of the exile from the Garden of Eden, by a life of penance and service to a God of certainty. Some put it into their work, their art, their music. Some become super-rational, flying from their feelings.

And some just fumble their way through life, like a child searching in the dark for some big strong hands to reach down and make it alright.

UNREQUITED LOVE IS GOOD FOR YOU
20TH MARCH 2001

When you love someone who doesn't love you, it hurts. It's a hurt that can't be fixed, can't be healed. Paradoxically, I find myself celebrating it. It's not that I enjoy being hurt; it's that I'd rather feel such good feelings about someone than not. To not do so is to be empty, and I know I'm not empty. It's entirely illogical: it's what stops me from disintegrating, and yet, because it's unrequited, it threatens to bring me to my knees in terms of what I believe about myself, what I like about myself. For one can only love, truly, if one's love outweighs one's need.

Ironically, that's never more explicit than when love is unrequited. It's the harshest test. It's like the courtly love of medieval times; a knight fixed his attentions on a beautiful unavailable woman and wrote poetry for her, made her the object of his affections – but never was it intended that such love would be consummated. The joy of it, and its exquisite bittersweet pain, was that it was impossible.

Do I give up? Do I stop loving? It seems I'm unable to. Am I ashamed of that? I don't think so, although there are times when it seems sorely tempting, to concede that love is impossible, and adopt a philosophy that is closer to a rock-bottom existential state, in which one takes one's pleasure where one can, and expects nothing. Healthier, perhaps – but without hope, there's not much point in carrying on. But hope can be a killer too; the Buddhists are down on hope, believing it to be an escape from the moment. Perhaps they're right. But I'm an escapist – and I don't know anyone who isn't, to a greater or lesser degree.

As difficult as it is, something has changed or been changed in me and I can't unchange it. I've felt what it's like to be with someone who brings out the most sensitive feelings in me, and for a brief while they were matched. To wish to turn the feelings off because they sting is only natural; I will, in time, learn to find a way of opening up my heart in a different way, to someone else. But no matter how sensible it would seem to move on, it seems that I am powerless. I have let go of him, in that I have accepted the inevitable, and can do nothing to change it, but there is still left a well of warmth that surges up inside me when I'm with him.

For some time since we broke up, I've pretended that I am cool, that I'm able to withstand the implications of unrequited love. I think I can get back on the saddle and pretend that something fundamental hasn't happened. But I'm not cool. I can play The Game of sex with the best of them, but at heart I want to put all the roleplaying and toys and sexual intrigues away and stop playing, to rest instead of fight, to comfort instead of thrill, to relax and be close and hold hands instead of getting high on the testosterone stress of playing out fantasies. No matter how hard I try to be, how thick a skin I need to develop to join in, in the rough and tumble of the sport called gay sex, I am unsuited to it. My feelings leak out. I keep on being drawn to it, but it's a distraction, an ersatz intimacy, a mistaken attempt on my part to feel close and engaged with others, when the reality is that sex, as practised by so many gay men, is only fun when you leave your feelings elsewhere.

Well, my feelings are not elsewhere; they're fully present at the moment, warm, soft and full-blooded. And sad. And it's so hard to find others who share them – who are gay men. It's not that I discount the reactions of my women friends or heterosexual male friends – it's simply that, for those men who love men, it seems to be a tougher journey to try to position love at the top of the tree; to admit to vulnerability without it being seen as a weakness, or a symptom of a whining, self-indulgent, victim mentality, connected to the last time some bastard let you down. I don't feel let down. I don't blame him or anyone else for not matching my feelings. It's life. But then, am I angry at life?

In myth, one of the main gay characters in the Greek pantheon was Ganymede, the beautiful youth who was snatched up by Zeus, the bisexual philandering King of the Heavens, to be his playmate and cup-bearer. From his name comes the pejorative word catamite, or bum-boy in the vernacular. In looking up Ganymede's story, there is one fleeting glimpse of him, in another myth, when he is found playing dice with Eros, the god of love – who, of course, was playing with loaded dice, and cheating the hapless Ganymede. So it seems, in the lives of so many gay men that I know: we're unlucky in love, and learn to accept the roll of the loaded dice as they fall. Those that are lucky enough to find soulmates often find that they have to remove themselves completely from the gay scene to let their relationships flourish, for there is usually one of them who is likely to be tempted with The Game of sex, which is not the most conducive to long-lasting healthy relationships. Not necessarily, of course, but it's common sense.

But then common sense never really applied to love. It's impossible to control, impossible to force it in, or onto, another. Without the sting of it ending, we would probably be a lot more content; but it seems the sting of Eros' arrow is what brings us in touch with the highest qualities in us, if we don't let them fester in cynicism or bitterness. Yes, love hurts, but if what you love in someone else is good, then it brings it out in you, even if it doesn't work out. It's growth by osmosis; the aspiration alone, if it's done without selfishness, brings its own rewards.

But of course it's not unique to the gay experience, this "love hurts" business. I was dragged out of my depressive state last night by a very sweet young woman who brought me to a gig by Mark Eitzel, a delightfully morose American singer/songwriter, who during one song had the entire audience singing gleefully along to the chorus: "I – don't – know – if – I – will – ever – love again". He was at his funniest when he told us that he had no self-esteem issues – and proceeded to share how once someone shouted at a gig "I love you, Mark" and he heard the words "Fuck you, Mark" so he shouted straight back: "Fuck you too". Fab. "Welcome to my world," he said.

I know that world, and so did everyone else at that sell-out gig. The wonderful thing about artists like Eitzel is that when you turn pain into art, something healing happens: the misery of being alone is lessened.

BINDWEED AND THE CHILDREN IN MY LIFE
20TH JUNE 2001

It's quite something to be depressed on Prozac. It's proof that the human spirit, when determined and ruthless enough, can overcome all chemical inducements to bonhomie.

Andrew Solomon, in his elegant if overlong book on depression that I'm reading slowly, *Noonday Demon*, likens depression to ivy taking over a tree smothering it, gradually stunting new growth, until it gets to a stage that even if the ivy is cut at ground level, the tree doesn't have enough leaf-mass to regenerate.

That feels right, but for me it's more akin to convolvulus, or bindweed – that fast-growing weed with delicate white flowers that seems so pretty, but lasts only for a day. Trying to rid a garden of bindweed is next to impossible: for if you dig it out, each segment of root is capable of self-propagating – so the more effort you put in, the more you cut into it, the worse it gets. By first frost, the garden is covered with a dead brown matting of intertwined threads and tendrils. Then it is easily hacked off, the winter garden can be made presentable, and everything looks healthy again, if a little sparse. Come spring, and the flower-tipped shoots return with a vengeance, seductively entwining themselves around every stem.

At night, the flowers look particularly attractive. Depression is a night-feeling, of shadows and shades and increased sensitivity to compensate for limited sight. One's worldview becomes strangely like the image in the viewfinder of an infra-red camera: seeking out energy instinctively, the shapes one sees being primitive projections of one's own desires and compulsions, blurry Turin-like saviours, offering ghostly promises of redemption. Or is it confirmation of damnation? There is no light, no colour. A million shades of grey. A curious sixth sense emerges, fuelled by testosterone, where shadows take on the almost supernatural charge of symbol, and the world is ruled by a self-fulfilling prophecy: thou shalt encounter only those who are in the grip of the same neanderthal phallic Daddy-search, ready to lock antlers with the demons of your unconscious, primed for a futile unsatisfying scrap – unsatisfying, for the victory is against oneself. No real meeting happens. Or, the reality is of the bindweed kind – parasitic, suffocating, transient and overwhelming.

We see what we want to see; and those night-flowers of bindweed only last a day, but I can't get enough of them. I don't want to wake up and face the day, and deal with reality, for the light hurts my eyes, so used am I to seeing the murk in other people's souls.

Soul is the longing of the soulless for redemption, a friend of mine wrote in my Oscar Wilde fridge-magnet notebook, quoting someone he couldn't remember. Longing is the feeling I'm sitting with at the moment, if I stop running away from it and sit with it, which I am loath to do. I'd rather be involved in a nocturnal chase to confirm the ugliness of the world, to root out seediness and display it to demonstrate my perfectly-honed skills at night vision, at seeing what drives us all to destruction. Or to reconstruction, if we can manage to see beyond the symbolic death and see the birth that is imminent.

Last week, I spent a day with a five-year-old boy − brought him to the park, bargained with him over sweets, scared him with my anger when he ran across a road, shopped with him and cooked him pizza, removing the pineapple bits for him. At lunch, he informed me gravely that he wanted to go to the loo, and I had to wipe his tiny little bum with toilet paper, skin too soft, asshole too small to leave anything but a baby snail-streak of shit. In the evening, in front of the Muppet Pirate Movie video, he climbs up on top of me and starts stroking me, jiggling around on my body, hands stroking my stubble. I feel neither shame nor pleasure; just an awareness of terrible destructive power − an adult feeling. But this child's innocence soothes it, diminishes it.

He falls asleep when Tim Curry is let go into the darkness with the treasure in a leaky boat, his blond head on my arm, his body spooning against my torso. There is no escape then. I put him to bed, he squirms at the cold sheets, and then sighs and sleeps again.

There's a new report on fathering out*, which takes an overview of all the sociological and psychological research on fathers. It makes for encouraging reading − most importantly, it deepens our understanding of the nurturing and caring side of men, which is so necessary to balance the advances that women have made in the public realm. Among its findings are that men have equal sensitivity and reactions in heartrate and blood pressure to their crying or smiling children as mothers do, knocking squarely on the head the notion that women are biologically more suited to parenting. Fathers adapt and respond to children in exactly the same way when feeding them as mothers do − knowing instinctively how to match the infant's needs. Fathers and mothers give their babies the same amount of affection. Many studies show that the closeness between baby and father is almost identical to that between baby and mother. Linguistically, men are just as capable as women of speaking to babies in a way they can understand – although men, apparently, are more likely to use inappropriately complicated words. The report leaves it for us to decide whether or not this is a good thing – suggesting the possibility that it is through fathers that children stretch themselves linguistically, to try to understand them. The gender of parents is also irrelevant: same-sex couples have been studied, showing that it is more important that children have two carers (or more) than just one. The gender of the secondary carer is irrelevant in the child's later development; kindness and warmth are more important. The quality of caring by the father is more important than the quantity of time spent with children. Where dads are around and supportive before the age of seven, children are less likely to lead a life of crime; where dads are around and supportive between the ages of seven and eleven, children are more likely to succeed at exams, age 16. It is sad that the only scientifically measurable impact of fathering pre-adolescent children is whether or not exams are passed, but let's not dwell on the limitations of science when it comes to evaluating the fruits of love.

Each generation of fathers believes that they have discovered the joys of fathering; being a father is cited as the most important thing in most men's lives. Men have always been warm and kind, it's just that it usually takes a while for them to realise it, and to open themselves up.

I am not a father, nor am I likely to be, now. But there are children in my life, and I feel lucky. I'm the only man around in their lives – and so, without inviting it, I feel some sense of responsibility, although I guess it's a nebulous feeling. But their love for me is profoundly healing, the smiles on their faces when they see me are like a dawn chorus to my night-loving soul.

*www.fathersdirect.com

I'D LIKE MY LIFE TO BE DIFFERENT
28TH JULY 2003

Waiting for life to offer encouragement is a pathway to Hell. If, like me, you are sensitised to how other people feel, and if, like me, you live a fairly solitary life (over seven million people live on their own in these islands), then the outside world can become like a projection screen for your fantasies and fears. And the world is full of enough goodness and/or wickedness to support whatever mood you're in. You do see what you look for. People you meet or talk to in your day can have an inordinate impact on your life, and the amplification of feeling and meaning can distort and blow your inner speakers, and leave you reeling.

It's hard to get a relational balance, as it were, to lower your sensitivity to tolerable levels, to manage your feelings so that they don't dominate or control you. It's either pin drops or rock concerts. Neither are relaxing – the silence waiting for a phone to ring or an email to arrive can be vast and seemingly eternal, a recipe for panic, as the vacuum of loneliness can seem intolerably near. On the other hand, the cacophony of stimuli when you are with someone else can be intoxicating, addictive, and, if it's a sexual encounter, it can be like the most intense reality-distorting trip. And then, back to the silence, waiting for the pin to drop.

I'd like my life to be different. Where there is high-contrast, I'd like there to be a middle-ground, a blend. The trouble is, what I'd like involves other people, whom I've not yet met, which is tough, because if there's one thing I've learned in all my travels in psychotherapy, it's that you can't change anyone else, only yourself. So: I'd like to be the sort of person who lives with lots of people, with dogs, kids, adults of various shapes and sizes. I'd like to live in messy, raucous bonhomie with people who know about respect and creativity. I'd like to live, in other words, in Bohemia.

Another dream.

They say that when we cry, as adults, it's over an idea, rather than a direct expression of pain. In other words, if I were to suffer serious pain through an accident, for example, it would not lead to me weeping. Crying seems to be more to do with the visceral processing of an idea, an emotional high tide that leaves a watermark of acceptance afterwards, and often relief and some peace. The idea may be truthful: you are bereaved, someone has died, you will never see them again. Or, the idea may be false: you are single, you are unsuccessful at making new friends, you will always be single. Or, of course, it may be a mixture of the two: I have been single for most of my thirties, I'm frightened my forties will be the same.

The trouble with this sort of mentality – my sort of mentality – is that it can lead to the most awful self-pity, a smell that reeks through the cheesiest of smiles, and perpetuates the very issue that is perceived to be the problem. And it can lead to blindness; a narcissistic belief that I'm the only one who feels like this, the only one who is struggling with isolation. Which is of course total bollocks, and I wonder if I've lost some friends along the way for not having seen that their struggle is similar to mine. I do my best.

This is all prompted by an extraordinarily moving letter I received this week. I occasionally get letters sent to me from readers – all of which are appreciated, and some of which I reply to. I wish I could say I responded to them all, but my nerve fails me sometimes. This week's letter was unsigned, I do not know who sent it, but he had written to me once before, about eighteen months ago, and he sent me snowdrops and poetry.

I am lucky enough to have a stranger send me snowdrops and poetry. Let that be one of the top ten nicest things ever to have happened to me.

The sad thing is, this second letter was an apology. He was saying he was the "half-wit" who sent them to me, and that he was cringing about it ever since. He, like me, suffers from depression, and he was writing to explain away his extraordinary gift to me, as a manifestation of his depression. He had hit rock bottom, having recently lost a friend, and found himself in a churchyard full of snowdrops, and he thought he'd send them to me as a symbol of hope. He assured me he'd never write to me again.

Well, whoever you are, thank you. Symbol received and accepted, with thanks and love. To apologise for such kindness – well, that brings a tear to my eye. What we do to ourselves is often the cruelest thing.

CREATIVITY: IT'S COOL FOR CATS
23RD JULY 2004

The creative process – the worst part is the beginning. The Sitting Down. Ask anyone. Go on. The lengths to which a body will go to avoid the Sitting Down are extraordinary. It's as if it's a trap. An act of commitment, an "I do" in front of the priest, a cul-de-sac, no man's land. "I promise to be faithful to what I'm writing and not allow my attention to wander to anyone or anything else, however exciting or seductive". But that vow, sadly, just serves to invoke excitement and seduction from every corner. Phonecalls, emails, surfing the net. Newspapers. Sex. Shopping. Coffee. Food. Stimulation. Anything but Sitting Down to write.

In the end, after a day of complete success in avoiding Sitting Down, I give up. It's exhausting, the battle. I have dinner outside, in my little patch of courtyard. I open a bottle of red wine. Cheap Shiraz. I pour some into one of my remaining good wine glasses; the cats demolished two earlier in the day. I wish they would act their age, they're seven years old for chrissake. Oh. They're not kids, they're cats. Bugger. Bugger. Bugger.

The kids of the estate, who have been happy little monsters all day, their banging and shouting reverberating in the flat, have all gone in to watch *The Simpsons*, and it's blissfully silent. The weather is close and the sky is low, purple. Soon enough, it crackles with thunder and lightning, and the paving stones are spattered with huge drops of rain. The guitar player from across the way hears the storm and comes out to stand in it. Always with Elvis dyed-black hair in a quiff, he has a startling buzzcut on the back and sides, now revealing his grey, almost white, temples. We smile at each other. Once, years ago, he knocked on my door and asked if I was alright. He said he'd had a dream and something bad had happened to me. I said I was fine, but that I was touched he asked.

The truth is that he and I never know what to say to each other – we're from completely different worlds. We don't have anything in common, but a view of each other's front doors. Another truth is that I had been darkly depressed when he had the dream. Maybe that's something else we have in common. Depressed people often cannot bear to talk to each other. Only mere batsqueaks of greetings are possible; anything more and the feedback loop of despair threatens to overwhelm. I've seen what happens when he's had a few, and he shoves his girlfriend out of his flat, late at night, I've heard the hate. Smile and wave, keep one's distance.

The downpour lasts two minutes. The air is so humid it's like a greenhouse. I look up, and see a grey Victorian sky. I have to play 'Come Back To Camden' by Morrissey. Earphones, loud, private. (I live behind Camden Town Hall. He wrote that song for me. No one else.) It's heart-breakingly beautiful.

A couple from the block next door come into ours, and start calling for a cat. I've seen the note on the estate noticeboard, it went missing last night. I assure them that I haven't seen a tiger cat "like the one in the Bacardi ad", and that I'll be certain to let them know if I do. Soon after, a woman on her way up to see her friend on the top floor, to get her weekly stash, stops by and fills me in with the details about the cat – there is hell to pay, apparently. (Gossip is so satisfying when you aren't the subject of it). The owner was away for one night and her neighbours, this couple, were supposed to look after it. Had I heard the shouting earlier? Indeed I had. I thought it was a fight between working girls on crack, so vicious was the tone. Sadly, I live in a neighbourhood where I can make that comparison.

Take my cats. They're not human, I've discovered.

Next door, I hear my neighbour calmly dictating to his computer. Words come out slowly, drifting through the window, too slow to make sense of. He must be tapping something after each word, confirming the suggestions that pop up. He's wheelchair-bound, MS claiming his body to a degree I can't bear to think about. But his mind is crystal-sharp. He's a journalist by trade. He has loyal, witty friends, and his carers are invariably very pretty young men, which no doubt cheers him up. He's younger than me, taller (if he could stand up), more handsome. I am a bad neighbour to him. I smile and stop for a chat when I see him, but I can't do more. I know why. He never stops smiling. It breaks my heart. A smile can be a "Keep Out" sign, too.

I finish and print out a fan letter to an old acting buddy, who's in a play I saw the other night, that will be hitting the Dublin Theatre Festival in September, called *Shining City*. I've never seen a play that so beautifully captured the process that people go through when they come see a counsellor. But as playwright Colm McPherson says, it's not about therapy, it's about how men talk to each other.

Or not.

I think those who have no pretensions to creativity are blessed. There's a wonderful, maverick Jungian writer, by the splendid name of Adolf Guggenbühl-Craig, who bemoans the current notion that we should all be creative beings. Pointing out that there are very few really creative people on the planet − by which he means people who have created something completely new − he questions the modern, self-help, pop psychology creed that we all have creativity to unleash, if only we learned how to avoid the modern sin of dysfunction. It's a version of buying indulgences − but, instead of a promise of a blissful hereafter, if we do the work now, with our guru/therapist/counsellor/rebirther, we too will be truly original, and that bestseller/commission/Hollywood deal is ours for the taking. His response to all that is, more or less, "get real".

Perhaps the only creativity that is possible for any of us, is to be present as things unfold, to notice the newness of things. It's the hardest damn thing.

I go to bed and don't sleep well. I hear cats calling. I realise that one of them is one of mine, and I get up to let her in. Alarms go off through the night. It's how I imagine New York is in the heat of summer, the mugginess, the bad tempers, the discontent.

Later on, and I don't think this was a dream, I hear a young cat calling, a door opening, and a cry of joy, as the prodigal is welcomed home.

THE DISCONNECTED SOCIETY IS HERE AND NOW
29TH OCTOBER 2004

It was touch and go whether I'd go out last night or not. I had tickets to a show* and I couldn't get anyone to go with me. I'd spent a disconsolate day off work. A hoped-for morning coffee with a friend I hadn't seen in ages didn't materialise – it transpired that SMS messages weren't getting through. So I was left to my own devices, to unravel the fabric of my day, as is my frustratingly habitual wont. Disappointment is a fractal. It's not something I've really addressed. Maybe I should become a Buddhist.

I spent most of the day in front of my computer, inspiration for this article largely absent, writing emails, vaguely chatting, vaguely cruising, vaguely trying to fix a chronic software problem without resorting to drastic measures. A Bill Gates classic. The Microsoft engineer's bottom-line recommendation: uninstall and reinstall everything. That means a full day of muted anxiety, passively clicking "I accept" or "OK" every now and again, as the unstoppable process threatens to destroy all that one has created, in order to make one's working environment safe and familiar and efficient again. At the end of a chat session with a support technician called Evan, somewhere in the world (they're never allowed to reveal where they are), my frustration got the better of me. "Someday," I withered, typing very fast, "Microsoft will train their staff to apologise for all the time that their customers waste trying to fix problems that aren't our fault in the first place." He wasn't willing to engage. He sent me the standard "thank you for contacting Microsoft" paragraph and closed the session.

I wouldn't want his job. I'm lucky.

When I'm in that mood, plugged into cyberspace, I lose connection with the material world, with the need to eat, to clean up, to wash the dishes, to walk, to get fresh air, to talk. I need to connect. But I can't make connections happen.

Later, in the early evening, someone I have known for a year or so calls me. Number withheld, as usual. He says he's in the area, and asks, very politely, could he drop by? Erm, yes, do. He's sweet and tender and direct, with incredibly soft skin stretched over sinuous muscle. We take our time, and talk about how much better sex is with people you know, as opposed to strangers. For some reason I don't come — most probably my dissatisfaction with the day, a self-fulfilling prophecy. But he does, loudly and humorously, chuckling infectiously. He showers, he chats a bit, but he's not staying. He never does. That's the deal: what's on offer is only the affectionate physical contact, every couple of months or so, when he's "in the area" and I am at home. Do I turn him away? Hell, no. Why on Earth should I? I'm lucky. Am I not lucky?

With him gone, back to whoever wonders why he's late home from work, I realise I've five minutes left before I have to leave for the theatre, and I am still undecided. I look ahead at my evening, and it's more of the same: me and an electronic screen, either TV or computer. I figure my mood won't lift until I make an effort, so out I run.

A woman is on stage in darkness, sitting at a desk in front of a huge projected Windows computer screen. She's typing away. The microphone is directly under the keyboard, so the noise is oddly deep and rumbling, with scratchy overtones as her nails clip the keys. We, the audience, arrive in the middle of her composing a story, which is chaotic, slightly absurd. It turns out to be a dream — we find this out only as she saves it with today's date, and drags it to the folder on her desktop called "dreams". The Windows desktop has become a combination of performance area and cinema screen, inviting the audience in, to what is normally a private, solitary experience. I had fled from this, just an hour earlier.

We learn about her hopes and fears and past by watching her draft and redraft letters, to-do lists, business plans, dreams. It is such a revealing process, redrafting, editing; her mind is exposed to us in a way that seems shockingly intimate — it's as if we are in her mind, watching her. And yet she is utterly alone.

A message pops up: her disk is too full — she has to discard files, videos, photographs, memories, in a spring cleaning that is both comic and sad. Every five minutes or so, a webcam "security monitor" program interrupts her with a shot of outside the front door of her apartment, as if through a peephole. We learn that there's someone living upstairs, illegally, in the attic, who leaves the house at three in the morning to go shopping. He is a subject of fear and, ultimately, fantasy. He hasn't left the house in three days, and she knows because she's been watching for him. Slowly we see how she's been projecting her own fears and depression and isolation onto him, and as she makes ever-despairing attempts to deal with bureaucratic emails, feebly attempting to write a business plan, searching for jobs and trying to get a visa, we see how the computer world is keeping her imprisoned.

The show ends with her joining a webcam chat room, with various bits of inane chatter going on between buddies giving a good imitation of intimacy, rather like barflies passing the time. When she's asked how she is, she says "I'm in a dark mood". "Turn the lights on," someone jokes, and the banter continues, as the houselights come up. Gradually we realise that the show is over. No applause, no recognition for the performer/artist, whose face we now see for the first time, but only on screen, a little hovering window showing the image from her webcam. We shuffle out silently, as if we're trying not to disturb her.

As I write this, a new report comes out about children's lifestyles. More than two thirds of children now prefer to sit in front of the television or the computer on their own, than to play with others, according to a survey by Mintel. "Playstation children could be alone for life," says the headline. One of the authors says: "The risk is that we become a disconnected society. Quality of life depends on us relating to each other, and if we have no opportunity to do that and practise it as we grow up, we may settle for solitary lives, depending on television for entertainment and the internet to communicate."

That "disconnected society" is here and now. Perhaps this generation of children will not feel so disappointed when they grow up.

Maybe they're the lucky ones.

Or Press Escape by Edit Kaldor, was featured at the Riverside Studios, Hammersmith.

EVERY SHAG A SIGNIFICANT SHAG
23RD AUGUST 1996

I've had this really great idea. I'm sure it's going to catch on. I'm starting a campaign to encourage men to put the meaning back into sex. The motto will be: Every Shag a Significant Shag.

I am addressing all men in my crusade for considered copulation. Those of you who have sex with women will no doubt have stumbled into this arena before. But, brothers, it is not because of women that I urge you to join me at the teleological barricades. This revolution is for improving the quality of our lives.

It is gay men, however, who have spurred me into this action. Gay men, who without the influence of women's sexuality, have taken sex to its pneumatic limits. Gay men, who, when promoting free Rubberstuffers condoms on the back page of the UK gay newspaper *The Pink Paper* recently, give the following definitions for sex:

"SEX: 1. Short for sexual intercourse. 2. The insertion of one male's penis into another male's rectum which is followed by rhythmic thrusting usually resulting in orgasm. 3. Feelings and behaviour resulting from the urge to gratify the sexual instinct. 4. Stimulation of your or your partner's erogenous zones. 5. Any act of mutual pleasure resulting in an intense feeling of relief and euphoria. 6. Following an instinct that is not shameful or wrong but true, powerful and liberating. 7. A force that is life-giving but can be life-taking." The headline that follows this definition is : "Rubberstuffers – giving you the freedom to have sex".

This is catchy copy, designed to make condoms sexy by making sex sexy – "true, powerful and liberating". No clumsy human fumblings in the dark for gay men, it seems. Fair enough – this is advertising. But what really fires me up is how feelings are mentioned. According to Rubberstuffers, a registered charity, sexual instinct is paramount; feelings result from the urge to gratify it. This is a curious liberation.

This ad is but one example of the ethos and values of the "gay lifestyle" to which I supposedly belong, and by which I am becoming more and more disturbed.

I believe that the urge to have sex manifests when our feelings are stirred. These feelings can range from love to despair, from boredom to loneliness, from rage to joy. But they come first. Think about it. When you last had sex, how were you feeling? (And if you weren't feeling anything, what were you feeling before the first pint?) Did some unnameable primal instinct/force take you over just when you were about to settle down in front of the telly with a cup of tea? Did your cock suddenly begin to throb as you were feeding the cat?

Most probably, there was a context to your experience of horniness. In other words, you were with someone you felt something for. This seems to me to be obvious. But for consumers of the "gay lifestyle", this concept of feeling something for the person with whom you have sex is alien.

The ad states that sex results in a feeling of relief. Surely sex results in a relief of feelings? A relief from feelings? Or could it be – and we're getting to scary territory here – an expression of feelings?

This is where my campaign comes in. It has been said that AIDS brought about a change in the way gay men related to each other; that grief and fear has brought us closer as a community, and has made us value each other more. Well, this is an ad from an AIDS charity. The people who wrote, or at least commissioned, this copy should be representative of those gay men most influenced by this supposed change in our values. It appears not. What we get is a definition of sex that eschews the idea of men as emotional beings, with no room to include that ridiculously old-fashioned − heterosexual? − concept of making love. This is propaganda for candyfloss sex, insubstantial and sugary; this belongs to the same land where "The Real Thing" is a syrupy brown liquid. This is selling sex to boys, not men.

Men, we're in trouble if we don't stop this now.

Perhaps we gay men got into trouble with viruses because we wanted to believe that we could separate sex from feelings. Perhaps not. But in spite of, or maybe even because of, the grief of AIDS, we seem determined to keep feelings out of our sex lives now.

We're watching a new generation of young men grow up being taught by registered charities in respectable newspapers that all they need when they next get assailed by "the sexual instinct" is to put on a rubber and they'll experience what sex is all about.

We're raising perpetually horny creatures with the bodies of Gods and with hearts of stone. We're raising monsters.

I WATCHED A FEW MEN BEING PUBLICLY DUMPED BY THEIR WIVES THE OTHER NIGHT
22ND JULY 1998

Dating is an activity I've been trying to get the hang of recently. It requires a little confidence, and a good dose of maturity. Which is probably why I haven't done much of it before. By dating I mean meeting interesting men for a pint, with no strings attached, and going home alone, saying in parting that you'd like to see them again for a movie or something the following week. You know. What most human beans do. It keeps things light and entertaining and no one gets hurt; and if it gets serious eventually, then there's a better chance that it might work because you already have some idea about how you relate in social mode, on neutral territory. You have tasted the flavour of time in this person's company. Each person is different, and you have a sense now of what this person's differences might be.

I was going out with someone for a couple of months there, but it didn't work out. That's a bit coy, I realise, but I'm not going to kiss and tell. But while I was going out with him, it felt very relaxing to escape the hamsterwheel of my sexual nature as a single gay man. Nice thing to report is that instead of going crazy since breaking up, I've been bizarrely sane. I've dated a couple of guys, and that's been it. A reformed man, I am. Civilized, urbane, witty, you could bring me anywhere and I'd not look out of place. Well, nearly anywhere.

Something has been getting on my nerves, though. When I confess that I was the one that broke it off with your man, two things happen. One is that no matter how I try to explain it to my friends, I get overly defensive. The second thing is that a split-second image of Ally McBeal being literally dumped into a tip appears in my head. It's the image that she sees (and we see) whenever a man dumps her. I can't get that silly, irritating woman out of my brain. I know it's only a TV comedy, and I know I'm not supposed to take comedy characters seriously. But she's such an airhead, it drives me nuts. The fact that the series is written and produced by a man had me convinced for a while that she was the creation of some misogynistic queen, writing autobiographically about Unrequited Love For A Straight Man. (For those readers who never caught up with what was "America's hottest show," for, oh, it must have been all of two weeks, Ally McBeal is a lawyer working in the same office as the man of her dreams, with whom she used to be in love until he dumped her, presumably because she's so thick. Each week we see how much she's still in love with this wimp, and how much she's in denial about it.)

However, my usually reliable gaydar is not functioning properly. I see the show's writer happens to be married to Michelle Pfeiffer. How wrong can you get? But then, who's to say? Maybe Pfeiffer is an airhead when she doesn't have a script; maybe this man's world is like that. Maybe the world is like that. Perhaps we're all in denial about what we should be doing with our lives, and there's an audience watching us somewhere throwing things at the screen screaming "Do it, you moron".

Ah, TV culture. Sometimes I spend a lot of time watching it, and then I can go for months without really bothering. I always try and catch what is supposed to be the "hottest" thing because it's fascinating to see what values and personalities are in fashion. It says a lot about our society. Sometimes, though, you wish it would go unsaid. Take *The Jerry Springer Show*. As long as it entertains, an item of human misery and/or oddness is worthy of inclusion. I watched a few men being publicly dumped by their wives the other night; each thought that he was being brought on for a pleasant surprise. The twist was that the women were leaving their husbands for other women; that alone was reason enough, apparently, to put these men through the most public humiliation I have seen in a long time. Not since one Friday night in a leather bar in East London, but that's a different story.

The cuckolds put on brave faces, and none resorted to violence, though their hearts were breaking. One man even had his wife complain bitterly that his cock was too big, and that it had hurt her every time they made love in their marriage. He was flabbergasted, dismayed, shocked, embarrassed. The audience bayed with laughter as his erstwhile partner suggested that he cut two inches off of it. These men watched as their beloveds started cavorting around onstage with their new lovers in front of them. One man, the only one with children, vowed passionately to keep their children away from her, and I couldn't blame him. The queer party line is that no parent should have their children taken away from them just because they're gay or lesbian. But after watching that display of emotional cruelty, I would worry about children brought up to follow an example of a lying, cheating mother who gets off on boasting about it on international television.

The scorn that these women were pouring on their husbands was shocking to behold; all the more so because there was no evidence from any of them that the men were guilty of anything other than having been suspicious of them. The fact that they were entirely justified seemed to be unimportant. This was a ritualised Coming Out, but it was a process based on hate, not love. The part of me that feels a link with others who are lesbian and gay, who have shared the experience of coming out, is embarrassed.

What is disturbing is that I can't get away with saying that it reflects on American culture only; the other night *The Jerry Springer Show* was on three different channels on cable TV in London; I'm sure it's no different elsewhere in these islands.

I'm trying to find a positive thing to say about this nightly Theatre of Abuse and Degradation. The only thing I can think of is that we have all known that life is stranger than fiction; perhaps this is the first time that a pungent degree of strangeness is being publicly acknowledged, almost celebrated. But the contrast between sanitised, romanticised Hollywood and this world of barely coherent, mean-spirited, exhibitionistic, passionate and amoral people could not be more stark. Perhaps if our art, our culture, drifts away from reality, then people go to the other extreme to compensate. A diet of saccharine-sweet happy endings for the Beautiful People can only result in misery for real people, those of us who stare boggle-eyed at flickering screens at 3am, avoiding the reality of a cold, empty bed.

GIVING UP THE DAY JOB
19TH FEBRUARY 1998

Frankly Mr Shankly
This position I've held
It pays my way
And it corrodes my soul
I want to leave
You will not miss me
I want to go down in musical history

– The Smiths

I'm giving up the day job. By the time you read this, I'll have handed in my notice. I'm going to write that long-threatened play/screenplay/novel, carry on studying, and hopefully live off the proceeds of a couple of little businesses that started off as hobbies. It's exciting and terrifying at the same time; like taking a step off a cliff, not knowing whether I will land or take wing.

It's not been the worst dayjob I've had; in fact I feel indebted to them for being so flexible with the hours, so accommodating with requests for time off. I've certainly made good friends there. They've almost been so helpful that I don't notice how badly paid it is, or how the boss regularly forgets to pay us on time, or how Christmas invariably fails to have any effect on our pay packets. Almost.

That indebtedness has been a curious sticky trap, it has kept me there longer than has been good for me. It will be hard not to appear churlish or ungrateful to my colleagues when they realise what a relief it will be when I leave, how much I desperately crave an end to the banality and drudgery of office work. The resentment is not directed against them really of course; as the song says, it's something to do with soul. And the concept of soul is a hard one to keep hold of when you're doing the filing and packaging and answering the phone for a mail-order company.

It's a difficult thing for others around you to hear that you want better for yourself, better than what they have settled for. It can bring a frisson of implied criticism and condemnation. Begrudgery is everywhere, if you choose to look for it; only if you're very lucky – and/or if you've been careful enough over a period of time, do you find yourself surrounded by people who are willing to support you if you choose a path that implies that you believe you can do something creative.

I believe I have been lucky; perhaps the greatest obstacle I've faced is my own resistance, my own lack of faith in myself. But it's also related to the uneasy relationship between art and money, between the artist and society. Is art valuable only when someone pays for it? Is someone who claims to be creative entitled to support, to enable that creativity to blossom? To be honest, part of me believes that I shouldn't have to dirty my hands with filthy lucre; that someone should recognise my astonishing genius right now and become my patron. Or husband. But most of me acknowledges that I'm not living in the Star Trek century at the moment, that a living has to be made first, before I can get on with my own stuff. And I'm getting on a bit; the day I hope will be my last screechingly mundane day of employment is my 35th birthday.

I reached a stage when I feared my own stuff would never get done. I've been in a monumentally foul mood ever since Christmas; I blamed it on the shortness of the holiday, but it was more to do, I think, with the prospect of another year filled mostly with days in which I have to turn my brain off to survive them sane. As I'm sure many of you know, that's an exhausting occupation. At the end of each of those days, to try and get any serious personal work of any kind done is an uphill task. And when it mounted up, and I was frustrated by my inability to make any inroads into it, then I'd escape by picking up the phone and dialling S for sex. After a day in which passion plays no part, at night I would do my best to make up for it.

As I got angrier and angrier, I asked myself who, in my inner cast of thousands, was getting angry with whom. And when I looked, the angry guy looked rather like a combination of God and Morrissey, if that's not tautological. "The 21st century is breathing down your neck," he said. Who am I to argue with Mozza?

There comes a time for everyone, I imagine, when mediocrity makes you want to retch. Some people throw up, some, perhaps most, swallow it back down and try to forget about it. I've done it a few times in my life, most notably at school – but a fat lot of good that did me. If I'd studied for my exams then, I wouldn't be in this crap job now. Let that be a warning to you, dear reader.

I guess I'm about to throw up again. Let's hope I feel better afterwards. Perhaps the knack is in the timing. Maybe one should make plans for a serious bout of vomiting up mediocrity.

It should be taught in schools. Insurance companies should cover you for it: indemnity against illness, loss of a limb, soul corrosion and death. I'd pay that premium.

If I could afford it.

WHALESONG: A LITTLE BIT OF HEAVEN ON EARTH
10TH JUNE 1998

The Americans have been listening, with their redundant anti-Soviet submarine technology, in the waters now known as the Malin Sea. They've heard whalesong, which is not unusual – but for the first time in decades they've recognised the song from the Mother of them all, the Blue Whale. In the past couple of years, according to a newspaper report, five of these animals, the biggest ever to inhabit the Earth, have been spotted in this part of the world. It's been over twenty years since the last one was seen here, off the coast of Ireland. It was thought that the North Atlantic population was beyond recovery, and that they were surviving only in the Southern Oceans, far from the Japanese and Norwegian whalers, whose activities early in this century nearly drove them to extinction.

I've always been fascinated by these creatures; especially since they remain firmly in the world of my imagination. They haven't yet appeared on primetime, with David Attenborough's dulcet tones in earnest commentary, bringing them into the mundane world of recorded fact, reducing them to the size of my TV screen. I checked on the Internet, to see if anyone else had managed to film them. There are remarkably few images, by the standards of Internet culture; usually if you go searching for something, the choice is overwhelming. Plenty of material on every other type of whale, but not the Blue. There is mention of an American documentary, by a photographer called Al Giddings. He is quoted as saying that he had not expected to film close-up footage of the Blue in his lifetime. I found a photograph of a Blue Whale's dorsal fin and a bad painting of something looking rather like the Loch Ness monster. That's all I could find, in half an hour of surfing. I'm sure there are more images out there, but if photography steals souls, as some believe, then the Blue Whale's soul is still relatively free.

I've been greatly cheered by this news. It's too early to say whether these sightings, and soundings, mean that the population is definitely on the increase or that they've simply moved closer to us. In other words, we humans haven't a clue. At the end of this century of technological sophistication, I find that reassuring.

I know that this news has some impact on my life this week, but I can't quite put my finger on why. As I write, someone is putting the finishing touches to a fountain that he has built outside my window, in the courtyard. There's a magnificent gleaming nickel-plated fish poised mid-leap between two (currently empty) rectangular copper pools. Tomorrow the electrician arrives to connect the pump, the pools will be filled up, and I'll work to the sight and sound of trickling water from then on. That's a little bit of heaven on Earth, as far as I'm concerned.

There have been other activities in the courtyard this week as well. Yesterday, plants were delivered, hundreds of them. Whereas up to now there have just been earth patches, as bare as the builders left them, flattened by kids determined to ignore their parents' injunctions to stay out of the mud, there are now verdant banks of evergreen shrubs and trailers. Half of them are still in their pots; if I get a chance, and if I finish this in time today, I'll plant a few more. I helped the gardeners yesterday for a few hours, in the pouring rain. I've blisters and a sore back to prove it, not to mention a chesty cough, which is lingering longer than it should. I didn't do it for payment, and I didn't do it because it was right outside my window. It wasn't that the gardeners were women and they needed a man to help them move and plant some trees. It's true I will get great pleasure from my environment being green and pleasant, but it would look the same whether or not I helped.

The word I think I'm struggling towards is community. It's a dubious concept, at the best of times. The rules for each community differ, and they are largely unspoken. Here, in the centre of impoverished King's Cross in London, there is a taste of 1970s counterculture in this refurbished Victorian tenement block. The residents organize a festival every summer, with circus acts and rock gigs and tea and biscuits for the local pensioners. That was my job for a couple of years running, persuading the old dears to be civil with each other while I made countless gallons of tea stew with an old Burco boiler. Obviously, they couldn't stand each other, but they turned up anyway.

The kids aren't too pleased at the moment, especially the older boys in

World Cup time. The gardener has dictated that there's to be no more football in the main yard, because of the plants. They are complaining bitterly about grown-ups being unfair to kids. I am delighted with the new rule, because three of my four potted plants have been broken by footballs slamming into them, and it is impossible to relax outside when a ball is being kicked around. I have to smile, though; for when I was their age my hate figure was a neighbour who banned football in the cul-de-sac where we lived. My mother had to use her most persuasive charms to dissuade me from picketing her house with a "Boys' Lib" sign. The world keeps turning.

But the kids are excited by the new fountain; the older ones are holding up the little ones to explain where the water is going to spout from, where it will go, and they all want to touch the glistening fish. A resident designed and made it all; it was paid for by the residents' association. But I know he can't have been paid properly for the work he put in, merely the cost of the materials plus expenses.

A community is as rich as its members want it to be. It's not about money, it's about whether people want to put something into it, without expecting anything back in return. If the number of people willing to do that reaches some unknown critical mass, then the world becomes an infinitely better and more pleasant place.

I'm sorry, I know that this is turning into a whimsical green eco-friendly save-the-whale ramble, but there you go. Warm-blooded animals, with hearts bigger than we are, are circling our islands again, forgiving us for our previous crimes. And I'm learning about what big-hearted gestures of community can do, if enough of us make them. I'm going out to plant a few more shrubs.

LET IT OUT: NOTHING'S TOO LURID FOR THE NEW AGE
24TH NOVEMBER 1999

I want to be on *The Jerry Springer Show*. I want to parade my darkest secrets on international TV, for all the world to see. I want all those who have cheated on me, and all those I have cheated, to enter the studio, in turn, on cue, to face my wrath and/or my pleas for forgiveness. I want the screen to be filled with colourful captions about my life, such as "Tainted Love – You used me, you Rat!" or "I'm addicted to sex – I want to come clean!" The audience, hyped to a frenzy, know what to expect; and they're on my side, bellowing, and urging me to do what I gotta do. To give Good Television. Nothing else matters.

I want all remnants of poison and guilt to be purged from my system, in one colossal shameless eruption, spewing up my stored-up vitriol on all around me. I want to scream and shout and pour abuse, in raw untreated Anglo-Saxon, on all those unremitting shits who have done me wrong. I want the syndicated audiences across the world, from Lagos to Manila, from Perth to Reykjavik, to see my mouth move in foul, contorted obscenities, to the sound of a continuous beep. I want to rent my clothes like I'm possessed by a particularly sleazy god, and show off my frenzied body, pouting, preening and swaggering, roaring till my voice is shot to pieces. I want to punch and kick and punish the air for separating me from the objects of my gloriously righteous rage. I want five mountainous men to hold me back and restrain me from inflicting serious damage on all those within my grasp. I want the audience to stand up and grunt and holler and yell their approval, every time I make a run for it and strike another blow for vengeance.

I want to hear their roars of approval as I dig the knife into that low-lying scum of a cheatin' ex-lover. I want to see those who have swindled, and lied to, me stand and blink in terror, as the crowd hisses at them, outraged at my sorry tales of sordid betrayal. I want to hear blood-curdling moans of hate rumble from the crowd, as some smug bastard throws my flowers away and refuses to accept my apology for having done him wrong. I want the audience to chant my name ecstatically as I pick up those flowers and try to shove them up his tight bony little ass, foiled only by being sat upon by two hefty bodyguards in the middle of the petal-strewn coliseum.

I want the show to end with the stage full of all the characters in my life, with me in the centre, bedraggled but reborn, while Jerry gives his homily to the world on the nature of forgiveness, with his (still obligatory) tone of dry distaste, as he patronizingly wishes us, his guests, happier lives. As the credits roll, and my fifteen minutes is done, I want to leave the studio with people shaking my hand and clapping me on the back, for having done the performance for them; for having spoken what they daren't speak; for having felt what they daren't feel. I want the rawness inside to fade, to be replaced by a sublime contentment. I want to know that there's nothing left inside to conceal, to fester. I want to feel that I've confessed to the world, and that the world has tuned in, in their millions, to give absolution. After such global redemption, there is no more room for the heavy baggage of shame.

Others may feel ashamed for watching the show, disturbed by its amoral exhibitionistic narcissism, and perturbed by the way in which television has eroded the concepts of modesty, of discretion, of privacy, and made them appear to be synonyms for prudishness and shame. In the new century, where feelings are judged only by how well they translate to the small screen, expressions of hate and lust and envy and greed, once the great deadly sins, are now prime-time fodder. It's good to feel bad. Let it out. Nothing's too lurid for the new age. Forget all Victorian concepts of neurotic decency. The new plebeian morality banishes patrician pretence in favour of an unvarnished, ugly candour, a primeval display of animalistic passion, uncivilized and grotesque. To the ever-increasing class of folk who gain their emotional literacy from daytime soap operas (the same the world over, from Brazil to China, with clearly defined villains and heroes, infused with a western obsession for ostentatious wealth), *The Jerry Springer Show* offers the opportunity for catharsis that is as far removed from the psychotherapist's couch as is possible to imagine. Whether such emotional purging is self-indulgent and destructive, or liberating and necessary for good mental health, is a moot point; but both Jerry and the shrink perform the same function.

After years of the dreary drip-drip-drip of listening to my own neuroses reverberate around a room to an audience of one in therapy, I long to get it all over and done with, and let Jerry work his special voodoo on me; to feel what it's like to have my preposterous pretensions to bourgeois decency come tumbling down, to the ecstatic roars of approval from the great unwashed, who have never been taught that their feelings should be tamed, like wild prairie-bred horses, broken in for market.

THE BIGGER THE DREAM THE MORE PAINFUL THE LIFE
13TH MARCH 2003

Mother will never understand
Why you had to leave
But the answers you seek
Will never be found at home
The love that you need
Will never be found at home

– Bronski Beat
'Smalltown Boy'

I was 21 when I first heard Jimmy Somerville's extraordinary voice pealing the words to 'Smalltown Boy', a siren call to my soul to move, to leave, to find the answers I sought, away from home. Practically all of my gay friends left Dublin in the following years, for London or the United States. I was the last to go. The trajectory of leaving towns or villages to find love in Metropolis, common to so many gay men, is archetypal in this period of our history, in this part of the world. Themes of bullying and shame and loneliness and ostracisation inform the beginning of the journey. At the end of the road, the proud rainbow, is the pot of gold, the trinity of the big job, the trendy loft apartment, and the dream lover, the one that couldn't be found at home. If not for any other reason than statistics. Go to where your kind are congregating, ease the existential isolation and dive into the pool of queer humanity.

I'll never forget my first London gay pride festival – the sweet humbling of being one of a crowd of tens of thousands. The bewildering visceral pleasure of realising all these handsome and stylish creatures were the same as me. I yearned for sameness, to let the bruises of difference fade. Not only safety in numbers, not only strength in numbers, but hope in numbers. Somewhere in the crowd; there's my man. Maybe. Maybe this time.

Glamour, urban exoticism, the sexual experimentation of the huge gay scene took me out of myself, made me relate differently, enabled me to connect with others in a specially intense, charged way, which bridged the gap I felt existed between me and the rest of humanity. Especially after I'd been hurt in love. Part of me believed that all I had to do was be seen by enough men and of course he would appear – love at first sight, immediate certainty, dream come true. Each time that didn't happen, I licked my wounds and comforted myself in devilishly urban ways. I wanted the piercing focus of erotic attention to reach the parts of me that hadn't been reached before. I wanted to banish feelings of being an outsider, a maverick, the last to be picked for football.

Of course I wanted someone to look after, and I wanted someone to look after me. But it took me some time to realise that leather-clad, jackbooted and shaven-headed men weren't the most likely to offer kindness or consideration, however much my libido cried out for that creative expression, that contact, that limit-expanding dance with sexual power. In Metropolis, sexual play is a rough contact sport, and not for the faint-hearted. An actor, I thought I could play the part – but underneath the leather I'm as soft as butter. As is every other "hard" man I've met. Trouble is, "hard" men don't thank you for seeing their softness, for naming it. Too intimate. Too close for comfort.

Metropolitan lifestyles, for smalltown boys, are tantalising because they offer the excruciating hope that you can have it all. The sexually experimental, faithful and endlessly fascinated (but not clingy) lover being top of the list. Being men, hot sex is part of the expectation – the fantasy is so similar to heterosexual men's fantasies of women being both madonna and whore that, to all intents and purposes, there is no difference. Same sex drive, different object. To this end, gay men work hard to ensure they don't miss out on the dream: perfect bodies, perfect attitude, perfect gear. If it's not happening, it's because they haven't been to the right club or taken the right drug or got their sixpack well-enough defined. Along the way, the search for the dream lover becomes extraordinarily blatant; it becomes reason enough to dump men out of your bed and life because "it's not working out" –*i.e.* you're not perfect, you haven't given me enough attention to make me feel special, and even if you did I don't believe you did it because it was me, but because you wanted something for yourself. It's a narcissistic feedback loop, a dismal manipulative dance of trying to get the other to care.

And what of our Jimmy Somerville, mascot of the queer metropolitan? On his website, he jokingly has Captain Kirk as one of his heroes, and one of his dreams was to leave Glasgow and find his own Captain Kirk. He wryly notes that he still hasn't found him. I met the wee Scot once, on a surreal night of drowning my sorrows in my local dive after a particularly harrowing breakup – he was unhappily pissed and rageful and obnoxious. The smalltown boy hadn't found what he hoped he'd find, away from the smalltown.

I think there's a rule of emotional contentment that goes something like: the bigger the dream, the more painful the life. Big cities offer big dreams. They attract the powerless, offering dreams of power. Dreams of heroes to whisk us away from ourselves, to rescue us from our plight of enduring our own company. But we can't command others to love us. If we're lucky, and we don't fly so high that we burn up along the way, we may discover that location has nothing to do with loving ourselves. Love, like charity (and regime change), begins at home. Smalltown, Big City, or country boy.

IT'S WAR OUT THERE, I TELL YOU. WAR.
12TH MAY 2003

Wrong side of the bed today. I'm going about my business and the world seems abysmal. Hypocrisy and falsehood rule, and every encounter seems fraught with spiky hostility, with misery. The soundtrack to *Magnolia* is running in my head, that fiercely beautiful dirge.

The headlines on the tabloids speak of the "Baghdad Bounce": Blair's the comeback kid, the polls are looking good for him. Britain is an alien land to me again. I feel about this government the same way I did about Margaret Thatcher's. I could not move here as long as she was still in charge, and I do not think I can live in Blair's Britain much longer. There is a collective blindness here. The emperor has no clothes but there is a dismal failure to acknowledge it. The arrogance, the conscious determination to ignore history's lessons, the absence of integrity, the obscenity that a passionate self-sacrificial (and therefore self-justifying) appeal for war could ever be seen as a moral argument are skated over. The lies, the self-delusion, the curious way that this seemingly rational country permits its leaders to live in a bubble and go mad with power ("we are a grandmother") to make decisions that are contrary to what its people actually want, to surround themselves with sycophantic courtiers to anaesthetise them while democratic principles are surgically removed – all this is permitted. And the British people seem willing to forgive him his folly. Putin calls his bluff and he's shocked. Reality stings. Expect anti-Russian bile to hit the tabloids soon.

What Kofi Annan says is dismissed as irrelevant now by the British media – it's as if the government's amnesia has infected them, a pernicious little virus. But the truth is probably simpler: people like to forget.

Walking to the tube this morning, past the emaciated working girls standing by the post office, the raddled crack addicts selling their heaven with threat pulsing through their veins. It's Kings Cross. That makes a difference? Why? Geography? Tolerance? Tradition? Fuck knows. It's here every day, every hour. Down three levels into the grimy station, crowds flowing stream-like down man-made courses. In the middle of the hall, a man stops. He slowly reaches down with one hand and uses a can of lager as a stilt. He's crumbling. A knee goes first, to the ground. He still stares forward, his free hand waves gently in front of him. His other knee touches the tiles now, and he slides out onto his side. He has half a smile on his face, but he's not really present. People hurry past ignoring him.

A staff member saunters by and doesn't notice the man on the ground. I stop him and say that someone's collapsing. He looks over and irritation flashes across his face. More work for him.

Every single day, in Ireland, a man kills himself. It's the leading cause of death in young Irish men. 70% of men who kill themselves, were known to have experienced depression before – it's hard to establish what the rest were feeling, but it's not likely to have been much different. One in five people gets to suffer from depression, but most of them fail to recognise it, or get help for it. It's a difficult thing, this life. Hard to get a grasp of it, squeeze out its essence. Hard to get conscious, to think from a place that is balanced. It changes every day, like the weather. I don't see the life I know, anywhere in the media.

We see what we look for, this much I know.

I read on the tube that an octopus in an aquarium died of a heart attack because some imbeciles took flash photographs of him, ignoring the sign that says "No Flash Photography". I hate people so much sometimes. I hate ignorance.

The evening, after work. I'm less angry. A man in his fifties, with wild grey hair and gardener's hands, stands in the supermarket aisle. He's facing the shelves full of men's shaving paraphernalia. He has two different brands of shaving cream or gel in his hands, and he's staring at them: a reverent gaze, as a paleontologist might hold a couple of bones. As I pass him, he asks in a polite voice: "Excuse me, I wonder could you help me?"

I have the sort of face that beggars like. I get asked, if I'm in town, at least once, more often twice a day for something. I've decided the best way to react is simply to look people straight in the eye and shake my head, smile ruefully, and walk very quickly away. If you speak, you're a goner. Engage with a guilt-tripping maestro and you'll always come off worse. The worst ones are those who have mastered the martyred, putting-on-a-brave-face, intensely cheer-filled "have a nice day anyway" retort – a nasty little weapon. Such words can pierce the heart, like shrapnel from cluster bombs that the British and American people have left in fields for Iraqis to walk on. It's war out there, I tell you, war.

But this guy is different. He is asking with the tone of someone who has never asked a question like this before. Not a pitched-just-right tug on the heartstrings, not an East European ululating whine that bores into the root canals, but an expression of bafflement.

"Yes," I say. I stand beside him. He looks at the two canisters. I look at the two canisters.

I read recently how friendships can be made in India between men. You go up to someone and stand beside him. You don't have to do or say anything. Just watch the world go by together. If he moves on, he has said "no" and is not interested. If he stays, he's enjoying your company, and you could be friends for life. It's subtle. It's like music. There are ninety-six words for love in Sanskrit.

But I'm not in India. I'm in a supermarket in central London. The staff may have Indian features, and Philippino, and Malaysian, but the culture is English. Don't talk to strangers, don't smile with your eyes. Get on with your grey day. God, it's a punishing city, it pisses on the last embers of warmth in your heart if you let it.

Gillette foam or gel? "I've never used any of these things before. They say this is what I've got to get. I've always used a brush before, and soap, you know?" Yes, I know. "But now I've to get one of these."

We survey the ranks of painted aluminium containers, with their plastic tops. "What do I do?" he asks.

I explain about aerosols and squeezing a little bit into the palm of your hand. "And then what?" he asks. "Then you rub it on your face," I say. "If you're used to the sort of suds that come from a brush, then try the gel, it's more like soap – the foam goes a bit frothy and dry". "Oh. OK. Thanks," he says, and I go off. Ten minutes later as I go past the aisle again to get to the checkout, he's still there, reading the label on a can. You've got to get these things right.

I get home, eat, and write this. A spam email arrives with the subject line "Monster cocks tearing girls". It's in my mind before I can delete it.

I want to shout again. And do.

TV IS A LOVELESS MEDIUM
16TH DECEMBER 2004

Big Brother, on Channel 4 here in the UK, went "evil" this year. It reached new depths of depravity and violence, all in the name of entertainment, as the hapless wannabees flailed around in the mud that was being thrown at them, each climbing over one another to escape the quagmire, to get their fix of the poisonous drug called celebrity. Everyone's favourite Big Momma, Davina McCall, abandoned all scruples, to salaciously reveal to the mauled, exiting competitors that Nadia was – get this – a man before. Watch those guys squirm!

Reality TV is, increasingly, coming out as overtly sadistic, from *I'm A Celebrity, Get Me Out Of Here*, with the astonishingly perverse Ant and Dec (in hushed, awed tones, breathless with cruelty: "... and there's another crocodile in the water now, mate") to *Changing Rooms*, with participants wracked with guilt as they slavishly follow a despotic designer's plans to ruin their friends' home. Simon Cowell on *Pop Idol* or *X Factor* relishes every opportunity to demolish people's fantasies about themselves. Trinny and Susannah are cruel to be kind to their victims, of course. There's Queen of Mean, Anne Robinson on *Weakest Link*; Frank Skinner's malicious humour, or the half-time moment in every episode of *Wife Swap* when the wives get to impose their vengeful will on their new family. And of course, Jerry Springer. We lick our lips and salivate at the hunters going in for the kill. And we don't have to get off our fat asses to do it.

We are all becoming armchair sadists. Watching TV is a strange activity in itself, a passive state, where we plug into a different zone in our minds, one which is not about human relationship, but which enables us to avoid feeling alone. At its best, of course, it is informative, moving, challenging and inspiring, and I know that my life is richer for having seen many superb dramas, comedies, documentaries and news programmes over the years. But when we sit down and watch these people on our screens, we unconsciously take ownership over them. The press exploits this ruthlessly, gleefully exposing every human flaw in the personalities of those who place themselves in front of a camera. They're all "fair game". We punish those who entertain us, we do not forgive them – because they have surrendered their privacy for us, and offered themselves up for inspection: they have presented their pretty arses to us in submission, and we can take grisly satisfaction in shafting them in the comfort of our own lonely homes.

The relationship between the inspector and the inspected is a powerfully charged one; the Marquis de Sade made this explicit in his writing. He, of course, had no concept of television, nor could he have imagined its constant companions, the baying hounds of the tabloids, ripping into the flesh of its denizens, but were he around today he'd have no problem recognising that what goes on in every living room is exactly the stuff of his tortured imagination.

Inspection – the objectifying gaze, the act of turning people with hearts, minds and souls into visual and imaginal objects, things for our own pleasure – is part of human nature. The interplay between those who offer themselves up for inspection and those who observe and objectify is powerfully charged. It may be part of an important creative function, one which testosterone develops (remembering that both men and women have this hormone coursing through their veins). In every sexual relationship, there are degrees of this dynamic at work, for without a degree of separation, of objectification, the erotic takes a walk; but without a degree of compassion and warmth, of seeing the other as a person rather than an object, love takes a walk. TV is a loveless medium, masturbatory, manipulative and isolating. We are impotent and silent, passive and controlled, slaves to scheduling and advertising. In our bondage, we get our kicks from a misguided sense of revenge. But if the TV or computer screen were to change suddenly into a mirror, we'd see our slack-jawed inertia and dead eyes, and, with a shock, might be propelled to start living instead. The best revenge is not to get off on sadism; the best revenge is to live well.

There are exceptions on TV that prove the rule, of course. In watching the recent final instalment of *Musicality* on Channel 4, I was touched on a deep level by the stories of the participants trying to win, each one overcoming a lack of experience with impressive amounts of bravery, talent and hard work. It was a compassionate programme because everyone involved was supportive and encouraging, the judges' unfavourable criticisms were regretfully delivered, standards were high but fair. It is not only because I am a former actor that I recognise this to be characteristic of theatre folk in general. Actors know some of life's home truths that can elude many others: life is difficult, unfair, unpredictable, and unstable. The fickle finger of fate is a reality that has to be dealt with, without rancour. Life is better with teamwork. And dreams can come true, if you work at them.

But theatre also serves another purpose, which television cannot reproduce. I do not propose that all TV should abandon cruelty, and adopt the comfy, huggy tones of *Musicality* or, my other favourite, *Faking It*. Life isn't like that. We need our shallow reality exposed, dissected, examined; we need to look at our own greed and emptiness and hunger for fame, we need our soap star scoops and tales of murder and pettiness, our farcical competitions and our meretricious exhibitionists. Otherwise we cannot know that this is what we have become.

But theatre is a collective, ritual experience, a participatory one. Its origins were sacred. As television and the internet dominate our lives with pap, are we becoming increasingly isolated, disconnected from a sense of participation, of community? Are we capable of greater cruelty when we are sitting on our sofas at home? For every time we sit down and watch a sadistic reality TV show, we are encouraging more of its ilk to come.

Seeing Marina Carr's magnificent reworking of the Medea story in *By The Bog Of Cats* in the West End recently, witnessing a tragedy unfold in a way that had myself and everyone around me wet-faced with grief at the end, I felt shattered, sore, and ultimately uplifted. We had watched together an extraordinary tale of sadism and masochism, love and hate, murder and despair, and in our rapturous applause at the end, we came through the darkness and into a shared sense of joy. It touched a place, deep down in our guts, that television never could.

Cruelty is part of life. But we need to know when we're being cruel, we need to see its effects, we need to feel for those who suffer. We need to think about it, talk about it, come into relationship – or relationships – with it. But unconscious cruelty, when we slip into the amoral world that is SM TV, is the stuff of nightmares.

3: LET'S TALK ABOUT SEX

HER SHAVEN HEAD EXPRESSES MORE
THAN WORDS CAN SAY 25TH AUGUST 1993

Admiring the beautiful shorn features of Matthew Devereux on the cover of *Hot Press* recently – mischievous, curiously boyish and teasing – I wanted to know whether the skinhead image appeals erotically to women as much as it does to me. I'm not sure why, but it seems to me to be, in essence, a homoerotic image, enlarging our canon of male pin-ups to embrace wit and honest-to-God deviousness. I wonder, however, how much of his choice to transmogrify into a skinhead was influenced by a conscious decision on the part of his group, The Pale, to adopt an image that is currently fashionable, and how much is his own self-expression. I imagine it is a mixture of both, as in most things.

Once, when someone I had trusted dumped on me, I shaved all my hair off, and went with fire in my belly on the hunt for anonymous sex with as little emotional contact as possible. I was hurting, in a very inaccessible place, and instead of seeking reassurance in the presence of someone kind and generous, I sought, and found, scenarios with men immune to feeling that night, who found the image of the skinhead horny, and the ultimate in sexual object. I became a non-person, a plaything. And when, at dawn, I found myself walking home through the streets of Dublin with grim satisfaction that I had got what I wanted, I wondered what would have happened if someone had shown some kindness, some curiosity as to what had led me to such depths, and not colluded with me in my ritualistic voyage of humiliation. But then perhaps I needed to get it out of my system. Who is to say? It was all safe sex – but it was as devoid of humour and humanity as a man can manage.

The symbolism of the appearance – the bald head, the shaved, pierced and tattooed body: fascist or queer? I'm sorry, I can't tell them, me, us, apart and I can't escape. Didn't fascists annihilate 600,000 of us, the forgotten holocaust? I am in a nightmare fantasy, but it's real. The nightclub is full of watchful eyes in hard, shiny-pated faces, skintight jeans, 14- or 21-hole Doc Martens with white laces. Excuse me, what do white laces mean? "Well, if you're a 'straight' skinhead, it means you're a fascist, a Nazi. If you're a gay skinhead, it means you're into rough sex." How can you tell? "You have to find out for yourself."

A stunningly beautiful dark-skinned man, 6'4" and built like a tank, is being beaten by a smaller white man with a pinched face and boots up to his knees, with an audience of hungry eyes. Afterwards, I watch the two of them having a drink and a laugh. Later still, the Adonis is on his own, his Master nowhere to be seen, and he is looking for more abuse. Or is it sex? Or is it love? Or is it possible to say? For if you stand very close, after a whack of the belt, you can hear the whispered "is that alright?" from the "abuser", and the "abused" nodding in assent with eyes on fire.

Violence is the undercurrent of the skinhead image, as far as I am concerned. It rages in all of us, only some live it out more visibly than others, instead of repressing it, and letting it operate on less visible levels in our psyches. What this identification does to ourselves as feeling human beings is not for me to say, except to suggest that if it is done without being conscious of the resonances, no progress can be made, and the patterns of abuse are perpetuated *ad infinitum*, becoming an essential part of the sexual experience. A man I took home once said that he couldn't come unless he was whipped. It put a dampener on the evening, I can tell you.

Power and impotence: perhaps they are two sides of the same human principle. And the skinhead is to be found on both sides, blurring distinctions. That most vulnerable of suedeheads, Sinéad O'Connor, whose wounds have entered the public domain, finds herself reviled and loved in confusingly overwhelming ways. Her image is achingly resonant of the terrible damage that the human heart can be exposed to. She lives it out for the rest of us, and we respond according to our capacity to understand our own pain and impotence. Those who bitterly complain that if we had her looks and her money we wouldn't be unhappy are missing the point – she wouldn't have driven herself to such poignant creativity had she not been through the experience that she has. It is part and parcel of her life.

What is bewildering, perhaps, for her is that she has the potential to wield considerable influence now, as a world figure – but as someone who has good reason to distrust authority, she is apparently doing all she can to mess up her chances. She is caught in a destructive pattern, which in most of us goes unnoticed. I believe her shaven head expresses more than words can say about her life-experience, and taps into something far deeper in us than mere tonsorial taste should allow.

The story of Samson resonates to this day. Perhaps at some stage in the future she will emerge with flowing tresses, a pride in her own power as a mature woman and a capacity to enjoy it. And leave behind an image that has more to do with eschewing adulthood than embracing it. I hope so.

And what of the other extreme, the skinheads who are on the increase in fascist groups all over Europe, whose credo is hate? I believe they are expressing something not dissimilar – but without the ability or the desire to be creative about it, they externalise their hatred and project it onto others who threaten their shaky sense of identity, as Germans, Britons, or Irish people. But pain is the root of it. The pain of feeling impotent.

As for gay skinheads, we seem to cross an uneasy divide when we play around with power games, throwing into confusion the roles of abuser and abused. The thin line between both fades to insignificance.

THE JOYS OF BEING FUCKED
25TH JANUARY 1995

I was having an enjoyable pint or three with a friend of mine the other evening. When he asked me what I was going to write about this week, I found myself giggling helplessly. I had to retreat into the gents to gather myself, before going back to him, still grinning. For I had just been thinking how I was going to expound, to all you lucky, lucky people, on the joys of being fucked.

I looked at his open, bemused face and I realised that I had suddenly gone extremely shy. Although he is a dear friend with whom I could discuss anything, I sensed that, all the same, my laughter was of the nervous variety. As most laughter is, of course, so I'm not saying much. But it got me thinking.

There is a word that I have never used, except in quotes, when describing people, and that is straight. It is not only because the opposite is bent. It is because there are so many gay people I know who are so conservative and resistant to change that straight is the only *mot juste* for them. And there are also so many other people who refuse classification, not because they are bisexual, but because they see such definitions as inherently limiting. I happen to agree with them. But in that flash of nervousness, I realised that I was about to tell "a straight man" about something intimate and exclusive to my experience of sexuality, as a gay man.

The "straight man" occupies a strange, ambivalent place in the gay pantheon. At once the hated thug and the much-desired love-object, the archetypal Marlboro man's style is slavishly copied by most gay men I know, and quite a few women too. Jeans and check shirt, with at least a short back and sides. It is the uniform of the woodsman, the cowboy, the worker. Singular, independent, cold as ice. Ironically, of course, you can spot a gay man a mile away in that mandrag.

It's not authentic. It is an attempt to evoke a quality of distilled masculinity, which we imagine resides in the "straight man". But what I've discovered through my friendships with men of all persuasions is that the "ideal" remains elusive to us all. But it is only some gay men and some homophobes who worry about attaining it. It's a self-consciousness, a feeling of insecurity about one's image and what it says about us on the inside. When you get to know a "straight man" his individuality transcends any such classification, of course. That goes without saying. Doesn't it?

For some, the "straight man", becomes that obscure object of desire. I have met men whose sexual life centres on searching for previously 100% heterosexual men and having sex with them. It is a challenge, not without its risks. I once had to reassure a colleague of mine, a mother of teenage sons, because a gay man of her acquaintance had been saying to her that, given enough time, he could sleep with any man, including either of her sons. She was quite alarmed, and it would have taken a heart of stone to criticise her. I told her that he was probably boasting, and that if her sons weren't gay, then they wouldn't sleep with him, and she was not to worry. (What would you have said?)

I was thinking of the subject of being fucked because... No, scratch that. I was thinking of writing about the subject of being fucked because, earlier in the week, I had been debating with a heterosexual man who doesn't believe that the HIV virus causes AIDS. He supports a theory, along with quite a few others, that other factors, most importantly drugs of all kinds (including poppers and AZT), come into play to destroy the body's immune defences. He believes that one of the risk factors is (unsafe) anal sex *per se*, which has "unique inherent health risks" and that bodies "aren't designed that way". He insists this is a stance without any moral judgements on homosexuality, for he acknowledges that not all gay men have anal sex, and that not all people who have anal sex are gay men. He was asking for reassurance that he didn't come across as homophobic, that he wanted to befriend gay people, not condemn them.

In response, I found myself saying something like "All homophobes are obsessed with anal sex". A sweeping generalisation, I now concede, but not without its merits. I was thinking primarily of male homophobes, ("Save Ulster from Sodomy"), those who are freaked out by the idea of sameness, of getting close to another man. Especially those who are petrified of being receptive. Emotionally or otherwise. And what's worse, enjoying it.

I firmly believe that what we most despise in others is a reflection of part of our own character, and nowhere does this manifest more clearly than in repressed homosexual men. I watched a rugger bugger recently, who was so incensed by the sight of two queers sitting beside him that he had to keep up a tirade of tedious vitriol to "impress" his bored girlfriend. What was so threatening to him? I believe that we reminded him of a part of himself with which he couldn't cope.

I remember a *Late Late Show* a few years back which addressed the topic of homosexuality, and someone from the audience asked why homosexuals are obsessed with each other's back passages. Quick as a whippet, Gaybo asked "Why are most heterosexuals obsessed with women's front passages?" which earned him a few gold stars in my book. But the fact is – and it's taken me a long time to realise this – practically everyone who isn't gay presumes that when men have sex with each other there is always a "passive" and "active" partner, and that penetration always takes place.

Well, here I am to tell you that it ain't necessarily so. But when we do, we take a good strong condom and lashings of lubrication and...

Now I've gone all shy again. You guys just have to find out for yourself.

YOU KNOW THERE'S NOTHING TO BE ASHAMED OF
3RD APRIL 1996

Fetish *n.* inanimate object worshipped by primitive peoples for its supposed inherent magical powers or as being inhabited by a spirit; principle *etc.* irrationally reverenced; (*Psych.*) abnormal stimulus, or object, of sexual desire; hence ~ism.

Oxford English Dictionary

An older Oxford dictionary on my bookshelf uses the term savages instead of primitive peoples. How the English betray themselves. For what else is a crucifix but a fetish? But then, of course, it's rational to revere a crucifix. Nothing savage or primitive about the English.

It's easy to forget, though, that the cross is a symbol of grotesque torture. If Jesus was put to death in another culture or at another time, we could have grown up with the image of Jesus on a guillotine, or with a noose around his neck, or, perhaps, fried on the electric chair. Yet none of those means of execution involve the time-delay factor of crucifixion, which is the torture. They all seem quite humane in comparison. So for symbolic equivalence, a modern time-warped Messiah's iconography would have to have tastefully assorted images of handcuffs, whips, and chains added.

Nah. Too perverted. More importantly, you'd never see the detail on top of a steeple; it's just too busy an image. No wonder God's graphic designers went for the cross. Simple but effective.

OK. So we've established that all Christians are fetishists. What about Muslims? The Crescent Moon seems inanimate enough a symbol to me, and we in the West project more than enough irrationality onto it. Star of David? God only knows what we've projected onto that. Basically, when it comes down to it, all religions have their icons, their symbols, their objects of worship that are "inhabited by a spirit". When pushed, eccentric pagan that I am, I suspect a candle might have some symbolic resonance for me; but then so do forests and mountains and the sea. In other words, fetishes, in the spiritual sense, are all around us, if we care to look.

When it comes to the sexual meaning of the word, the Oxford definition is even more revealing of English/Western attitudes. For a start, it seems to drip with sickness. It's abnormal; it's derived from Psychology, inferring a pathological condition. In exactly the same way as the first definition refers to the object, the fetish, as something foreign and irrational and nothing to do with English sensibilities, the second definition implies that the only normal object of desire is animate. (And no, I don't mean sheep.)

Ah, normality. I've yet to meet anyone who's normal. If you believe you're normal, then please drop me a line, it would be nice to know what it's like. (A picture postcard from Courtown, Blackpool or Atlantic City springs to mind. I don't know why.) Although, as you are reading my ramblings, your claim to normality would be suspect from the start, I'm afraid.

My first memory of anything fetishistic is quite bizarre, especially for me. I was trudging up a very steep street in a small Welsh village at the age of thirteen or so behind a pair of black stiletto heels, being at the end of a pair of shapely legs, belonging to a Miss Corrina Thomas. I'm amazed I remember her name; I even remember the first line of her address, 24 Maes-y-Llan, although the village is lost in the mist. She was hanging around the older boys in our scout troop, dying for a snog.

I hadn't even begun to shave. We played 'January' by Pilot on the jukebox in the chippie. She was around fifteen, I guess. But I remember the electric charge of that walk, as she was clicking up that hill; it's my most heterosexual moment. And, for your interest, I've never found female drag erotic since: that was a one-off, a phase I went through.

One of the most interesting aspects of the gay scene is the way sexual fetishes are celebrated, from leather to rubber to uniforms to handcuffs to frocks to body piercing to business suits. As we shake off the yoke of "normal" sexual orientation, we also lose a lot of other inhibitions. Sometimes, of course, as with any human characteristic, it can be taken to excess. It can be a very convenient way to avoid getting emotionally involved with someone. If, for example, your particular fetish is for leather, then you can end up not caring who's behind it, as you flit from one leather queen to another. When the object becomes dissociated from the lover, then the lover becomes redundant. And as you devalue the lover, so you devalue yourself.

Or so the classic psychological approach goes. But I'm beginning to wonder. I occasionally go hell-for-leather into fetishistic sex scenes. Each time I do so, the Catholic/psychologist in me says that I shouldn't get so much pleasure from such sex with strangers, that it is an avoidance of relationship, a negation of my, and their, humanity. But another part of me knows that that is bullshit. Sex is, in essence, a wonderful, natural activity; its wonder lies in its unfathomable mystery; its nature being essentially dark. It is the one thing guaranteed to bring us down to our animalistic, instinctual natures, to remind us that reason and intellect and social status and good intentions count for nothing in the greater scheme of things. Fetishes remind us of this; they are symbols for that descent into the sensual world, be they stiletto heels or motorbike helmets.

In this culture, where we are so hell-bent on trying to rationalise and psychologise and understand everything, perhaps there are some things, like sex, which cannot be grasped in that way. Maybe the way to deal with sex, and the objects and activities that are sexually charged for us, is to follow the link that exists in the double meaning of the word fetish.

Celebrate sex: imbue your fetishes with a sense of mystery, a spirit of adventure, and a "savage" magic. You know there's nothing to be ashamed of. Deep down.

SOUNDS OF ZIPS AND GROANS AND SLAPS DRIFTED THROUGH THE NIGHT AIR
26TH JUNE 1996

"I want you to find happiness, and stop having fun."
– Marilyn Monroe, ticking off a list of rich eligible bachelors, to Jane Russell, intent on dating the entire American Olympic team, in *Gentlemen Prefer Blondes*.

Having fun and happiness: opposites on a romantic scale. Or so they say.

I had my eyes opened this weekend; I finally understood something about the London gay subculture, and I am currently wrestling with what I learned.

I went to Hampstead Heath, at night, for the first time. It's the sort of experience which is lifechanging, in many ways, for it explained to me something about the difficulty I have had in the past relating to Londoners. Or, more specifically, trying to maintain a monogamous relationship with those who have absorbed the values of the London scene. After living here for three years, I still hadn't quite appreciated the scale of competition that's out there to forming a real relationship; I still couldn't understand the way men treat each other here, after a sexual liaison. That is, with complete nonchalence.

Now that is not to say that I am an angel in these matters – but nine times out of ten, if I see someone I've had sex with before, I will try to catch their eye and smile if I see them in a pub or club; it is, it seems to me, only civilised. Time and time again, I've been frozen out of it, which I can't help but be depressed by. My mistake, I now see, was to take it personally. In the London scene, with the Heath as one of its major elements, at least during the summer, nothing is personal.

In my last major relationship here, I felt that I was constantly losing out to someone else, and that that someone else was anonymous. I had to deal repeatedly with the hurt I felt at his infidelity with strangers; my values were exposed, time and time again, to be out of kilter with his. Mine felt classically guilt-ridden and uptight and Catholic in comparison, those of a shrewish, possessive, clingy wife.

I have watched at close quarters young Irish gay boyz move to London, and observed how they come to terms with the prevailing attitude to sex. For some it is upsetting, but they manage to keep a sense of themselves, a sense of "decency", even though they are sailing against the wind. Others lose their inhibitions almost overnight, and dive right in to hedonism – and who can blame them? I certainly don't; you're only young once. I may worry about the price you pay – but I'm in my thirties. It's only natural.

And so to the Heath. It has been described to me as "the last great haven of unfettered guilt-free sexual exploration." I'll come to the guilt-free part later, but it is undoubtedly the most extraordinary sexual arena I've ever encountered. On a local pirate radio station recently, someone was interviewed in his role as the distributor of free condoms on the Heath. He was asked how many men cruised the park at night. The answer was that on a recent bank holiday weekend, under a full moon, there were probably thousands. They ran out of condom packs, after eight hundred.

The local police have recently come to an understanding with the representatives of the "gay community" and do not enter the park after dark, unless there is trouble. So, with this semi-official seal of approval, there are now stalls lit by gaslight at the entrance to the woods, staffed by volunteers handing out condoms to all who enter. The car park is constantly full. There's a doner kebab van on the main road, open all night, doing a roaring trade.

Having stepped down past the lights, I found myself quite blind, for about ten minutes or so. I gingerly trod my way along the path, banishing all thoughts of Mirkwood and Little Red Riding Hood. Standing off the track, waiting for my eyes to work, I became aware that the forest was teeming with men, trekking downhill on well-worn, familiar paths. As the shadows began to yield their secrets, I realised that everywhere I looked were men, standing, waiting, hunting. And these were not the singular furtive figures familiar to Irish eyes in parks late at night; these were men totally at home in this environment, sure to meet someone to fulfill their fantasies. And what fantasies they were! As I walked further and further into the woods, I was overwhelmed with the variety of men and their costumes. There were monstrous leather Big Daddies, and mean-looking skinheads. There were men in suits, complete with briefcases. There were cute little ravers in skimpy shorts, with glazed eyes; punks with teeshirts and boots and nothing else. There were bikers, somehow untouchable, with helmets and gloves, getting off on their image, but not apparently with anyone else. Sounds of zips and groans and slaps drifted through the night air, and when I looked up, there were the stars, silent and watchful.

As I waited for the night bus at 4am, along with about twenty others, dawn was breaking behind me over London. Around me were ordinary faces, tired, cold, sleepy. They had expressions on their faces not unlike those of cleaning ladies on the first bus into town – there was nothing burning now, just a dull, common humanity. The fantasies were spent; the demons that drove them there were vanquished. Drove us there.

Was it guilt-free for me? Probably. But someone I met disturbed me because he was so handsome, and we had sex smiling, which was heart-warming. Typically for me, at the end I was left wanting. Wanting to see him again, to know all about him, wondering how on Earth I could ever arrange my life to include the daily presence of such a gorgeous-looking creature.

But it cannot be. The implicit contract in such meetings on the Heath is that they are transient, anonymous and exploitative. The fact that they are mutually exploitative, and fun, is beside the point. He went off with a smile and a wave, and I shivered inside.

Never wanted to. What am I to do? I can't help it.

VIAGRA AND THE DIAL-A-PIZZA WORLD OF CASUAL SEX
29 APR 1998

There's a pill now that offers the promise of the permanent stiffy. Already, after only a few weeks, Viagra is the fastest-selling prescription drug in United States' history. No doubt its appeal will not be any less potent on this side of the Atlantic.

I know that I should tut-tut this development, bemoan the desire for the quick fix that seemingly affects every aspect of modern life. The argument goes that there's going to be a whole new generation of people who will use this pill to enhance their sexual prowess, who will then become so accustomed to it that they feel uncomfortable without it, and so a new addiction is born. It may not be a chemical addiction, for it may not work that way; but anything can be addictive, if it carries some symbolic meaning for the addict. Not only the obvious baddies like smack and alcohol, but the goodies, too, like food and sex.

Cigarette smoking is addictive for me in the psychological sense more than the physical; I use it as an odd kind of anger regulator. With every drag of a cigarette, I suck in my erstwhile ferocious temper, and although sometimes seeming a bit too much like Bette Davis, it works to give me a smouldering, pleasantly poisonous way of coping with my feelings. When I am not smoking, and I regularly give up every year for six months or more, I am noticeably quicker to rise, less tempered in my response to antagonism. I'm more in-your-face and a lot less charming and deferential to those who annoy me.

I'm a month off the fags now, again, and still at my most volatile. The other day, I was cycling down the street, in a cycle lane, and there was a kid walking along it in front of me. As I veered out of the way, into the main traffic lane, I roared out "Get off the road, kid!" in a blunt sort of fashion. As I passed, I realised that far from being a kid, it was a diminutive woman, four foot nothing, who had a temper to match mine. She roared back at me "KID?" and started picking up traffic cones to throw at me. She was apoplectic with rage. I yelled back at her that if she behaved like one, then she would get called one. Then she started running after me. I swear to you that I didn't use any other, more offensive, word than kid, dear reader, you know I would tell you if I had. I took advantage of my pedal power and cycled away as fast as I could. I've had a lot of encounters like that since I quit. I'd like to be calmer, I really would.

The other activity on which I am prone to being "hooked" is the dial-a-pizza world of casual sex, here in London. It's hard to explain to those who haven't experienced it just how easy it is to find a sexual partner if you're gay and you know which telephone numbers to ring, or if you know which IRC channel to visit on the Internet. It is mind-bogglingly quick. The other week I felt horny, picked up the phone, immediately got chatting to someone who was calling from his mobile phone just two minutes away from my flat; I gave him directions, met him outside, fancied him, and took him back for a no-strings-attached frolic. It was as simple as that.

That's by no means unusual, except for the fact that he was in my bed five minutes after I had picked up the phone; within an hour is the usual timescale. What's also possible, if you are prepared to forgo the immediate gratification of the local *plat du jour* in favour of a more exotic dish, is to find someone who's into playing out a particular fantasy that you share, or one that you'd like to try. The only limit is your imagination and even that will be stretched by the imagination of others, which never ceases to amaze. The problem with anything to which you are addicted, is that the last experience has to be "topped" by the next, otherwise the buzz isn't as intense. And it is the buzz that matters, gratification is King. The gambler has to go for the big one, risking everything for the last great chance for fortune. The E-head has to take five on the night instead of the two he used to take a few months back. The alcoholic's journey to numbness takes a half-bottle of gin longer than it did last year. A masochist told me recently, with a mixture of shame and pleasure, that his ambition as a human ashtray was to work his way up from cigarettes to cigars. I was glad I had given up smoking.

Mostly via the safe anonymity of the Internet, I've talked to guys into being "asphyxiated", beaten up, burnt, "raped", pissed and shat on, whipped and cuffed and put in stocks or wrapped in clingfilm and hung upside down for days. Each person has their own particular fetish, their own sexual metaphor that makes sense to them, that offers them release when it is enacted. I've been trying to establish what reasons could possibly exist for such distortions of the sexual impulse and I have drawn a blank each time. Each person's reasons are different, unique to them and most say that they don't know, it just turns them on. One guy, when a teenager, experienced someone accidentally falling over him, and winding him, at a party; the guy had landed with all his weight on his belly. His fetish now is to repeat that early experience of being winded, by being punched and/or kicked in the guts. He doesn't want sex; he can get that with his boyfriend; he just wants, every now and again, to relive that adrenaline rush. Another guy I've talked to always played with plastic bags as a child, enjoying the danger and thrill of near-suffocation; it's part of his sexual repertoire now. He thinks it's a bit sick, but keeps on doing it anyway. He doesn't know why.

Some guys aren't into being psychoanalysed of course, don't take kindly to my questions, and tell me to fuck off and I'd be lying if I said all these discussions were undertaken in the spirit of journalisitic research alone. I have been a horny bugger and played some interesting games recently; each time parting with a kiss and a smile after doing some things that would make your eyes water. But now I've called a halt. Most importantly, it is to test whether I can or not, to wonder aloud if I'm addicted or not. Strangely, it feels rather like quitting cigarettes. I feel like chewing on something. Can't imagine why.

I am near forgetting the mystery of another human being, the joy of slowly getting to know someone, the attraction of letting sex follow feelings, letting it be an expression of them. As with anything, it is hard to resume a normal relationship with a substance or activity after you've experienced addiction. The alcoholic can't just have a glass of wine with a meal; the gambler can't just buy one lottery ticket; it remains to be seen whether I've strayed too far down the soulless cyber highway to do a U-turn.

As for Viagra, I think I'll give it a miss. I like limp dicks anyway. Those who are going to get hooked on it are probably those who would get hooked on something else to "assist" their potency, such as pornography. Getting hooked is one of life's mysteries: everyone does it in some way or other. There's a gap in everyone that can't be filled, no matter what we do.

SADO-MASOCHISM AND THE PRINCIPLE OF CONSENT
11TH NOVEMBER 1998

I went to hear a woman called Pat Califia speak this weekend. She's lesbian, an SM activist, poet, pornographer, and counsellor, from San Francisco. She was speaking as part of a weekend organised by SM Pride, the organisation that used to be "Countdown on Spanner", which was formed to defend the men jailed for consensual sadomasochistic sexual activities. The weekend was being filmed by Channel 4 – no doubt in a few months' time some of you will be able to watch it at 2am or some other "safe" time, to protect the children from corruption. Other events on the agenda included workshops on Japanese rope knotting techniques, and a seminar on watersports

– and I don't mean scubadiving.

I was greatly impressed by Califia's humour and her candour. I blame my mother, of course, for introducing me to her writing. She had an essay included in a collection called *Dick for a Day*, in which a number of women were invited to imagine what they would do and how they would feel if they had a penis for a day. As I was borrowing her copy to read, my mother said something about how the only one of the women who seemed to have any fun was Califia, in her essay 'Dildo Envy and other Phallic Adventures'. When I read the book later, I found I agreed with her; but I was also was highly amused at the fact that my mother had picked out the most pervy story of the lot of them. There's life in the old girl yet...

Califia's speech was intended to set an agenda for what she called the "SM community". Now she herself admits that she's a political creature, who cut her teeth in the feminism of the '70s. Americans seem to be more able to define themselves in terms of groups or communities than Europeans; it seems to be a splintered, tribal thing. As for me, I find it difficult to reconcile myself to the "gay" community to which I supposedly belong; I look around a pub full of gay men on display, looking as cold and indifferent as they can be, and I want to be beamed up, so alien do I feel. I went to a leather club that night, where I noticed a very tall man standing moodily in the corner for ages. I went up to him and asked him if he found that people were intimidated by his height, and did anyone say hello to him? (He must have been six foot seven or so). He smiled a lovely smile, but then said "That's not the best way". I didn't know what he meant, so I left it, standing beside him like an eejit. I should have said "what is the best way?" – but I can never think of smart ripostes in real life, only on internet chats. Ten minutes later he was chatting to a gym bunny in a rubber suit, and I thought to myself that some things will always remain a mystery to me: what looks plastic and generic in my eyes seems to be highly attractive to others.

Califia's belief is that people who are into SM are, just like those into more straightforward or "vanilla" sex, unable to change their sexuality. She therefore believes that it should not be pathologised, or seen as sick. For some of us, the fetishes that get us going are related to control, humiliation, submission, domination; for others, experiencing pain is a distinct pleasure. For so long, I've wondered about the healthiness of indulging in acts which seem to have nothing to do with love. I've met some severely fucked-up people who centre their lives on a particular fetish, to the exclusion of everything else. I've seen one guy who has lost his house and job because he's so obsessed. I simply haven't encountered many sane individuals who are into SM. But perhaps that's simply because they are riddled with shame and self-loathing because of society's attitudes to their sexuality rather than anything intrinsically damaging about their fetish.

I really don't know. I believe that there's a raw, existential truth to sadomasochism: life can be humiliating and painful, we may be powerless, we can get dumped on all the time. By eroticising these experiences we may feel that we triumph over them. Certainly everyone who's into SM is highly sensitive; some, too sensitive for this world. The thicker the leather, the softer the inside. Sometimes I believe the hunt for fetishistic sex is about a need for something transpersonal, almost magical, to happen; the costumes and the paraphernalia add to what is essentially a theatrical, ritual performance. Perhaps the disappointment that most of us feel when romantic love fades into friendship happens when the magic goes. The leather/rubber drag of SM can be Magick, a hypnotic celebration of the taboo pleasures of the senses. It is only in the West that SM exists; in other cultures, you have to look to spiritual practices to find a similar preoccupation with the experience of pain. But for them, there is a deep meaning behind each act, as a Fakir pierces his stomach with a sword or a Filipino gets crucified at Easter. In the West, as with most other things, the sense of meaning can go missing from sex. Perhaps this new SM "community" is part of a new wave, in which some fundamental issues to do with being human are being addressed; issues of power and sensuality and meaning; and, most fundamentally, the principle of informed consent.

Fine in theory, of course, but in practice fantasy has a habit of fading. Unless one is actually having sex with someone you love, not for how well they play the role of master or servant, but for the type of person they are, then their richness as a human being can't be enjoyed. And that's one of the dangers of roleplaying; one can become less interested in people, and only interested in how well they fit the role of the fantasy playmate. That search never ends, and can end in despair.

So many times I've put the cart before the horse when it comes to sex, searching for the frisson of intense sex rather than finding someone loving with whom it would be fun to play. Trouble is, that's not something you can conjure up. SM sex is but a means to an end, like most sex; a personal, private, consensual act of trust and feeling between two people. Too often SM can be seen to be the end in itself. That way lies madness. Or so I've been told.

IF I WERE MONICA I'D HAVE BEEN ON MY KNEES IN A FLASH
20TH OCTOBER 1998

"Sometimes a cigar is just a cigar" – Sigmund Freud

The lack of sophistication of American culture is at once both its most endearing and its most depressing feature. The zeal with which they test the limits of their legal system to absurd extremes in the public arena, believing that it is a symptom of a healthy, open, just society, beggars belief. Instead of being a system of checks and balances in the service of justice, the law has taken on a life of its own, a feral parasite strangling its host, starving it of the oxygen of common sense and moderation.

The laws against sexual harassment are based on a number of blinkered assumptions about the nature of sexuality. The connection between power and sex was always assumed to be a one-way street: those in power would abuse their position to "take advantage" of those in their employ by suggesting or instigating sexual relations with them. I don't for one moment deny that such abuse of power takes place in the workplace every day, but my interest is in sexuality and how it's defined, not unfair employment conditions. Having sex is not in itself unfair – but power and powerlessness can be very sexy.

The phallocentric assumption is that a sexual relationship between two people of unequal status is always instigated by the boss, placing the lower-ranked individual (assumed to be a woman) in an invidious position. She then feels pressurised: she may not be able to cope with the pressure to start or continue or end or refuse a relationship for fear of damaging her employment prospects. It is assumed that her "active" employer would be the only one to gain from the liaison, enjoying the buzz of having a "passive" employee in his thrall. That any pleasure the woman may have had could not be taken into account, because only relationships between "equals" are valid, so the law infers. Any responsibility she may have for her part in the relationship is assumed to be suspect because of the inferior socio-economic position of women; it is assumed that she is denied the dignity of full adult responsibility because of her femaleness, and the law is there to protect her against him and against all Bosses. Victim Woman, economically enslaved, sexually objectified, lost in the machinations of a patriarchy that disregards her humanity – this is the pathetic creature the law is designed to protect. But bizarrely, this is the sort of woman it creates, too. With such a definition enshrined in law, it serves to rob women of their responsibility for their own actions, in the choices they make to keep a job, to have sex, to be in emotional relationship. Any choice she makes to place emotions or passion ahead of her career is deemed to be irrelevant; she should not be in such a position in the first place, therefore she needs to be protected against herself, against making such an "unwise" choice. Women in the workplace are immature girls needing a shield of legal armour to protect them from the big bad world.

The fact that it is framed in gender-neutral terminology, allowing for employees of either sex to take action against bosses of either sex, is a red herring here; it is assumed that the sex-roles of the active partner and the passive partner are allied with the hierarchy of their employment status. This actually enshrines a patriarchal view of the world in law, as opposed to eroding it. Far from being revolutionary and liberating, such anti-harassment legislation fails completely to encompass the full spectrum of sexual expression, serving to hobble sexual independence and equality instead of promoting it.

I know this is not the conventional view, but in power terms, Monica Lewinsky was in charge in the sexual relationship with her boss. She initiated the sex. She was the pursuer, he the pursued. She had the power to destroy his reputation and his marriage, she was the one who lied to him about keeping their relationship secret. That she told eleven people directly about the affair implies that the whole of Washington must have known about it.

I'm not saying that Clinton was the victim of a scheming, manipulative woman. That would be far too queer of me. I am saying that sexuality can't be defined as a one-way street of active person in power "doing it" to a passive impotent person. The sex between the Starr-crossed lovers became the matter of public enquiry because of the assumption that all sex between powerful people and their "minions" is symptomatic of abuse, instead of being the most natural thing in the world. Lewinsky's complete lack of discretion reveals Girl-Woman at her most naïve, playing an adult's game. She may have revealed a powerful unconscious urge to destroy the man she claimed to love, but this was well matched by his flair for self-immolation. At some level, she knew that by telling her friends about the affair that she was asking them to lie for her, possibly in court, given that the atmosphere at the time was heavy with the Paula Jones lawsuit. He knew what sort of child she was, but still he succumbed; although he has more willpower than I could ever imagine possessing, by resisting her aching pleas for him to fuck her. I'm sure if he did she would have conceived within the hour.

I suspect Bill Clinton believes in his hair-splitting legal definition of what constitutes sex. The fact that he didn't fuck her, when there was no practical reason not to, implies that in some way the split was real for him. He's a redneck Southern Christian: perhaps he learned about sex from a Southern gal or two in his youth, assuring him that it was alright if they didn't go all the way. I imagine he must have thought all his Christmases had come at once when Monica started her striptease for him; here was excitement from an unexpected source, and he didn't have to do a thing except let it happen.

The President played the passive role in this sexual encounter, something anti-harassment law didn't bargain for and that has given him the loophole through which he can defend his porkies.

I'm trying to see how my sexual morality would hold up if I were in either Bill or Monica's situation. Immersed in the no-holds-barred hedonism of the London gay scene, my world and theirs couldn't be more different. And yet sexuality is universal; as Woody Allen says, all sex is shameful and dirty, if you do it right. I know a gay couple who are involved in a loving relationship for over a decade; they do have sex sometimes with other men, but only what they call "hand shandies" in a park or sauna; they reserve fucking for their relationship alone. It's a double-standard, but it's their double standard.

If I were Monica, and I knew my boss fancied me by the way he met my gaze, I would have been on my knees in a flash, but I would most certainly have treasured the memory and kept it to myself, and not sullied it with any dreams of romance or commitment. I've had sex with too many married men to have any illusions. Although I bet Bill would probably have wanted to get shagged; most married men in my experience do, at least once.

If I were Bill, in a stable relationship, and some handsome youth lingered behind in my office with doe-eyes and a bulging packet, I don't know what I would have done if he'd started to show me his jockstrap. It is quite possible I would have just wanked and watched, not touching, attempting to keep some boundaries intact. But probably I would have gone wild with the buzz of danger, and devoured his young body. Then I'd have transferred him to Hawaii.

But my cigar would have remained in its box.

THE MOST DAMNING INDICTMENT OF MEN I HAVE SEEN SINCE DACHAU
14TH JUNE 2000

I saw a pornographic video involving children recently. I can't go into great detail here: the tape is now with the police. I've never before "shopped" anyone, and it goes against my nature to do so, but in the increasingly amoral world that gay men have created, especially with new technology, the twenty-first century seems to be becoming one in which we each have to make our own moral stance and stick by it, and pay the price for it, if necessary. The "wild frontier" in cyberspace is the shame barrier; it has been blasted to pieces in the name of liberation, of progress, of commerce. The price I may pay now is getting involved more than I want to, associating myself with an issue that is so highly charged that rationality is very hard to maintain. And the police are not known for their sensitivity; the difference between pederast and homosexual is not one that is obvious to the average detective, I imagine. But what is disturbing to me is that gay men who are only focused on erotic pleasure may not be clear on the difference themselves, and such blurry vision is not acceptable.

We, as gay men, seem happy to allow the borders of the old morality to be airbrushed away, in the name of tolerance and sexual diversity: acceptance of all sorts of sexual activities is now the norm. Now don't get me wrong, I'm glad that whatever I get up to with other men is not subject to outside scrutiny or the law. I am my own worst moralist when it comes to sex; no one else judges me as harshly as I do, and I have yet to free myself of a whole pile of guilt on sexual matters. But, when it comes down to it, it's my choice whether I choose kindness and warmth or cold perversity – and if it's the latter, it's always with consent and always with a sense of trust in the man, which has, I realise, yet to be abused. My biggest mistake has been perhaps to mix the two up, but that's another story.

Children can give no such consent, for they may not know how much their trust is being abused at the time, until later on, when they try to establish a healthy identity as a grown man or woman, and attempt loving relationships. It's a brave few survivors of abuse who can emerge into adulthood as warm and kind people; not seeing themselves as victims; unlearning the lesson that love, sex and trust involves humiliation and manipulation and feeling like an object, a plaything, instead of a whole, loving, confident person with a will and a soul. (But that takes bravery for most sensitive people, regardless.) Some may eroticise their feelings, and turn old rage into new pleasure; but pervery offers diminishing returns, and keeps emotions stuck exactly as they are. It's hard to contain it in a loving relationship, for there are two different forces at work. Love and rage erode each other; if there is enough love, the rage will wither; if there isn't, rage triumphs, and love is destroyed.

Some survivors may bury their pain through drugs or alcohol, or unsafe sex, and destroy themselves slowly; they may become "escorts" because they might as well make a living out of what life has taught them; questions about what it's doing to their inner life are met with a philosophical shrug. No one cared about their inner life when they were children, why should they start now? Prisons are populated with those who were abused sexually as children. Some may simply end it all with suicide, because the pain is unendurable. And some others may shut it all away and pretend nothing happened, until, as parents or guardians themselves, they find themselves repeating the abuse down the generations, for they associate childish love with sex, and some part of them has never come to terms with it, has never grieved for the loss of their innocence, and does not value it in others.

The tape was appallingly easily available, and was being offered via a medium that was not overtly pervy; it was just gay men looking to meet or chat with each other. The pornographer was a mild-mannered, easy-going man. I took a great risk in getting involved; my (perhaps naive) intention, when I realised what was on offer, was to do an undercover job to discover just how easy it was to obtain, and, if it was really child pornography, to do something about it, but I didn't know what. In the time it was in my flat, for about 12 hours overnight, even with the covering letter to the police written, and the envelope addressed to them, waiting for a stamp, I was aware of how my career and reputation were extremely vulnerable to destruction, with a knock on the door and a search warrant. Even writing about this now is sailing close to the wind; but it's too near to my heart to ignore, and it cuts right to the core of what my beliefs are.

I did consider destroying the tape and forgetting about it; but the faces of the children involved would not let me. Yes, I watched it. I am not sorry I watched it. Men can do the most appalling things in the name of pleasure; the tape was proof of how men can switch off feelings completely, the most damning indictment of men I have ever witnessed since I visited Dachau as a teenager. But this tape was more chilling, in a way, in that the children had to look as if they were having fun; it was in the close-ups on the young faces, waiting to be told how to act, being trained how to please, that the full horror became apparent to me.

This new world, this 21st-century nation that we inhabit, is not Ireland or the United Kingdom; it is global and anarchic, and not subject to any enforceable laws. While debate goes on about how constitutional democracy is under threat, with fewer and fewer people bothering to vote, the real challenge is far more serious: that voting for a parliamentarian is becoming increasingly irrelevant. Every type of abuse that governments try to control is happening on the Net now, or in the burgeoning, unmonitored world of telephone communications.

The government of Albania fell recently due to its endorsement of a pyramid-selling scheme; but every day I receive spam emails inviting me to take part in similar get-rich-quick scams. Computer virus writers threaten the global economy, which becomes more vulnerable to attack the more it depends on the Net. Who could have foreseen that global disruption of our banking and telephone systems, as happened recently, would depend on whether a country like the Phillippines had an up-to-date law, with the whole world waiting for a judge in Manila to get out of bed and acknowledge the importance of what was happening?

Terrorists, the most anti-democratic of individuals, gain comfort in finding like-minded people all over the world, and obtain their information on how to make bombs from the Internet, as baby-faced David Copeland did when he was planning to murder gay men in Soho and black people in Brixton and Asians in Brick Lane last year. He saw no shame in what he was doing; he was as insulated from morality as the men I saw in the video tape with those children.

There have always been immoral people; the danger is now that the Internet brings them together and they develop a discourse, a framework that justifies their thoughts and actions, without any challenge or debate, or thought for the emotional impact of their actions. Morality is unfashionable now, especially among gay men, and most especially when we are looking for sex. The old moral order was nation-bound, formal, institutional, religious, shame-based. Twenty-first century morals have no external authority to support or enforce them, in cyberspace, which is our new space, the matrix which is increasingly becoming the world's nervous system. We can only guide ourselves – and I, for one, am woefully unprepared for the world in which I find myself, for I still harbour sentimental illusions about how the world, my world, should have been.

The answer lies, perhaps, in education; a way of encouraging children to educate themselves about how to live in the new millennium, where anarchy reigns, and to teach them ethical responsibility, developing their own conscience, and to make fundamental decisions for themselves, aware of the implications. All old notions that the world is a safe and comforting place will have to be discarded; we may fondly wish it were, but it does children a grave disservice to be ignorant of the world's shadow.

I do not seek to remove innocence, but to protect it. The computer in the bedroom or schoolroom is a portal to every possible seduction that exists on this planet, more threatening to innocence and love than any dirty old man in a raincoat hanging around a park late at night. We can keep children in at night. But the devil is within, more than he has ever been before.

PERVERTS, THROW OFF YOUR CHAINS!
26TH MAY 2000

I've been immersed in meaty psychoanalytic theory recently, which has stripped away all sentimentality with regard to sexuality. About time too, I hear you say. In particular, a book called *Perversion: the Erotic form of Hatred* has given me a lot of food for thought. Allow me to vomit it up for your delectation, in easy-to-digest little pieces. But make sure you take no pleasure from it.

Gay men are so nice in public, aren't we? We dress well, we take care not to offend, we're kind and understanding; we're every mother's dream, we're a girl's best friend. Wistfully, women will remark how we're "such a waste": we're such wonderful companions that surely the sex thing could be overcome, if we put our mind to it. They imagine that we'd be fumbling and kind and earnest in bed, for we would not be like the brutish heterosexual men who are so cold and aggressive and run at the first sign of commitment. We do a good line in self-deprecating humour, and we sure know how to party. We're entertaining, artistic and charming; we may be moody, but we're forgiven easily, because we're so sweet.

When we get upset, we have little hissy fits, rather than getting angry, because we're so sensitive. We're like pre-Suffragette Victorian ladies, swooning with attacks of the vapours. We're so unlucky in love that we gain sympathy easily, as we regale our friends and colleagues with stories of the perfidy of men, that will have most women nodding in understanding. But we bounce back, ready to fall in love again the next weekend. It's all a bit of a lark, isn't it? And, slowly, imperceptibly, it doesn't seem to matter that we fry our brains with ecstasy, or that instead of the occasional drink, we find ourselves "popping in, to see who's around" in the pub every night, accustoming ourselves to evenings made fuzzy and warm with alcohol. For at night, in our private lives, away from our public daytime personae, we play dangerous games with our feelings, seeking perverse pleasure wherever it can be found.

Perversion is everywhere, says the author of this insidious but persuasive little book, Robert Stoller. Every time a man (for it is mostly men) look upon a person as a sex object, it is perverse. Every time a man uses pornography, or gets turned on by a stiletto heel or a Doc Marten boot, it is perverse. Every time there is a seduction as opposed to a courtship, perversity reigns. I'm sure you're getting the idea. Every man is a pervert, and quite a few women. He's describing a universal state, the capacity to get turned on by actions or objects or things that have nothing to do with making love with a person, and everything to do with sexual gratification. But he's more interested, naturally, being a shrink, in the more extreme perversions − sadomasochism, fetishism, gender confusion, and, from his point of view, homosexuality. If I were politically correct, I would shun his book like the plague, screaming homophobia − but then I abandoned political squeamishness a long time ago. I'll try any label on for size − gay, queer, sex addict, pervert − see if it fits, and then discard them all. Today I'm wearing my pervert hat. A natty little number, don't you agree? No? Tough shit.

He wrote the book in the 1970s, and his tone is enquiring, not judgmental. He freely admits the ubiquity of heterosexual perversity, thereby rendering his inclusion of homosexuality as a perversion as a nonsense. We are not responsible for the sex of the people we find attractive, but we are responsible for the way we treat them, and ourselves, sexually. In this, he has helped me realise that many ways in which we relate to each other sexually as gay men are deeply perverse; indeed, the whole gay male subculture has centred itself commercially and socially around the maintenance, if not celebration, of perversity − escorts, phonelines, and saunas fund the mainstream gay press.

But far from being rebels and anarchists, most perverts are deeply conservative in public, and keep their perversions, their rage, to themselves. Yes, rage: scratch a pervert and you'll find a furious little boy. That is, unless scratching him turns him on; if so, find another way of getting under his skin. Layers of leather and rubber serve to protect the most thin-skinned of souls.

In perversion, the fury of a wounded spirit is turned into a private game, a pleasurable re-enactment of old hurts. There is a sense of triumph when we persuade someone to play a perverse game with us; we have won, made ourselves or the other parties into objects, to be played with, hurt, humiliated, or treated with cold indifference. Oh, oh, oh, stop! I'm coming. Horny, nice one. Who can I play that game with next? Oh yes, here's another who knows the score, who can pretend with me that what I'm doing is fun. It's just horny, that's all; it means nothing. Mmmm, you play that game well. But don't take it seriously, right? It's only a game. Jeez, I'll see you around. (Heavy, he's taking it too seriously. Doesn't he see it's only a game?) Next!

And so it goes on, the script stays more or less the same, but with different characters; we get stuck in a play that we are condemned to repeat, a queasy, familiar nightmare. Sometimes we change the words, take different roles; but the finale, the drumroll leading to orgasmic applause, is when we watch that knife go in, and someone gets to feel just like an object, not a person. Roll right up, take your seats please for the next performance of The Victim's Revenge, for the theatre is empty and we can't watch it go dark. That would feel too lonely. Today, our hero will play the part of the Victim, and the part of Persecutor will be taken by A.N. Other. Or is it the other way around? No matter. It's all in the script. Who writes this shit, anyway?

We may be surprised to discover that as long as we keep our theatrical performances private, it is mainstream society that most stands to gain from the way we have sexualised our suffering, and keep it to ourselves. If perverts were to stop getting distracted by the pleasures of the flesh, to tear up our customised scripts of The Victim's Revenge, stop the endless search for new cast members, something dangerous might happen.

We might start getting really angry. We might allow ourselves to feel powerful. We might threaten those who have hurt us – we might even threaten to hurt right back. We might find the courage to stand up and be counted and work towards changing the rotten state of affairs that exists in this world, in the gay scene, in the way women treat men, and men treat women. We might challenge the institutions that have wreaked such havoc in our personal lives: the church, the education system, the claustrophobic institution of the family, the government. The pharmaceutical multinationals. We might disturb a few people, shock them with the evidence of how hurt and angry men can get. We might offend our families or our neighbours; we might make life less comfortable for those who seek to defend the family as the model for healthy child-rearing. We might dare to draw the link between how hurt we were as little boys and how scared we are as grown men; it might dawn on us that we don't have to be victims any more. But hey, that's too radical; that might take real courage. There's no script to tell us what to say. We might fail. Now that's a real challenge.

The Christian church has long had a tradition of masochism, the denial and flagellation of the body, to attain spiritual ecstasy; the symbol, the cross, of Christianity is a grotesque instrument of sadistic torture, an emblem of suffering, martyred flesh. It is no accident that homosexuality as a construct, and sadomasochism as a practice, is predominantly a Western phenomenon, a Judeo-Christian inheritance. The tighter the grip a fundamentalist, Christian, body-hating ethos has on an individual or society, the more prevalent the underground reaction in the form of perverse sexuality. The pervert is the shadow of Christian morality, and therefore inextricably bound up with Christianity; take away Christian aversion to pleasures of the flesh, and the pervert loses his *raison d'être*.

The pervert and the priest, in other words, are two manifestations of the same archetypal principle, and are more alike than either would care to admit. The *status quo* is maintained as long as the pervert keeps his life secret, for that keeps the priest in his pulpit. When perversion ceases to be private, that's when real social change happens. In Ireland this began to happen when it was reported in the early 1990s that a priest died in a gay sex club in Dublin, and was given the last rites by two other attending priests. Along with other clerical child sex abuse scandals, when priests were discovered to be incapable of following the strict moral code of the church, this served as an engine for social change, loosening the choking grip that Mother Church had on Ireland since its foundation. But that started with an accident, an old man dying of a heart attack where he shouldn't have.

Far more interesting is George Michael, who was outed as a pervert when he was found, as he knew he might be, flashing his bum to a pretty police officer in LA. Instead of disappearing into shameful silence, he shocked us all with evidence, hitherto invisible, that he had a sense of humour, with his mocking video for 'Outside'. In interviews that followed, he displayed a thoughtfulness and a maturity that was light years away from the closeted, precious creep he had been up to then. Public nice boy, private pervert. Public pervert, grown-up complex man.

Perverts, throw off your chains. Stop being nice. There are real battles to be fought, and real injustices to be righted. Shock the world, for the world needs shocking.

THE GAME: MAGIC OF A DIFFERENT ORDER
8TH JUNE 2000

He was tall – very tall, about 6' 5" – and lean, with a broad back and yet he obviously didn't go to the gym; he had a cute little paunch. He was topless, and wore close-fitting cream chinos, hanging low, showing his Calvins and his pert bum; he had a shaved head, and deep eyes, and a lovely smile. I was watching him in the club; there was something about him that was magnetic. It wasn't just his height, it was something else I couldn't put my finger on. He was chatting with someone; I watched him from behind as he leaned gracefully down, like a giraffe, to his shorter companion; his smile was sweet. He was about 28.

He left the shorter one to go to the backrooms; I followed. He caught my eye; the look that was exchanged was direct but without heat; it was clear he didn't want to play with me, but it was also clear that he didn't mind me around; I would have sensed anything else. Neutral. Fair enough by me; I was getting far too much pleasure watching, to ignore him. Soon enough, he had found someone to play The Game with: a short, stocky, tattooed cropped and noseringed guy in his forties. In the backroom, Tall Guy played him to perfection, using him for his pleasure, mixing domination and gentleness in an easy, confident style. Gently, but firmly, he pulled Nosering's nipples, until he squirmed; slowly but firmly he forced him down to suck and gag on his big cock. His wide hands enveloped Nosering's cropped skull and stroked it. Tall Guy pushed him down further to hold him in a vice-like grip between his thighs, and wanked over him; the other guys in the darkroom tried to intervene, but Tall Guy was focussed on his fellow player, and was giving him his masterful attention, which continued for about twenty enthralling minutes. I stood beside him, watching and enjoying The Game being played so well. Eventually, Nosering came up for air, and they went out to the bar to chat. I got a drink, and came back to observe them, but things obviously weren't going well for Tall Guy. He was keen to keep on playing, but Nosering had had enough; probably his nipples were too sore. Nosering had been playing The Game for much longer than Tall Guy. Backrooms were his playground; he didn't do breakfast.

Tall Guy was being really persuasive, but Nosering was adamant and left, with a smile; but of course no telephone numbers were exchanged. I watched Tall Guy take it well, standing on his own at the bar; in one very familiar gesture of disappointment, he wiped his face with his hands. Was he going to go home, or was he going to carry on with The Game?

He carried on, as of course one does. It's hard to get off the rollercoaster mid-ride. I watched him play with various men in the backrooms, but none matched the fire of the first round and eventually I found him at the end of the evening in the back of the room being fucked by a big black guy. I moved through the semi-darkness; it was like wading through the sea, hands fluttering against my body like seaweed. I slid my own hand down to check that a condom was being used, and it was; I felt surprised and relieved. I stroked Tall Guy's back for a bit; then it was over, and he got out and composed himself for leaving.

It was just another night in a sex club in London, one of many such places in this city. I didn't have sex that night; I tend to give it a miss if there's someone I fancy there who doesn't fancy me back. As the place emptied, I watched Tall Guy leave; he caught my eye, but again the neutral, non-hostile exchange of looks.

It was only later that I realised why I was so fascinated with him. I remembered that we had met, about four years previously. His shaved head had thrown me, and also I didn't recognize him with his clothes off. When we met before, it was because we had liked the sound of each other's voices on a phoneline, and decided to meet for a pint. We talked and he was in bad shape. He had just completed his training as a policeman; he graduated on the anniversary of the death of his father, who had also been a policeman. Since he joined a station, he had found the experience unendurable; it was more racist and homophobic than he had found it at training college, and he was suffering badly. But he had kept his sexuality secret; I imagine everyone of a certain generation there having known his father hadn't helped.

He went missing for a few weeks, without notifying them; took to his bed during the day and slipping out of his mother's house at night to play The Game. When he turned up again to work, he faced disciplinary charges, but the authorities were asking him: "Is there anything you want to tell us?" It must have been screechingly obvious what the problem was, to anyone with a brain. But he couldn't come out. He was given an official warning. I met him during the second time he had gone AWOL and he knew that he faced the end of his short career. He felt trapped and unable to muster the courage to challenge his father's authority in his mind, unimpeachable in his grave. In the few phonecalls to me that followed, he told me how he was doing, which wasn't good. Eventually he stopped ringing me. He did say how nice it was to talk to someone who treated him like a human being, but then that's because we hadn't played The Game together. And, like me, he was drawn to playing it, like moths dancing around a flame.

What is The Game? I've written about it many times; I've looked at it in forensic detail, trying to understand it from a psychological point of view, trying to explain it to people who, for the most part, I imagine, don't play it. Probably, most times I've oozed shame and Catholic guilt about it; and I haven't been, as they say in this subculture, sex-positive. I tend to wail in despair at the way people I meet here in London relate to me and to each other – but the time has come to accept that I haven't given The Game its fair dues. Some part of me has been very ashamed that I should have sexual pleasure, and is reluctant to write about it in a way that is purely celebratory.

The Game is a trip, a heady flight of pleasurable imagination that is second-to-none in my book. It's akin to the high that gamblers must get; like gambling, it's a numbers game, and it's a matter of floating with opportunity; taking advantage of the moment; my friend and I call this surfing the waves of sex a rollercoaster. Sometimes, when you're playing The Game, whether it be out cruising or on the phonelines or on the Net, it can seem that the air is filled with the sound of jackpots, a heightened sense of ecstasy, as people queue up to play with you, with similar rules; other times it can seem like one is down to the last penny, when you're tired, and the fire of imagination has faded only to reveal the dinginess of your surroundings, or the lack of real company.

But company, funnily enough, is not what The Game is about – at least not the company that friends or lovers can give you. Sometimes, depending on the medium, it's not only breakfast that's skipped. The fantasy is paramount, the other person is secondary. In The Game, it's preferable sometimes not to cum, for that is when a man is at his most vulnerable, most likely to forget the rules. That's often left for afterwards, in a private reliving of the scene. Some varieties of The Game even skip actual contact – a particularly juicy sex fantasy shared on the phones or the Net is perfect in itself: why spoil it with the potential for disappointment by actually meeting the guy? And, if The Game is particularly intricate, playing with power, it's even part of The Game that the person stands you up; the point has been made, the rules are known, and he's won. It's an internal headtrip, that comes from allowing a particular kind of horny magic take hold in your mind and in your loins; it's creative fantasy that is collaborative, and almost psychic. It's psychic in the sense that so much of what goes on between gay men cruising is highly intuitive. A level of trust is in operation that is rarely in evidence elsewhere in life. All the times I've been hurt, it's been because I've brought my feelings into The Game, which is not where they belong. As an emotional man, it's been hard to accept this.

If it didn't give so much pleasure, we wouldn't be doing it. I can call it addictive, and see it as a pathology – but then I end up denying the part of me that wants, maybe even needs, to play. I know it's perversity, in the way that it's not about love, but about a smouldering fury, a compelling imaginative drive towards fierce independence and imaginative control and potency, albeit masked with camaraderie and often a sense of humour. My urge to explore the reasons why people do things is part of who I am, but, with sex, it's not so easy: reason alone does not make something less horny. It's like a part of the brain that crackles to life in bright, cobalt neon when The Game is on, when the adrenaline and testosterone are pumping; once you've felt the electricity of pleasure, it's hard to then be a Luddite and say you'd rather sit in the dark. Not when you're young enough to still play The Game and win, as I've been recently rediscovering.

It's a sport of hunting, of discovery — that's why rematches are so rare. Once two bodies have been discovered and enjoyed according to your (shared) rules, then the reasons for repeating the experience lessen. There is more interesting territory to be explored elsewhere. Sometimes, one person can share new experiences with you a few times, with new rules; but it's hard to play The Game with someone who doesn't offer the buzz of the unknown in some way.

Players know, or should know, that romanticism doesn't belong in The Game. Just because someone matches your ideal look, or does that thing to please you expertly, doesn't mean anything but that they're good players. It's where I've gone so wrong in the past. Too often I've fantasised that the people I meet while playing are potential boyfriends. For potential boyfriend, read: someone who can take the sense of loneliness away from me. This need spills out and spoils The Game. Successful gameplayers are always those who keep their feelings compartmentalised, safe, protected. Those who fail to do so, as I have done in the past, get badly burnt. And, of course, hell has a place specially reserved for those who pretend to be romantic from the start, and all the time have been playing The Game.

Ironically, however, the most successful players are those with boyfriends, in relationships of varying degrees of openness. There was a time when I used to lament this, bemoaning the lack of faithfulness in this gay world, and therefore, by implication, seeing a life of betrayal ahead of me whenever I got involved. But I've been recently reconsidering, for I've been seeing my life in terms of a very conventional morality. If I see betrayal, I find betrayal; if I see it as a life being lived fully, then that's a different kettle of fish. Gay male sexuality here is too explosive to be contained in a conventional relationship, I suspect; except for those who have reached a certain age and have decided The Game is not as enjoyable as it once was for them, or for those who have never had those inclinations in the first place, whom of course I hardly ever meet. Then, a different pleasure awaits, if they're lucky, that is more about companionship and affection. But does love come easier to those who play The Game or not? I don't know. I know love is rare, and comes when you least expect it. Perhaps relationships are more difficult to maintain when one or both are players, but that's not the same thing. Long-term relationships to the end are always between friends, however they start.

But playing The Game throws up paradoxes. I said yes and no to two different men recently, when they called to ask to see me again. One was a troubled, intense, emotional and creative man, gorgeous to behold, and with lashings of juicy Jewish guilt, which almost puts my Catholic variety in the shade. I had had a lovely time with him, but then he broke The Rules: he started bemoaning the state of his 10-year relationship, now sexless. He talked of cuddling up with me in front of the sofa, and going out for meals, and he gushed how he hadn't felt like he felt with me in such a long time. And it was mutual; there certainly was a strong connection there. The other guy was a cool, arrogant, gentle but firm player of the most exquisite sort: black, confident and sexy, and highly sensuous. As for his feelings, I'm left none the wiser, but he sure hits the spot erotically with me. So I said no to the man who offered (conditional) warmth and cuddles, and yes to the cool guy who offered nothing but pleasure – because I knew the former would break my heart, being emotionally unfaithful to his lover, and leaving early to be with him; and I knew that the latter, although emotionally opaque, would not touch me inside. Except physically.

The Game is not for lovers. The attitude that one brings to The Game is totally different to that which one brings when dating someone attractive, someone you've met socially or through work; it's almost as if once you've decided to play The Game, and seduce, in a designated place (real, cyber or telephonic, it doesn't matter), then there is no point in pretending that there is anything else on the cards with that person, for the original motive is selfish, not loving: to hunt, not to meet a soulmate.

To make love with someone, to be truly in love with someone, one needs to know the whole person first. It's totally different to the implicit contract between players of The Game, a magic of a different order.

Some people only know one or the other; I'm lucky enough to have experienced both. I know that finding love again is out of my control, but I also know that being ashamed about what games I play for pleasure is not likely to find me a lover either. Shame and insecurity are the real enemies to love, not playing The Game.

VISIONS OF BEAUTY, OF POWER, OF PERFECTION ARE HARDWIRED IN OUR BRAINS
9TH JULY 2004

I've been going to the gym since Christmas and have just had a fitness test. I'm in tip-top condition, and have lost 8 kg – that's well over a stone, in old money. I feel much better, I've more energy, and in the last month, people have begun to compliment me on how well I'm looking, how much weight I've lost. I never realised that people are so aware of weight. Or how obvious my weight-gain last year must have been.

Anyway. The gym I've chosen is one across the way from where I work, and it's a well-run, friendly place, a little on the expensive side – but that just tends to act as a spur to keep going. I'm determined not to waste my hard-earned dosh.

As with all gyms, it's a case study in narcissism, with quite a few muscle-bound peacocks strutting around. But it's not a cruisy gym at all – it's predominantly men in their thirties and forties keeping fit, playing squash, working off the spare tyres. Mostly married, they are in the main a genial but non-invasive lot. The staff have a good sense of humour. It suits me fine.

About ten years ago, I used to go to a gym that was full of gay men, and the atmosphere was very different. It was both exciting and, at the same time, deeply frustrating, for it was a highly competitive arena. The exhibitionism was relentless, and the intense stares of cruising gay men got me down, undermined my confidence. The excitement of lingering a bit too long in the sauna or shower, the games of peek-a-boo and the subtle or not-so-subtle mating rituals of men rutting, were compelling and distracting. I ended up forgetting the reason I went there; in the end, the main purpose of going – keeping fit – seemed boring, pointless.

This time around, I'm a man in my forties, and it makes a big difference. I don't take health for granted any more – and I've had to work hard to get to these levels of fitness and energy, and even then my knees give a twinge every now and again, and I have to take it easy. What keeps me going is not narcissism (although that doesn't mean I'm tearing up my membership card to Narcissist's Anonymous quite yet), it's fear of getting old and decrepit. Simple.

Last week, though, someone put on a show in the gym changing room that disturbed me on many different levels. A young man with an enormous dick was displaying himself, in steely provocation, unsmiling, almost hostile, challenging everyone there to look at him. No one could miss it – he was standing squarely in the middle of the room, holding his ample hose and fingering the end of it, as if to rub a bit of fluff from the end, nonchalantly. He had shaved every bit of hair off his body – he wasn't that tall, but he was very defined and lean. He had a pinched face that could easily have come from inner-city Limerick or Glasgow, with hard, tiny eyes.

Normally, when someone puts on a show like this, it's aimed at someone in particular, and of course I thought it was me, at first. I locked into his gaze and felt myself churn inside, that heavy deep tug in the guts that signals an end to rationality. But it soon became obvious his exhibitionism was global – he demanded that all present admire him – and also, perversely, completely insular, in that it he was doing it all primarily for himself. We, the observers, were irrelevant. He was the provocateur, queering the pitch. The rest of the men in the changing room feigned ignorance, as, I suppose, did I. Nothing was said, nothing happened. On the surface.

I wonder what it would have been like for those men if a naked, nubile Amazon had stood there in the middle of the room, with shaved pubes, fingering the nipples on her enormous, perfect breasts, with the same insouciance? What would the guys have done then? I suspect that, probably, they'd have broken into a collective cheer. I suspect, too, that there would have been a humourous reaction, some way of discharging the electricity safely, for most men are gentle, in my experience. But I also imagine there'd have been some undercurrents that weren't so pleasant. Because I was experiencing a lot of really unpleasant feelings, watching this young man flaunt his phallic power.

I hated the way his actions ripped through my composure, as if he'd poked an anthill under my feet, and I was crawling with lust and irritation and envy and admiration and pleasure and, ultimately, with a sense of rejection. I wanted to possess what he had. And it wasn't just his cock – he had a stunning body, and a pair of buttocks that would bring tears to your eyes. I wanted to command him in the same way as he was commanding me. I hated feeling so powerless. I wanted revenge. I wanted him to stop. I wanted to punish him. In a flash, I understood the impulse in misogynistic cultures to make women conceal their bodies, to forbid the exercising of this primal power.

I wish I could have just admired him, or ignored him. But he was beaming out loud on my wavelength, and my speakers were blown.

I felt light-headed. As this was not a gay venue, the rules were not obvious. As he gazed at me it felt like a heavy cruise, the like of which in a park or a club would have me on my knees in an instant. As it was, I found myself doing the worst possible thing: I smiled.

Will I ever learn? Smiling and this sort of sex do not mix. This was hard sex, horny sex, and his life was probably highly tuned into the power he wields with his enormous knob. Perhaps he was on the game. Anyway, my smile was a sort of "I know what you're doing and it's outrageous and I'm interested but I'm not playing the game and why don't you smile as if we're being friendly and snap out of this trance?" kind of smile. But he stared through me, as if my smile meant nothing. The urban cruel-cool. I then immediately felt like a fool. Again. For by taking the smiling route and failing, future interaction became impossible – the opening gambit had been trounced. Victor to the aggressor. The only thing to do was to retreat, lick my wounds, and to try to forget about him.

I spoke to a colleague afterwards about the way I'd felt. He used the language of sex addiction, saying that this guy had "triggered" something in me, my addiction.

He meant well. But I do not know a man alive who would not react at some level in the same way to such provocation, by a member of the desired sex. That sort of power brings us to our knees, in fantasy or reality, and it can overwhelm us like nothing else. I'm not sure that women react in the same way to such visual stimulation. I know some women who would feel the same, but I also know more women who would think along the lines of: "silly boy, put your toy away and stop showing off."

Addiction is not the right discourse to describe this interaction, this lightning bolt of eroticism. It's too universal an experience for men. Such visions of beauty, of power, of perfection are hardwired in our brains. They challenge us to our core, they bring out the best and the worst in us.

Again. And again. And again.

WELCOME TO THE SCENE, JIM
10TH APRIL 1997

I met someone last night for a pint. Jim is 35, has recently separated from his wife, moved to London, and has begun his own exploration of this "gay" life. We started talking to each other on one of the telephone lines that are proliferating in London; it's getting so that one can order sex in this city faster than a pizza. I've experimented with a few over the years – in the interests of journalistic research, you understand. For all my conscious intentions to remove myself from the objectification game, I still occasionally succumb to the lure of the phone, the possibility that the next delivery could be a deep dish. Although exotic, it's a fast food menu; wholesome nourishment is not on offer. And yet, of course, the occasional human bean with a story to tell turns up, like a 24-carat nugget in a mountain of Fool's Gold.

His ad interested me because he described himself as bisexual, and he sounded down-to-Earth. I've come to appreciate bisexuality more, recently – primarily because if someone has had a relationship with a woman, there's a better chance that he might value emotions more. This of course is not a rule I would stake my life on, but Hell, I'll see the positive in anything these days. It's Spring.

We got chatting, and because we live in the same area, I suggested a pint in the evening, with no strings attached. He sounded nervous, and for a while I thought he was going to chicken out, but he rang later to confirm our date, and we met outside the local library. He had described himself as someone who was neither Tom Cruise or Quasimodo, someone who would blend in with the crowd. I found that a strange thing for anyone to say, evidence of low self-esteem perhaps; but after spending an hour in his company I realised the extent to which my values are coloured by the image-conscious gay scene. He was not being self-deprecatory, he simply didn't set as much store on looks as on personality. He liked himself, he said. Now, there's a concept. He reminded me of Timothy Spall, the actor in Mike Leigh's *Secrets And Lies* – a decent, genial Englishman, unpretentious, kind and direct. And emotionally strong.

We found ourselves in one of the new chain of Irish pubs in Britain called O'Neill's. I watched it being renovated from scratch a few months ago. With a queasy feeling I saw the "Player's Please" sign being painted on the wall outside, the artificially-dusted faux-antique stout bottles being placed on the window sills, the pine floors and wall panels being stained a smoky oak. The soundtrack is high-decibel *céilí*, the toilets are *fir agus mná*. But if you examine the tables and stools, you discover that it's all premoulded MDF, with designer woodworm and cigarette burns. This is high-quality, mass-produced, franchised Irishness. They trace shamrocks in the Guinness. Authenticity *mar dhea*.

It was an apt venue to hear his story. Having decided to explore his sexuality, he visited a few gay pubs and clubs, with no joy. He describes himself as painfully shy. He found them full of pretentious, shallow young people, and couldn't connect with anyone. So he decided he would pay a visit to a group he saw advertised in a newspaper, the "Gay Professionals" group. He figured that it would be as good a place as any to meet new people, preferably of his own age group. He rang them up, and was told that they happened to be meeting that night, and that they would leave his name at the door.

So Jim mustered up the courage to knock on the door of the club later that evening. He was let in. He got himself a drink, and sat down. There were plenty of men around, all in suits, and they were of all different ages. But he realised that no one was talking. Halfway through his pint, a man came over to him, and handed him a business card. Jim looked at it, not understanding; it was an ordinary business card, with nothing written on it. He looked up, but before he could say a word, the man had turned on his heels and left the club.

Nonplussed, Jim finished his drink. Then someone else came over, and offered to buy him another. He accepted, and was pleased: this was going to be his first proper conversation with another gay man. The stranger returned with a pint for him, and then to Jim's astonishment, he proffered his business card. Again, before Jim could say anything, he did exactly the same as the first man; he turned and walked out the door of the club.

Bewildered, Jim sat there for a while, trying to figure out what had just happened. He decided to get out of there. But before he did, someone came over to him.

"Why did you do that?" he was asked.

"Did what?" said Jim. "I didn't do anything".

"Exactly," was the reply. "Why didn't you follow them out?"

It turned out that Jim hadn't read the rules of the club, which were spelt out on a blackboard near the door. Apparently, if someone offered you their business card, it was an invitation to have sex. If they handed it to you face up, it was a signal that they would meet you outside and take you home; if it was face down, you were to follow them into the club's backroom. The person who proffers the card is the active guy, if you accept a card, then you are agreeing to get fucked.

Jim fled. One of the men was still waiting for him outside. Jim explained that he hadn't known about the rules, and apologised for messing him about. He asked him if he could give him a call, seeing as he had given him his card. The guy agreed.

So, the next day, Jim rang him. He told Jim that he was free that lunchtime; that Jim was to get himself ready to get fucked at 1.15.

Jim hung up the phone.

As he was telling me this story (and he told it well, revealing a wonderful sense of humour), I was glad to be in the company of someone who was seeing the gay scene for the first time, and reacting with such vigorous incredulity at the coldness and absurdity of it all. I immediately felt less of a maverick.

He can laugh about it now, and probably will dine out on the story for the rest of his life; but it was not lost on me that I was probably the first person he could tell. What is sad is that he's been put off going to any other groups now. My insistence that not all groups are like that one seemed somewhat forced. In Dublin in the '80s, I'd know where to send him to make some new friends; in London in the '90s, madness is in the air.

This "gay" world has a culture which, wherever possible, conspires to dispose of all traces of personality. *Stepford Wives* is a reality. The chilling reason why the men of Stepford got rid of their wives and replaced them with brainless, beautiful, erotically supercharged automatons ("because we can") is the same reason why clubs like the Gay Professionals exist, with their preposterously contrived conventions designed to eliminate the need to utter even a word of greeting.

In some ways, I'm not the best person to give Jim advice, because I've learnt to swim with the sharks; sometimes I'm indistinguishable from them on a dark night. He spoke of losing his innocence, of becoming worldly-wise in a few short months, in ways he could not have imagined in his previous life. He has taken refuge in the phonelines to suss out what it's all about, at a safe distance. He's been shaken, disturbed, appalled, bewildered and bemused – and sometimes he's felt exhilarated by what he's heard. The values of his previous suburban, married English life have taken some serious knocks. He's determined not to lose them.

But it's going to be tough. Until he connected with me, he had not met one man who wanted to meet him, to have a chat, without expecting him to drop his trousers in the first minute. He's someone who knows that sex pales into insignificance compared to making love. He wants that for himself, in his new life.

I believe that it's possible; but I have no evidence to back it up.
It's an act of faith. I guess.

KEEPING CLEAR OF EMOTION
20TH FEBRUARY 1997

One of my favourite entertainers on the scene is a woman called Jean T who, with her glamorous sidekick Robert (The Bimbette), hosts a regular pub quiz/gameshow night at my local. The other night was the end of an era, of sorts – it was the last night they were playing on Wednesdays. The act is being shunted to Mondays; I got the distinct impression from the stage that they were less than delighted with the prospect. Whatever the reason, I'll not see them as often, for Monday evenings are when I sit down to write this letter from London.

It was a memorable night, but not necessarily in the way Jean and Robert would have liked.

They started off with "Mister and Mister". Onstage were a couple of guys – let's call them Steve and Jeff. Steve was the younger of the two, a beautiful young man with a shaven head and a gleaming smile that could melt the coldest of hearts. His lover Jeff was a bit older, but not by much; he was outgoing and cheerful, and a pub regular, with lots of friends in the audience. Again, he was shaven-headed; they both were into boots and Fred Perry T-shirts and combats – in other words the gay/queer skinhead look with which I flirt ambivalently. Jeff was sent upstairs out of earshot, while Steve was asked ten questions about him; after they were answered, Jeff returned and they counted up the score as to how well they knew each other.

Steve and Jeff won an impressive 9 out of 10 points, although Jean was a tad more lenient than is her wont on this occasion; perhaps she was determined to give as many prizes away as she could that night.

The questions were trashy: who was the bigger slut when they weren't seeing each other, what was Jeff's most unusual sexual experience, and so on; Jean had managed to worm out the most gory, intimate details of their lovelife from their friends beforehand.

Jeff was asked to demonstrate the position he took in this most unusual sex scene; surreally enough, he got down on his hands and knees and explained that he had – more than once – been used as a coffee table for a couple of hours. Naked, of course – but I don't need to tell you that, do I? In answer to the question as to which of the two copped off with other men the most when they weren't seeing each other, Jeff guessed correctly that Steve had confessed to having that particular distinction. The round of questions ended a bit lamely. The last one concerned an embarrassing moment when a houseguest had used a towel to wipe his face, which had just been used to mop up Jeff and a partner after sex. Jean's eyes went wide, and she asked what was on the towel. ("Was it poo?" she asked, hopefully.) After a few lame answers, it turned out that it was nothing other than make-up. Apparently the partner was from Manchester, which seemed, by an inexplicable consensus of the entire pub, to explain it.

Am I getting across to you the trippy sense of unreality here? I swear I was drug-free. But wait, it gets better.

After they had been given their bottles of plonk, and were halfway off the stage, Jeff confessed off-mike to Jean that five minutes before the game had started, he had just finished it with Steve. So, Jean told us, gobsmacked; this was greeted by the crowd with laughter and cheers. They hadn't wanted to spoil the game for her, so they carried on. Jean, rendered speechless for once, announced a break before the next game, and asked for a round of applause for Steve and Jeff, thanking them for being such good sports.

The next game, ten minutes later, was Blind Date; and of course, being single again, Steve and Jeff were contestants Number One and Two. (If you weren't surprised by this, then you're getting a sense of my world. You're welcome.)

"What's your name, Number One, and where do you come from?" Steve was asked, and on went the show. But it wasn't until Jeff's turn, when curiosity got the better of Jean, and she asked him why he had ended the relationship, that the words were uttered that still haunt me.

"I fell in love with him," was the quiet response. Jean, instantly recognising a potential moment of non-entertainment, moved swiftly along to contestant Number Three. The game went on, an impossibly pompous Ac-tor in a tuxedo was brought on as the Mystery Man, who, at the end, chose Number Three, although my memory isn't reliable. I was a bit preoccupied.

Did Jeff realise that Steve would never return his love, and so ended it in self-preservation? Or had he decided against emotional attachment, because it wasn't fun anymore?

Whatever the reason, it seems to me that the same theme keeps on getting hammered home to me in this life, in this London, among men who love men: above all, keep clear of emotion, of attachment, of taking the real risk of commitment.

THEY DO IT BY FUCKING WITHOUT A CONDOM
22ND JANUARY 1998

I had a very interesting conversation today with a man called Adam Crosier, who is author of a new report from the British Health Education Authority called "Life On The Scene". It's a survey of sexual practices among gay men on the scene, interviewed in bars and clubs over ten years from 1986 – 1996. It's emphatically not a survey of gay men in general. He estimates that two-thirds of all gay man are not on the scene. They may be celibate, or in monogamous relationships, or they may be men who have sex in places like parks or cottages or saunas, or via telephone lines or small ads, or when they get pissed with their mates. It's impossible to know. However, with all those caveats, it still made fascinating reading. Like it or not, I am "on the scene" in London. It shouldn't be a surprise to you dear reader, if you've been paying attention, to learn that I don't like it. So this is a statistical analysis of the world I inhabit, often resentfully, for want of a man to take me away from it all. If a year isn't mentioned, the figures are for 1996.

Let's start with the good news. The number of gay men on the scene who say that they always use a condom when having anal sex with a new partner stands at 68%, a figure which has increased over the previous five years. For those having sex with regular partners, the percentage, although lower, has doubled in five years, from 22% to 45%. When asked about the most recent sexual act prior to being interviewed, only 6% of those questioned admitted to having had unprotected anal sex. Adam urged me to look at another statistic: over the year, none of those interviewed said that they had unprotected anal sex on a one-night stand. However, given the fact that a mere 18% had sex with only one man in the previous year (if they had sex at all), this is not quite as rosy as it seems. Regular partnerships do not last long on the scene – only 10% of the sample were in a monogamous relationship of longer than 12 months' duration. (On the other hand, this could also be explained if couples retire from the scene after a year on the scene together. Unlikely, but in the absence of more information, one can dream.) The vast majority of men on the scene, 64%, have sex with less than 10 different partners every year. For a good 43% of them, this figure is less than 5 per year.

Those who are heavily involved on the scene are, not surprisingly, more likely to have more sexual partners over a year. A small group, 8% of those questioned, have sex with at least one different person every week, on average. The sexual activity of this group accounts for half of all the sexual encounters recorded in the survey. They have sex with so many people that it greatly distorts the average. This small group, including some who report over 100 partners in a year, are the ones who are most likely to have had high-risk sex in the previous year, with 36% of them admitting to having fucked someone without a condom. And there's more bad news. When questioned about their last sexual encounter, the majority of all respondents had taken alcohol and/or drugs during it. It's not really surprising, since everyone was interviewed in licensed premises, but what is surprising is that over 60% of respondents say that they use drugs. This figure rises to 92% of those who are highly involved on the scene. The majority of those who have sex while they are on drugs have anal sex, and a good 40% come more than once each time.

Condoms, in such circumstances, are hardly likely to be properly used. As the percentage of gay men who engage in anal sex is rising every year, this must be cause for the deepest concern. Even more alarming is that the number of people who admit to having unsafe anal sex in the previous 12 months is rising. In 1991, 19% admitted to fucking without a condom; in 1996, the figure is 28%. That's more than one person in four. Adam urged caution in interpreting this figure; he said that there was no information about the quality of the encounter, for example this may have been with a partner in a regular relationship, or it may have been two HIV positive men believing that condoms were redundant. Of those interviewed, at least one in ten are HIV positive. Over two-thirds know someone who is HIV positive, and 59% know someone who has died from AIDS.

"Although the epidemic hasn't taken off among the general population, according to the predictions of ten years ago," says Adam, "the epidemic among gay men remains fierce". It is reported that 1,500 − 2,000 new infections are reported each year in the UK, and clinicians are reporting that a lot of young men are seroconverting. "It's very difficult to make sense of," says Adam, "all we can do is offer the information, let them know the risks, and let people make their own choices." The survey shows that 92% of those questioned were aware that condom use can considerably reduce the risk of infection.

It is my conclusion that more and more gay men on the scene are making an informed decision to subject themselves and others to a disease which most of them know, through first-hand experience, is fatal. They do this by fucking without a condom. Of those who do use a condom, most do so while under the influence of alcohol or drugs or both, and the proportion of gay men on the scene taking drugs is at least 60%, and rising every year.

Have I stupefied you with too much information? I'm not sorry. Too often I have the feeling that I write from a narcissistic perspective, that my world appears crazy because I am crazy. There is some truth in that, I won't deny it; indeed the writer in me would claim that I am crazy because the world is crazy. But I digress.

I am a creature of extremes. Having not had sex for four months recently, in the past few weeks I've attempted to make up for it, with a plethora of unprintable shenanigans occurring between me and a number of nice men of my acquaintance. I went from preaching from the pulpit on the virtues of celibacy to a gleeful surrender to my rampant libido in one fell swoop, relishing each experience with a sensuous, heady intensity. It was good while it lasted, but now I'm calmer, the storm has blown over.

For all my excesses – and there are plenty who would argue that they are a mark of imbalance, of disturbance, of not being quite whole (and I would argue that myself, sometimes) – I have not fucked or been fucked without a condom in over six years, and then it was only once, and before that it was another four years. Ten years using condoms, in spite of the repeated offers I have had from men who want to have "bareback" sex with me. Ten years with only one burst condom that I know of.

Perhaps I am unusual. Perhaps I am fixated on only one aspect of safe sex, the most obvious one of fucking, and I shrug off the risk of any other activity. Perhaps I am in error to do so. But so far, I am lucky enough, or sensible enough, to remain negative. I may want to explore the mysterious, further reaches of sexual pleasure at times, but at heart I want to survive.

I have some experience of how sex can be obsessive, of how it can take you over, especially when you are feeling hurt inside. I've certainly gone on sex binges when I've discovered that yet another man is a lying shit, when I've taken a risk to go out and meet someone only to discover that he's got a boyfriend at home. I may act out the hurt through a good dose of mutual objectification; the jury is out as to whether this represents a triumphant exercise in the eroticisation of humiliation or an escape from real relationship. Or it could simply be a jolly good adventure. All three are possible.

Until reading this report, however, I had an idea that this struggle with my sexual nature was peculiar to me – or that it was a classically Irish Catholic activity, to play with myself and confess my shame to you, my readers. However, this report shows just how crazy the gay scene is, how at its core there appears to be something akin to a deathwish, or at least an addiction to Russian roulette.

I hope that it's acknowledged. Adam said to me that the question why people deliberately take such risks is not known, and he genuinely seems concerned and puzzled. I believe the answer is psychological. I believe the answer lies within each one of us. It's that part of us that craves danger in order to experience the thrill of being alive; the part of us that values immediate gratification over longevity; that part that perhaps doesn't like ourselves very much, and wants to shuffle off this mortal coil. That part, the part that hurts. You know it.

Adam and his co-writer, Dominic McVey, adopt another perspective in the foreword.

"Time and again, health promotion research has demonstrated that theories of health-behaviour based on assumptions about individual rationality, are not reliable in predicting health-related behaviour. This is true in the area of unsafe sex among gay and bisexual men, as it is in the areas of smoking, diet and alcohol use. In the case of HIV prevention, there is now greater appreciation of the importance of values other than health – such as desire, trust and love – which are associated with behaviours defined as 'unsafe'."

It's a somewhat poetic position, bearing in mind that it's the only instance of the word "love" in the entire document. As much as love may be blamed for the choice to dispense with condoms, I would suggest that a lack of love would also contribute to a similar recklessness. Those who take the greatest risks, the scene queens who fuck a stranger or two every week while off their faces, are perhaps slaves to desire.

Ultimately, statistics fail us. I suspect there are as many reasons why people dance with death as there are dancers.

Apropos of nothing in particular, I rang the London Gay Spiritual Group today, to find out more. He sounded like an enthusiastic vicar, inviting me to tea to meet his other parishioners who were "very friendly indeed", although he said he wasn't really into religion, and that there wasn't any particular religious standpoint expected of the members. I made the mistake of asking him why he started this, having people over to his home every month, running a newsletter, going to all this trouble. He told me that it was channelled by his higher being.

Ah well. Enough said.

THE SOHO BOMB: THE PERVERTED LITTLE FUCKER KNEW HIS EXPLOSIVES
10TH JUNE 1999

"My mother says that she didn't hear a bang. It was a couple of whooshes, she says. I was chatting to her on my mobile. 'What was that?' she asked. I told her it was a bomb, I had just watched a bomb go off across the road from me, and I had to go. She asked if anyone was hurt. I told her I couldn't see anything, it was all dust. Everyone was quiet, that was the really scary thing." He was speaking in a strained guttural voice, trying to hold back emotion, forcing the words out. "I couldn't see in for dust, I couldn't see in at all. But did I go in and help? No. No one came out. No one came out. And what did I do? I called in to work. That's what I did. I just dialled the news desk, on my mobile, said I was live at the scene of a bomb in Soho, and they put me straight through, live. I described what I saw. I don't remember what I said. What good did that do? I didn't help anyone; I just watched and talked. I was talking to my mother. She said it was like a couple of whooshes. There wasn't a bang. I don't really remember."

I'm glad I'm not a news journalist; I'm glad that it is not my job to sniff out disaster and put an angle on a story of human suffering. I'm glad I don't have to maintain a pretence of objectivity, to hide my feelings in front of a camera or in my written words.

He was speaking on Sunday, two days after the blast that ripped through the Admiral Duncan in Soho, in the centre of London. We were in a club. We had met over the Internet originally, chatted, exchanged photos, flirted with each other when we recognised each other in real life in Soho, but nothing came of it. We only bump into each other every few months. He's a big cuddly man, with sad puppy-dog eyes, and he probably drinks too much. On Saturday, we got chatting online, and he started to pour his heart out. By the Sunday evening, he was fit to burst with unhappiness. We were out in the same club. He had not been hugged since the explosion; I told him he should immediately sack all his friends, as he collapsed in tears in my arms. By the end of listening to his story, I had to seek out one of my best friends, who happily was there too, and I bawled my eyes out in his arms.

My ex-boyfriend, too, witnessed the carnage. He rang me late on Friday night in numb distress, more worrying than any tearful ramblings. He spoke softly to me of horrific wounds and grotesque burns, of pieces of flesh on the ground, of blood everywhere. He had left the building next to the Admiral Duncan, which houses Kairos, the spiritual centre, only moments previously; he turned the corner, and the bomb went off. His bicycle was destroyed in the explosion. I can't deal with his pain. I couldn't when I was going out with him, and I can't now. I had thought it was my pain I couldn't deal with. Perhaps it's both.

The last time I was in the Admiral Duncan was on a blind date. I answered an ad, we met outside a tube station, and we went for a drink. The Duncan was a small and crowded pub, with no particular type in the ascendant; just a noisy, cheerful, casual place. It was a safe space to get over the nerves of meeting someone new, or so I thought – but my date couldn't relax. He wanted to be with me on my own, but the neutrality of the pub is what I needed, to feel safe. He was nervous, unfortunately he covered it over by laughing at everything I said. I'm not that funny. I went to the loo. When I came back, he was chatting to a little Italian film student, who was amusing, in a Woody Allen-ish sort of way.

I relaxed because I thought my date was easing up on the pressure. But it turned out he couldn't wait to be rid of the student; he hadn't known how to rebuff the little guy's advances. Even though I didn't fancy the Italian, I found I could talk to him easily; we chatted about films and European cities and Dublin and food and the art of conversation, leaving my taciturn English date, unused to café or pub society, miserable. In retrospect, I didn't treat him very well; but then I felt so uncomfortable with him, I childishly said to myself "Well I wasn't the one who got picked up the moment the other went to the loo". Outside the pub, it was awkward: the Italian was all set for a night on the town with his new friends, having just arrived in London and my (by then quite surly) date was pressurizing me to go off with him on his own. I wanted neither experience, so I told them both I had to go, and I left them standing on Old Compton Street.

What's insidiously disturbing about the bombs in London is the number of people who rang in to claim responsibility for them. What's saddest is that the little fucker whose perverted mind thought up this plan, knew his explosives. Even the IRA, with all their paramilitary training, botched the job frequently on their last London campaign. It's not easy to kill, really. It takes a lot of hate.

On the day of the bomb, with warnings appearing in the gay press and on the Internet, I had spent a few adrenaline-pumped minutes in the bath daydreaming, imagining that I spotted someone leaving a bag in Old Compton Street; how I'd chase after him, use my newly-acquired karate skills to apprehend him; how I'd "persuade" him to come back and defuse the bomb to save the day, and become a hero.

They were vigilant in the pub. As soon as a bag was spotted, the manager went over to investigate. And it blew up in his face.

HURT LITTLE BOYS NEED TO GROW UP AND MAKE A CHOICE
4TH FEBRUARY 1999

"Our stories are important," he told us. "For too long the stories, details, and desires of gay men have been ignored. We owe it to them to let our voices be heard."

So spoke the leader of a writing workshop for gay men that I've been attending recently. He did preface his remarks by saying he was getting political, almost sounding apologetic at first. Nasty politics. But his conviction shone through; his commitment to a sense of community among gay men was sincere, his passion evident in his dedication to the group itself.

I had joined the group for a number of reasons. Primarily, there's a play in my head that needs to get out; and as the world's worst procrastinator, I thought joining a workshop would enable me to find a midwife or two to get the labour under way at last. For that reason alone, of course, it didn't have to be a group of gay men, and I have been part of another writers' group before, where sexuality was irrelevant. But it's also part of my journey in getting back to a healthier way of relating to gay men, outside the meat-market of the scene or the fantasy world of cyberspace and phonesex. If you only meet people in a sexual setting, or in the frenzy of a sexual fantasy, then only part of you is seen, and that's not the whole of the moon.

This is so simple and self-evident that I am amazed to find myself writing it; it's as if I'm confiding in you, dear reader, the startling fact that air is cleaner in the mountains.

But life is full of discoveries of things we already know. It's a different kind of knowing, perhaps.

I've been digesting his exhortation to write because "we owe it" to those whose voices were previously unheard. I'm not sure whether much good comes from a sense of obligation, a sense of duty, a sense of indebtedness, when one hasn't consciously chosen to take on the responsibilities in the first place. If one accepts that sexual orientation, the way one's compass points, is not changeable by force of will, then to go through the process of coming out only to discover that there's a plethora of people whose sacrifices have to be honoured, whose achievements have to be rewarded by further effort, whose deprivations are used as a guilt-inducing persuader, strikes me as rather similar to growing up in a family where one or both parents complain bitterly "after all I've done for you" whenever the child dares to grow up and challenge their authority. Such a dynamic disempowers, for one starts off in life not with a clean slate, but in debt. New, all-improved, pinker-than-pink Original Sin.

What I am about to propose instead may sound similar, but there's a subtle difference. Somewhere along the line, I think it's important to choose to be gay. I don't just mean acceptance of the fact, although God only knows how difficult, sometimes impossible, it is to accept that one is different. (For some, of course, their bisexuality precludes any such acceptance, for their compass veers from one point to another at various stages of their lives.) I mean at some later stage, one chooses to join the tribe of those like you, and take on the privileges and support and responsibilities of being a life-long member, as if it is the most precious thing in the world to you. For what draws you together is not that you share similar tastes in shopping and fucking, but the capacity to love. Looking at the way gay men get together now, and especially looking at gay media, you may be forgiven for forgetting this. I certainly forgot it. I'm trying to remember now. I don't mean the intoxicating fix of adoration and idealisation that is mistaken for love so often, the ecstasy of casual intimacy, "falling" for objects of lust and being disappointed when their sheen rubs off when the dirty deed is done, when the hoped-for magic hasn't happened, when the gay shaped hole inside hasn't been filled. That's not the love that heals, that helps, that warms, that makes the world go around. It's the love that destroys, that undermines, that sucks you dry, that owes more to obsession, control and hurt, rather than caring and tenderness. Both are undeniably aspects of love, of being human; I am not in any way arguing for the eradication of such passion. King Canute springs to mind.

What is lacking at the moment is some counterweight to the powerful commercial clout of the gay sex industry, the saunas, the phonelines, the prostitution. Not a banishment of it. I am not anti-sex; rather, I'm against the way gay sex has become commodified, packaged, exploited and corrupted, so that love and affection appear to have been written out of the picture. To many ears, this sounds like a Christian message, as if I'm preaching from the pulpit the values of traditional heterosexual sexual morality. It can be met with a hostile reaction, as if I'm aping an outdated traditional model, that I'm trying to turn back the clock and put sexual liberation back in its box where it belongs.

However, I believe the liberation clock has got stuck on sex, and needs to get past it. How? Perhaps the concept of tribe is a way forward. What if, at some stage, gay men could choose to join a queer clan or a fag fraternity or a benders' brotherhood? What if a newcomer was asked to say the following before being accepted by the tribe?

1. I choose to join this tribe of men who love men, freely and willingly and with all my heart.

2. I promise to treat other members with the same respect with which I ask them to treat me.

3. I promise to take care of my body, and not to damage it with drugs, alcohol, or unsafe sex.

4. I promise to celebrate my sexuality with passion, dignity, responsibility, and fun; to avoid demeaning myself or others in the process; remembering that at its best, sex between us is a deeply spiritual experience. In my relationships with other members of this tribe, I promise to play with honesty and courtesy, engaging in safe, sane and consensual acts.

5. I promise to share my feelings with others, and to encourage others to share them with me, in a world in which men's feelings are denigrated and often mocked.

6. I promise to love the woman in my soul, and to be open to the riches in the hearts of those outside this tribe. Our enemies are not women or heterosexual men, but ignorance and hatred of difference.

7. I promise to support other members who suffer from injustice, discrimination, and homophobia, and also to discourage feelings of shame, bitterness and victimisation, which can destroy self-esteem as effectively as any outside oppressor.

8. I promise to support other members, who are in committed relationship, to help them stay together if that is their wish, and to work towards the time when such relationships are as respected and honoured in society as any other.

9. I promise to value the friendship of other members, and offer the hand of friendship where possible to those who are on their own, who are ill, or are elderly.

10. I promise to work towards the time when no one, within the tribe and without, through ignorance or lack of self-love, infects him- or herself with HIV or any other disease. I acknowledge the extent to which AIDS has caused such suffering and loss in our tribe, and dedicate myself to healing that wound, starting by understanding all the ways it has affected me and those that I love. Through healing ourselves, we may be better able to heal others, who have suffered in a similar way.

11. I offer my creativity and imagination and support as gifts to the tribe and to the world outside, and honour the gifts that those members living and dead have given to, and for, the tribe before me.

12. I look to no one for leadership, but follow my own conscience; no one speaks for me, and I speak for no one but myself. My tribe is no secret society; I promise to work towards it being a shining example of solidarity and companionship to the world.

The concept of a group of people, especially men, banding together in such a way can provoke the most intense opposition, with talks of ghettoising and exclusion and elitism. Many gay men would shudder at the idea. The reaction to the Million Man March a few years ago in the States, when black men organised themselves, is one that springs to mind. But I know of no other group that needs to get its act together as much in our society as gay men; there's too much self-hatred around, too much loneliness and illness, objectification, co-dependency and addiction. Too many young men commit suicide, probably members of our tribe. We were born like cuckoos, most of us — aliens in our family and schoolyard, with feelings we weren't supposed to have. Hurt little boys (of all ages) need to grow up and make a choice, and take on responsibility for our own well-being, supporting each other.

Want to be in my gang?

AM I REALLY LIKE THAT?
15TH JANUARY 2003

Sometimes I wander through the world and it's as if I'm looking for reflections of me in other people's eyes, in other people's lives. Echoing the melancholic lilt of Peggy Lee's 'Is that all there is?' the question that scrolls through my mind, like a marquee screensaver of the psyche, is "Am I really like that?". It's a search for something. Identity? Community? A pantomime horse with two front ends, I want to be both as individual as possible, and as tribal as possible: to belong to somewhere, someone.

Like this gay thing. I go to a nightclub in London, a place where there's performance art, and edgy cabaret, and lame quizes on The Smiths, and DJs who deliberately do not mix — they play a record (like T-Rex or Bowie or Souxsie) and then it stops. And then they put on another one. Like it was when we used to play singles in our bedrooms. The crowd is casually dressed – no designer labels here, a deliberate anti-gay atmosphere. I feel at home and alien at the same time. Not an unusual experience. I look around. Am I really like that? Men in their forties with Goth-like, dyed-black, long hair and intense stares piercing me through their fringes. Little fat skinheads with glitter in their No. 1 crops. Like members of an African tribe, a group of piercing afficionados sport their body modifications, penny-sized holes in their earlobes, barbells through the bridge of their noses, tattoos elegantly snaking around the napes of their necks. Tall, patrician artists of a certain age trying not to look like Francis Bacon (and failing) stand with their G&T's in the corner. Post-lipstick chic dykes – drop-dead gorgeous women not bothering to camp it up anymore – stand in a warm huddle. A bearded Italian on E gestures in mock-seductive body language to me to smooch with him. I smile and demur politely. E-heads so much more pleasant to deal with than drunkards. The one face I recognise in the entire club is an ex of mine. Unhappy ending, why exhume the corpse of the relationship by saying hi? We embarrass each other when we talk. So I don't say hi. Am I really like that? Do I not keep in touch with my exes?

The cabaret, a mini stage-musical featuring the music of The Smiths, done solo with puppets and a Casio keyboard, is fun and too short, and, distractingly, involved baked beans being dumped on the stage. The club promoters, unusually friendly and kind men, are the ones who have to go onto the rickety stage with dustpan and brush and clean up the mess. Later on, the artiste wanders through the crowd in '70s glam rock gear. Having been an actor, and knowing the life-saving necessity of hearing ego-boosting praise after a performance, I say "well done, enjoyed it" to him as he passes by. A face like murder barely nods acknowledgment. Later he's standing beside me, smoking a joint while I dance to Talking Heads. But he doesn't look. He's not really there. The performer has no friends. Am I really like that?

I think of all the discos I've been to in my life. School discos, head-banging to Thin Lizzy's 'Dancing In The Moonlight' and Horslips. Early gay discos, the sweet shock of seeing two men embrace for the first time. The performance of dance, the quest to surf the rhythm of the theme to *Midnight Express* or 'Love To Love You, Baby' by Donna Summer. The sweat of it. The older clones with moustaches and hankies and poppers, ignoring me, all dead now. The standing against the wall, watching, hoping to be watched, nonchalant outside, dying inside. The walking home with ears humming. And the drunken tears of self-pity, nobody loves me, it's not fair, I don't know how to make connections. Boo-hoo-sodden-hoo. Am I really like that?

Am I special enough to get attention in the crowd? Am I ordinary enough to be accepted by the crowd? Do I dress in a way that sets me apart, or shows that I'm the same? Have I any hope of anyone getting me, the point of me, in a room full of people hell-bent on keeping up appearances? Can I get a grip on people coated with Teflon? Do I need to get a grip? Am I really like that?

Do I not appear just as supremely confident and self-assured as everyone else? How is anyone else to know what's inside? Oh, play another Smiths song, why don't you, it doesn't matter anyway.

Community matters to me, and in a huge metropolis that's oddly hard to find. What memories I have of the gay scene in the '80s in Dublin are fond. It wasn't perfect, nothing is, but there was a sense of people giving of their time to help out, politically, socially, creatively. Later on, I discovered the warmth of the Dublin theatre community − gregarious, social, generous. I could walk into any one of three or four theatre pubs in Dublin of an evening, broke, and be sure of a pint and a good evening sorting the world's problems out: because I'd do the same, when I was working, for anyone else in the same boat. It's about give and take. I miss theatre people enormously. Perhaps it's the actor in me that goes around wondering: "Am I really like that?" Or, perhaps with a more professional slant, "could I be like that?"

I've discovered a community that is meeting my needs now for exploring this polarity of difference/sameness, individuality/collective. It's called OUT*, and it's online. It's for gay men, and it's unusual in that it explicitly disallows predatory sexuality, proudly declaring that it's for Zero

Exploitation. Oddly, it works. Not that it's fluffy and cosy – the discussion groups can be extremely polarized and contentious. And most members are, of course, people sitting on their own in front of a computer screen, which has its own ramifications – self-selecting isolationists without a full social life, adapting the strange beast that is the Net into something that at least curbs the worst excesses of untrammelled libido. But OUT encourages people to organise social activities in their area, to get out and meet each other and find people on similar wavelengths. At its best, there have been long public discussions between members about relationships, depression, spirituality how to cope with the strangeness of the gay scene, full of compassion and understanding. And some of the funniest banter I've ever read.

For young guys, especially, I can't imagine anything more encouraging and supportive than discovering something like OUT. Like every community, you get back what you put in. And OUT seems to be something quite rare in the gay community – a place where young people can make friends and talk about their fears and hopes and get advice from older people who aren't after their bodies, but who have been through it all themselves. The advice recently given to a 17 year old asking "How do I pull or be pulled?" on the noticeboards was met with some of the most empathic, considerate, human and encouraging advice I've ever seen given on the Net, to any young person. The only way a community gains in wisdom is when experience is passed down from generation to generation.

When I read that advice, given to a teenager in a panic wondering basically what being gay is all about, going "am I really like that?" and the answers that come are generous and kind, then someone is learning that being gay – being a man – need not just be about getting your end away. And that's the beginning of grown-up community.

Out is at www.outeverywhere.com .

5: SOMETIMES IT'S HARD TO BE A MAN

EVERY SPERM IS SACRED
20TH JANUARY 1995

There is something slightly ridiculous about semen. In most men's daily lives it is the messy evidence that must be dispensed with after masturbation. It seems that in this society, where sex is rarely celebrated, that the furtive association won't go away. The embarrassment of stained sheets as a thirteen- or fourteen-year-old boy stays with us. Spilt seed, waste, mess, stain, the wet patch. A war is being waged against it to prevent its spillage into others by latex barriers and spermicidal gels and creams. It is the carrier of death and unwanted pregnancies. There is a safe-sex ad which consists of a picture of a man's torso in Y-fronts crossed out and the word "Poison" with a skull and crossbones emblazoned across it. The demonisation is complete. The male as rapist, pillager, poisoner. Waster. The embodiment of all that is lethal and destructive.

Research has been undertaken recently into certain abnormalities in wildlife in which the sexes of the animals (alligators, fish, birds) have become grotesquely distorted. Males have partially-developed sex organs, or none at all. Their sperm levels are low to nonexistent; females give birth to sterile eggs, or are unable to conceive. Scientists have discovered that there is a chemical which is in everyday use in certain plastics which, when it leaks out into the water table, behaves chemically in a fashion similar to oestrogens, causing the mutations to occur. In some lakes and river systems in Northern America, entire species of fish are thus affected, and therefore a few short years from extinction. There is I have read, a similar increase in such abnormalities in humans, with more and more children being born of indeterminate sex.

The sperm count in the human male has decreased by 50% in the past fifty years. It appears to me that we can't afford the luxury of being embarrassed about the subject anymore, for if the rate of decrease continues, the last human children will be born in another fifty years. My statistics may be a bit dodgy, but it surely must be a matter of when the human race ceases to reproduce, and not whether it happens or not. That is, if we don't pour millions into research to ascertain the reasons. This process has been described by journalists as the "feminisation" of males, which seems to me to be an obscenity.

A heterosexual man I know, who is involved in the men's movement, spoke of this "feminisation" with a hint of satisfaction. His background is in helping men to get in touch with their own feelings, regaining pride and strength in being men. Bringing back a sense of dignity to being a (heterosexual) man, in the face of overwhelming opposition (not to mention evidence).

Now I am all in favour of men getting in touch with their feelings. It is a recurring theme here. But the men's movement, as propounded by Robert Bly and others, seems to me to be in danger of making fundamental errors in its approach to the subject. It is specifically a heterosexual analysis of emotions, in which women are assumed to have certain basic traits and men to have theirs, and in the union of the two, the *coniunctio*, human beings achieve that mystical and mythical union of opposites, the embrace of the Other, and so achieve wholeness.

It strikes me as dangerous that certain feelings and qualities that are essentially human should be attributed to a particular sex. Iron John, the noble savage, is not an exclusively male story. I know of women, mostly lesbian, some not, who have the same qualities of wildness and courage and earthiness that the Grimms' story describes. It is part of their nature, which of course goes against what is deemed to be female in this culture. Similarly, I know of men, mostly gay, but some not, who are creatures of exquisite sensitivity, grace and charm. The myth of the Princess and the

Pea, in which a real princess can be discovered by her sensitivity to the presence of a pea underneath layers and layers of mattresses, describes a quality that they possess, and that is essentially part of them. Sadly, they too are misfits in this culture, by virtue of the fact that they are male.

Danish and British scientists are working on the theory that the pesticides, which are universally used in food production, may be among the culprits in the decrease in human fertility. They have found that a group of organic farmers and their families who have partaken in research studies are producing semen which is twice as fertile as the average. In other words, back to the level it was fifty years ago. It is a marked difference – and yet, because the study group was so small, they cannot draw firm conclusions yet. But they are working on it. If their conclusions are validated, I hope that we act on them, before it is too late.

There is a danger that viewing the world through sexually polarised lenses will cripple us instead of empower us to change. If industrialisation and militarism are seen as solely male provinces, if men alone are seen as the enemy, then a lot of energy will be wasted. More and more women are gaining political and industrial power, and yet the destruction of the human race seems to proceed regardless. It is our values we need to change, not only the sex of the people in power. It is ironic that it may be a threat to men's health that will force the change to a more ecologically minded society, when it is the women's movement which has been most insistent on the dangers of irresponsible industrial "progress". But there is also the possibility that this self-same threat might be ignored, because of men's dissociation from their own bodies and feelings.

Alarm bells should be ringing all over the world, for it is a Doomsday of sorts. If we don't wake up and care for our bodies, male and female, we deserve to die out, and leave the world to creatures who will husband her as she deserves.

MEN ARE DAMAGED TOO, YOU KNOW
30TH MARCH 1995

I read a book* recently in which the author lists what he calls The Eight Secrets Men Carry Within. Although written from a psychoanalytic perspective, I think they're worth reflecting on. I'll try to explain the jargon as I go.

1. *Men's lives are as much governed by restrictive role expectations as are the lives of women.*

I think this is readily understood by most men. Most importantly, male roles preclude a healthy ability to talk about feelings, or to have really close male friends. These roles are reinforced in so many subtle ways that they are impossible to detect sometimes. The phrase "male bonding", has recently achieved common currency, but it seems to me to mask an uneasiness with the fact that men need other men as friends. We can't simply acknowledge this, so we use the new age lingo with a jokey self-deprecation.

2. *Men's lives are essentially governed by fear.*

I know this to be true in my bones. I remember starring as one of Santa's little helpers in a shopping centre grotto, where a drama was played out every fifteen minutes to hordes of little darlings and their harassed parents. There was a moment in the show in which the baddie appeared, the lights flashed and the music rose to a crescendo. Invariably, some of the youngest kids would take fright. Seven times out of ten, the kids who got so frightened that they had to be brought out of the grotto, were boys. The parents treated boys and girls in the same way, except for one subtle difference. Some mothers, and most fathers, if they were present, couldn't help but exude a feeling of embarrassment that their son was so frightened. It was never voiced, but it was there nonetheless. The parents of the little girls had no problems with their crying child – for there was no cause for concern. She'd get over it. And indeed she would, often going back for more. But the misery of the crying little boy quite often wouldn't end; for he was getting disturbing reactions on that subtle wavelength of which, so often, parents are unaware. Men's fear is about failing to play the role of being a good little boy. Men fear loss of control, of being swamped by their feelings. Men fear losing. Men fear anything, especially relationships, which will expose the crying little boy inside them, who learnt how to feel shamed by his own feelings.

3. *The power of the feminine is immense in the psychic economy of men.*

This is jargon for the fact that there is male and female in each of us, regardless of our sex. I believe that there are far more than just the stark opposites of male and female at work in our psyches, that we all have many different sub-personalities inside us which may be male, or female, or neither, or both. But because "feminine" values have become so devalued in Western society, they are all the more powerful in a man's interior landscape. Men who can't deal with the feminine in themselves have serious problems in relating as equals to women in relationships, leading to misogyny, homophobia and violence.

4. *Men collude in a conspiracy of silence whose aim is to suppress their emotional truth.*

Watch a group of men together to test this. Emotions are rarely talked about. This holds true, surprising as it may seem, for gay men as well. We were brought up to be men, after all. It is only when men get together in support groups, sharing a common wound such as alcoholism or having been abused as children, that the collusion ends. Indeed growing up gay, in a homophobic society, is often damaging enough to get men to talk about their feelings. But only in certain controlled situations. And rarely, if ever, in public.

5. *Because men must leave Mother, and transcend the mother complex, wounding is necessary.*

This gets complicated. He is referring to the archetypal Mother, and not to the individual woman who gave birth to him. The archetypal, or symbolic, Mother may be represented in someone's life (and this goes for men as well as women) as his real mother, his wife or partner, or as an institution like Mother Church, or a nation like Mother Ireland or Queen Mother England. The relationship an individual has towards that which offers containment and security is resonant with the relationship an individual has (or had) with his or her mother. To call it a mother complex implies that there is something abnormal about it. But it is the curse of psychoanalysts and doctors to view the world in terms of sickness and imbalance, because that is what they meet and have to grapple with in their clients. That said, the relationship between Irish men and their mammies is undoubtedly highly complex. The wounding he refers to relates to his belief that, behind the structures of patriarchal defences, it is men who are the psychologically more dependent sex. To break free of such a close, interdependent bond as exists between a son and his mother is deeply painful, for both. But it is necessary if we are to become healthy, self-contained men.

6. *Men's lives are violent because their souls have been violated.*

It is my belief that, to a very large extent, men's violence is a direct result of damaging psychological experiences in their formative years. This is not to say that rapists and murderers and queerbashers should be let off because their father beat them or their mother needed them to stay infantile. But it seems to me that there is a strong link between disturbed boyhoods and adult male criminality. It is a violation to bring up young human beings to be ashamed of their emotional natures. But we do it all the time, almost in spite of ourselves.

7. *Every man carries a deep longing for his father and for his tribal Fathers.*

If your father is still around, give him a hug and tell him you love him. Break the pattern of male silence, which has been passed down from father to son for generations. He will be grateful for it. Even if he's indifferent, it will almost certainly do you a power of good.

8. *If men are to heal, they must activate within what they did not receive from without.*

Women's groups have always known this. It's time that we started taking the really courageous steps of admitting how frightening it is to be a man. If we're big enough to do that, and to admire that in others, then perhaps it will filter down to the next generation, and the vicious circle of male shame, the root of so much pain and violence, can be laid to rest.

Under Saturn's Shadow – The Wounding and Healing of Men
by James Hollis
Inner City Books Toronto

FLOWERS ARE FOR GIRLS
10TH MAY 1998

The other day I had had a strange encounter with a little boy that bemused and saddened me. I spend a lot of time watching kids at play these days; my flat is on the ground floor overlooking a courtyard in a Victorian tenement block, recently refurbished. It took two years, but now, happily, the builders have left, and the local saxophone player is back, crooning away as I write, and if I shut my eyes I can remember what the place was like with trees and atmosphere, before the bricks were sandblasted and the rents were doubled.

With the lengthening Summer evenings, the shrieks and cries of the hordes of children playing make it hard to hear yourself think. It helps that I love children, but it is exhausting just watching and listening to them; I can't imagine the strain it must involve to actually be responsible for one. Anyway, one bright spark came up to me and pointed laughingly at my T-shirt. He's a loud, rebellious, Dennis the Menace type of kid, with a cheeky grin and a penchant for kicking. And he's only four. "Flowers are girls!" he scoffed at me. I didn't know what he was talking about. I looked down. I was wearing an old black T-shirt, with a fluorescent, green, grungey flower sprayed onto it. It was advertising something; I'm not quite sure what. It was one of the "here's-an-old-one-you-can-borrow" kind, offered the morning after a party when I stayed over at a friend's place a few years ago.

Flowers are girls. It took me a while to let that sink in, and to appreciate what sort of boylogic would produce that statement, and why he would direct it at me. Old memories of being teased as a pouff at school resurfaced and stung for a brief moment, but I banished them as soon as they arrived. I'm a six foot tall man in his thirties; I'm not a likely target to be teased by four year old boys. Nevertheless, I think that's what he was attempting to do. It's not the first time that kids have unsettled me like that; I remember a highly intuitive girl of about five asking me once while I was having coffee with her mother: "Are you a man or a woman?" She freaked me out because she was seeing me inside, and not judging me by my appearance, which couldn't have given her any cause for confusion.

In the British *Independent*, which is what I read most days here, there has been an interesting spat between two of their columnists, Suzanne Moore and David Aaronovitch. It's being billed by the hype-conscious new editor as a "Sex War", but that's putting it a bit strongly. If you want to see a Sex War, try and get your hands on the documentary *Town Bloody Hall*, an extraordinary historical document, a film of a passionate 1971 panel discussion on feminism in New York, capturing, among others, Germaine Greer and Norman Mailer engaged in battle with gloves off. Meaty stuff.

The current so-called "War" has nothing like the same vigour or clarity;

it feels more like a mere squabble in comparison. It started with Moore commenting on the latest (quintessentially English) scandal about an old man of wealth and influence and pompous morality being caught with his pants down, with some "Miss Whiplash" or other — the details are irrelevant, for you've heard the same story many times before. She wrote, in quite a glib, lighthearted piece, that "the repertoire of male sexual behaviour is so limited, (she) could almost feel sorry for them".

Aaronovitch took offence at this, pointing out that if he said something similar about women, he would get nothing but abuse for it. She said that if she made a flip remark about men, its effect was not to denounce the whole of male behaviour. He disagreed. And then she said in response "You cannot be such a little flower".

Again, I was receiving the same message, from a completely different source. Flowers are girls, or for girls; boys can't be flowers.

There is such a powerful resistance to men talking or writing about their feelings, to expressions on their part of sensitivity and hurt. There is a special tone of ridicule reserved for men who dare to take that risk. For some of us, touched by the fickle finger of fate, our transparent sensitivity exposes us to that tone from an early age. We may dismiss it as homophobia, but that misses the point; the same thing happens amongst four-year-olds, for whom sexuality is a blissfully distant prospect. Sensitivity is the thing that has to be extirpated. A boy in my school was called Puffty all his years there; it had nothing to do with his sexuality, just his gentleness.

That was in the 1970s. What disturbs me is that in 1998, a four-year old boy mocks a man for wearing a flowery T-shirt, and listens suspiciously when he is informed that there are boy flowers as well as girl flowers. Who taught him to be so scathing of men wearing flowery T-shirts, to be so aware of old stereotypes of masculinity and femininity? He must have been on the receiving end of it already in his short life, to be so quick to attempt to shame someone else now. That four-year-old has already learnt to be ashamed of his "flowerness". The more shame there is around expressions of feeling in his childhood, the more likely he is to find ritualised expressions of it, a la Miss Whiplash, more attractive, when he "grows up" to be a man, just like his dear Papa. In my humble opinion.

GETTING IT WRONG, EVERY TIME
16TH JUNE 1999

I blame the air conditioning. It isn't working. The hall is so hot that I can feel my skin redden and cover itself in a film of sweat – not glowing but drenching. My white karate uniform, wet through, clings to me. My anxiety level soars. I know it's a self-fulfilling prophecy; I believe that I get stupid when I get hot, therefore my mind ensures that it happens, each time. Self-consciousness alone will do it, I suppose; now *there's* something which, occasionally, I'd like to lose, but certain base elements simply cannot be changed.

Stupid, wet, red and hot. Great. We've been warming up for about half an hour. There are profuse apologies for the heat, but they don't make me feel cleverer. I check my breathing, to see if I'm hyperventilating or anything else alarming; no, I'm in the peak of health and fitness. Bugger.

We are asked to pair up. To my horror, I end up facing one of the black belts, and me just a beginner. Immediately, I'm back to being the clumsy shy last-to-be-picked-for-the-team little boy, stuck in goal, praying that no one comes within a million miles of me. I shrink in size, as I wipe the sweat from my brow.

He, on the other hand, seems to assume Goliath proportions. No one knows much about him. He trained for most of his adult life in karate; once, stuck for conversation while ordering drinks beside him, I asked him had karate changed him. "Karate is my life," he said. And that's all I could get out of him. A loner, he is bigger and more skilled than anyone else in the hall; so much so that he's let do his own thing sometimes, for no one matches him.

He's a striking figure, as he goes through the motions of the advanced *katas*, or ritualised fights, in front of a mirror. He's probably very shy, but it's a close call, because he could be simply appallingly rude; he doesn't look you in the eye. You don't know whether he's seething with ill-concealed resentment at the plebeians he's forced to consort with, or whether he's burning up inside with exquisite, crippling shyness, and karate is the only thing that has given him the confidence to exist in the world. The romantic in me would, of course, imagine the latter – but there are no clues. Romantic? Oh yes, I forgot to mention. He's the sexiest man I've seen in a long time, in a rough, raw, animal sense. Practically everyone in the group goes silly over him, but no one has managed to get close to him. Blond and blue-eyed, he drives a fuck-off sports car, and works in the City. And that's the beginning and end of the gossip I've heard.

And so, dear reader, this is the man who is standing in front of me, his eyes averted, he's standing, breathing like a bull. I cannot do what I usually do, which is exchange a smile or a look, to see if anyone's home; this unsettles me even more. I cannot remember which is left or right. The basic stances and moves, which I knew the previous week, have deserted me. The leader calls out what we're to do; and he might as well have called out Bingo numbers, for I cannot connect the words with actions. I follow what my neighbours are doing. It's my turn to "defend". It's fairly simple, supposedly; I simply repeat a blocking move as my partner attempts to strike me. And he proceeds to do so. Ten times in a row. Each time, I feebly respond, as his fists come thundering towards me with the force of a train, stopping a hair's length away from various parts of my body, accompanied with the most intense guttural yell. Somehow I manage to cope with the onslaught. Then it's my turn to "attack" – and my world begins to melt. Each time I lunge, he grabs and yells and pushes me. And then he tells me I'm not doing it correctly. I'm standing in the wrong way; I'm not punching from the hip; I'm forgetting the basics. Gamely, I persevere. And still I get it wrong.

And he's right. I am forgetting at least one basic thing. I'm as transparent as glass, when it comes to how I'm feeling. People can read me like a book; it shows on my face. Despite the fact that I believe I'm doing the best I can, others nearby begin to take an interest in what we're doing. The leader asks me if I'm alright. In what I believe is a calm voice, I assure him that I'm fine; but, of course, I'm beetroot red and about to float away in a river of my own sweat. So no one believes me. Someone offers to take my place, to face Goliath; but this is not the done thing, in karate. His offer has me twice as self-conscious as before. The focus of the group's attention, I decide to carry on, as my brain gives up the ghost and goes home. I cannot remember a thing, except that the last time I faced such naked violence was when I was queerbashed and had my nose broken and my teeth chipped. The memory keeps floating back. I know that this time I'm not in danger, physically, but the sounds and force emanating from my opponent are horribly reminiscent.

I stubbornly decide to continue, coming unstuck every time. I dream of a moment, sometime in the future, when I've got over this brain-scrambled ineptness, but there seems to be nothing I can do now. I know it's not going to go away if I stop; I'd like to master it. But it seems that I have an affect on people around me; it seems that people want to step in, and stop what appears to be a total humiliation. I can't explain the reasons why people keep on intervening; they don't do it with anyone else. "I'm just a beginner, what do you expect?" I want to yell. But I don't. And I know the one thing that would relax me more than anything else, would be if Goliath would look me in the eye and make contact. I would feel more like a man. But he doesn't. And I don't.

The meeting ends. I don't remember the drink afterwards. I go home. At my door, a Spanish man, with whom I've dallied a couple of times, is there, leaving a note for me. I invite him in, put on the kettle, and put my feet up. I am as weak as a kitten. He doesn't know what to do with himself; he's in the mood for sex, and I'm not. He's classically macho, but with a saving sense of humour – and I've enjoyed having sex with him in the past. But now, it's the last thing I need. He sits on the edge of my armchair, smoking nervously. We chat for a while. After ten minutes, he says he's going; I get up to give him a hug; he doesn't reciprocate.

On Jerry Springer, meanwhile, another man gets thrown to the lions. Having professed his undying love to his wife, she then tells him he's a waste of space, and she's found love with her best friend Karen. His face is a picture of frozen cool.

Be a man. You can take it.

THE TRUTH IS THAT MEN ARE CHANGING
14TH OCTOBER 1999

Harrowing is the word that is most appropriate for the scene at Paddington station, just a few miles away from me. For some reason, I haven't felt inclined to watch television and see footage of the crash; nevertheless, I spent one sleepless night with a melancholy radio report haunting me. When the fire had died down, the sounds of mobile phones ringing plaintively, unanswered, filled the carriages.

It's hard to see why some disasters impact on consciousness, and others don't. Perhaps it's fire that terrifies me; my grandmother died as a result of a fire in her home. The impact of the bomb in Soho still lingers with me, although I have no real connection to it, except by association. One man I know, a witness to that bomb, has taken to drink to numb the pain, and has become impossible to be around, such is the level of his distress. He's jeopardising his career, because he's taking so much time off, and spends that time propping up a bar, smiling sweetly to anyone who'll listen to his tales of bitter self-lacerating rage, bearing witness to his shame about wanting to survive.

I notice, for the first time, that there's a different tone to the way the accident is being reported. There is, of course, the normal, and understandable, search for someone to blame; the kneejerk reaction is that it must be someone's fault, and that someone must pay for the assumed sins. Whether it's the train companies or the company that maintains the signalling or it's the Tory government, someone has to be the fall guy. I've always felt uncomfortable about this aspect of the media; for it implies that life operates according to strict rules of cause-and-effect. My experience, when anything goes badly wrong, is that usually, it's a sad accumulation of various disparate strands of incompetence or oversight or confusion, working together. To focus attention on the search for a scapegoat, on whose shoulders the media seek to lay all responsibility because it makes for a better story, is akin to a witch-hunt, and makes my blood run cold.

But the new aspect to this "story" is that the media are allowing other pieces of information to be included. An inspector of police talks about how two of his men had to be let go home, for they were too distressed by what they saw. Photos in the newspaper include shots of men sitting on the rail tracks, obviously wiping away tears, comforting each other. Now this may be simply feeding into my own agenda (but then, how could it otherwise, it's the only one I've got), but there is something unusual in seeing a responsible British officer of the law conceding without embarrassment or a hint of disdain, that members of his force have feelings. It's the '90s curse, I can hear some old-school, stiff-upper-lip voices saying; it's not a very British way of doing things. What's society coming to, if we let feelings get the better of our our boys in blue; what namby-pamby pinko ideas have taken hold? They should stick to their posts, it's what they're paid to do. What's next? Soldiers crying off when they see too much blood? It's the end of civilized society as we know it.

About time too, I say. The more we recognize how powerful feelings affect our lives, the better. Some reports claim that more American soldiers committed suicide after the Vietnam war than were killed in it. The mysterious "Gulf War Syndrome" that has afflicted so many people who were involved in that conflict may be put down to organophosphate poisoning, but it also has all the hallmarks of being a stress-related disorder. Again, the media emphasis has been on seeking a concrete cause, such as a poison, combined with a juicy bit of conspiracy theory to conceal evidence of that poison; but I suspect that the real truth is simpler and less complicated. More human, if you like. Men are slowly, gradually, and almost imperceptibly, admitting that they have feelings. The "rot" is setting in, but it's at moments of crisis, such as this awful accident at Paddington station, that we begin to see evidence of this shift.

For a few years now, it has been standard practice to report that "teams of counsellors" are on hand to support the bereaved, and other victims of disasters, both natural and "man-made". The line is drawn, between clearly identifiable victims, and those in the vanguard in the emergency services, who cope daily with such emergencies, who are somehow expected to be made of stronger stuff, whose role is supposed to be one of grit and endurance and stability. No matter what the emotional distress they may endure, it's part of the job, and they're expected to cope with it. No more. Perhaps it's because of the welcome presence of women in these emergency forces that things are changing; although, in the main, they still represent a tiny minority of those in the fire and police services. I suspect the truth is that men themselves are changing.

In my book, those two policemen, who said to their superior officers "I can't take any more" are brave. They are declaring that they are not prepared to sacrifice their emotional well-being for any cause; and, in so doing, they are also being responsible, for no one can do an effective job when they find themselves running on empty. They are declaring that their feelings are important, that their mental health is something that concerns them. Let someone new in, to take their place; let it be recognised that the job is not the man, and that the old codes of masculinity are being discarded. Let them not be ashamed. For too long, expressions of feeling, of distress, have been interpreted as weakness in men. If that old standard is changing, then even in the middle of this disaster, I am finding comfort.

For centuries, men have been at the forefront in emergency situations like this. Whenever a catastrophe happens, it is men who cut away the mangled ironwork to disentangle corpses, it is men who sift through the ashes looking for bones and teeth. For too long, men have been silent about the devastation that this must cause inside; and who knows what toll it has taken on them and their families, as their pain erupts later, in alcoholism, drug addiction, violence and self-destruction? This silence kills, just as effectively, but over time, and in insidious, indirect, and corrosive ways.

The more honest men are about their feelings, in the macho environments of the emergency services, the more chance there is that, in future, we can be less hasty in assuming that men can take anything that is thrown at them, just because they are men.

DOMESTIC VIOLENCE: MEN NEED ALL THE HELP THEY CAN GET
12TH APRIL 2001

Recently, I found myself in that age-old arena, the battlefield between men and women, and, in a heavily charged atmosphere, found that a new argument materialised in my brain, unexpectedly, when I was countering a very familiar shame-inducing charge from a feminist that women were disempowered in this society, and that it was not her role as a woman to socialize men. (Politically correct code for: all men are bastards.)

I responded by saying that men and women were "differently empowered". After the ghastly silence that followed my words, I was icily challenged to elaborate. I found myself saying that women were, or rather are, more powerful than men in one crucial area – emotional literacy. The more I think on this, the more fitting I believe it to be, in understanding the dynamics at work for men in relationship.

The context for this gladiatorial contest was a training workshop at work, on domestic violence – a subject presented very well by two women whose job is to support women survivors of domestic violence, and facilitate workshops for perpetrators who wish to change their ways.

In that context, it is hard for any man to listen to that material without feeling a queasy echo of collective shame, even those of us who consider ourselves relatively enlightened. I won't go into any detail about the training, as there are matters of confidentiality to contend with – but suffice it to say that what was presented was tough and hard-hitting. In the role-played scenarios, the men always resorted to violence, and the relationship difficulties, while avoiding overtly caricatured sex roles, were followed by questions solely focused on whether the man was justified in his physical retaliation. The didactic purpose was to get across the message that violence is never acceptable, at any time. In the end, of course I agreed, like everyone else there – it is never acceptable, except of course in rare examples of self-defence. There is no other possible conclusion to reach.

The disturbing thing was the obvious belief of these women that men need to be educated on this.

There are certain sections of society where violence is close to endemic – areas where there are few jobs, poverty, problems with drug abuse and alcoholism, and poor education. Women traditionally have been disempowered more by these circumstances than men, as escape seems a tougher option, with jobs for mothers, especially, being thin on the ground. The poverty trap can be vicious for women. Those women who have had a particularly tough upbringing may endure difficult or violent relationships because they don't believe that they have a choice, or in some way believe they deserve it, or that they will do anything to keep the family together, to protect their children from hardship. Recovery for those women is often long and painful, as they have to face their own part in their situation, and take steps to change their expectations and increase their self-worth – a difficult thing to do when mothering is so undervalued in our society, and the only jobs available for them are often the most demeaning and insecure part-time shiftwork. It is for these women, at the cutting edge of our society, that feminism has most to offer – for it is only by increasing self-esteem and educating themselves that they can set themselves free. And that of course requires government action, and social change, as well as grass-roots support networks.

But what about the men in these relationships? Except those who are psychopaths, all men, I believe, know deep down that a relationship has failed when violence rears its ugly head. Whatever the cause, be it alcoholism, depression, frustrated sexuality, or other psychological factors, when a man resorts to violence it is due to an incapacity to express powerful feelings in any other way. Once it happens, there is often no going back — both partners are stuck in dealing with loss of respect, absence of trust, guilt, shame, blame, and the catalogue of problems that are now classified as post-traumatic stress disorder. Emotional intimacy disappears, and both enter a stage of survival, attack and counter-attack, manipulation and control, from which it is extremely difficult to emerge.

I don't believe that men are innately violent. I believe that those who have learned violence as a language can only have learned one way — by being at the receiving end as boys and young men, from parents, elder siblings, school bullies and/or teachers.

I wonder what it would be like if boys were offered the same support and sympathy by their peers as women who have been victims of domestic violence. For young men to admit that they've been traumatised by being hit by anyone, especially in the more impoverished sections of our society, would certainly invite more bullying or, at the very least, ridicule. It is far more acceptable, sadly, to remain silent and take it like a man, or retaliate in kind. None of this sissy namby-pamby bleating on about hurt feelings.

Because they have learned to discount the effects of these traumatic episodes in their own lives, something is missing in their logic when they resort to violence in intimate relationships, when old unhealed wounds are reopened, when old buttons are pushed. There's a blind spot — they can't see the emotional repercussions to violence, for if they were to do so, they'd have to admit the extent of their own damage. It is not that men are incapable of this admission — I have encountered far too many brave men in 12-step recovery programmes or in counselling, coming to terms with their raw feelings in very moving ways, to suggest that. It is that they are not literate in emotional terms.

We are not taught the words to express our uncomfortable feelings, we are not encouraged to discuss them as little boys, we learn fast that emotional displays are a sign of weakness. It is often only when we are brought to our knees by a side-effect of our attempts to cover up these feelings, *i.e.* through alcoholism recovery, or treatment for depression, or through workshops for wife-batterers, that we have to start again and learn how to speak about feelings.

Even the two trainers I encountered in the workshop — wise and caring women both — could not resist a dig at the psychology of men. They joked that in order for men to begin talking about their feelings in the groups they run, they had to use a "macho" phrase like strengthening their "emotional muscle" to encourage them. The room was filled with laughter.

But not mine. Emotional literacy can be taught to boys and men in exactly the same way as assertiveness can be taught to girls and women. It's too late to teach either, when another couple need the intervention of social services, when yet another woman is battered and another relationship effectively ended, and another generation grows up with traumatic memories of childhood, and defective models of relating.

To only preach empowerment to girls, without redressing the balance by preaching emotional language – and yes, empowerment – to boys, is to perpetuate the split between women and men. It's a split that needs healing. It is not woman's role to socialize men – but in order for men to change, we're going to need all the help we can get. It is not man's role to empower women – but women need all the help that they can get, too.

Sisters are doing it for themselves. Brothers, where are you?

WHAT HAPPENS TO OLD QUEERS?
20TH FEBRUARY 2001

I love my postman. When I've overslept and am lost in a netherworld of dreams, of talking cats and the genetic code of poets, I hear the slap of mail on my hall floor and I know it's 9:15 am. His regularity is comforting, a gentle contact from a secure old world. In the UK, there's been some talk about taking postmen off their regular "beats", to supposedly increase efficiency in a privatise-and-socialism-be-damned world by pooling them and sending them out to different areas each day. So far, this has been sensibly resisted, and I still enjoy the benefits of my postman remembering the two previous flats I've lived in on this estate, and the circulars and fliers addressed there still get to me. Somehow, his kind attention to detail is reassuring, a human touch, even if the mail he delivers is oozing with ersatz familiarity, computer-generated seduction to lure me into purchasing another computer or having a snazzy new credit card the same colour scheme as my mobile phone.

When he's on holiday, I miss him; one of his replacements, a cute, fast young lad, runs on the job, balletically reaching out to each letterbox, popping the letters in the door with a twist of his constantly moving body, in his race to get to wherever he's going; it would only take the addition of a jazz soundtrack and a shift to seminal technicolour hues, to imagine him in an early Gene Kelly film, lithe and rhythmic. It doesn't really matter that his dancing often leaves in its wake a number of residents wandering out in our dishevelled morning leisurewear, to swap, with a shrug and a smile, the letters he's wrongly delivered.

Watching him in his sexy tracksuit and baseball cap, I try to imagine his mates in the staffroom or pub that he's so eager to return to at the end of his round, and am reminded curiously of the culture that spawns the worst of the English football fan thugs. I wonder why this thought pops up, considering that the last time he brought me in a sleepy state to the door, semi-naked, to hand me a package, I felt a cold fiery glance at my body. He left me musing hornily if he ever had nightmares, or dreams, of his mates bringing him off. Then I remembered someone else who had that casual look, David Copeland, who nursed his grievance that his parents thought he might be gay into a personal vendetta of hate and loathing, resulting in death and horrific maiming in the Soho bomb. I don't know why my thoughts run like this. I mustn't be getting enough of something.

But back to my main man, Lionel. He's Jamaican, black as coal, and sports grey sideburns and a gold tooth. He's slow and laconic and methodical, and chuckles at my jokes, saying "Alright, my man" when he sees me. He is without doubt a grandfather, although I've never asked him. There's something about his mirthful, comfortable demeanour that declares it. A sense of place in life that he carries around with him.

Perhaps it's just a symptom of getting older, but I'm becoming more aware of the richness that is family life, in all its complex, sometimes cloying, but usually resilient and supportive nature. This is difficult for many gay people, for too many of us have had our lives defined for us by being excluded, even vilified by our families, scapegoats for the ancestral murk. But too many of us also lack the balls to demand that we be included thoroughly, for the parts of us that doubt ourselves falter at the prospect of causing ripples, of breaking the mould, of taking responsibility. Armistead Maupin, creator of the *Tales of the City* series, was told how he came closest to persuading Rock Hudson to come out, while he was still at the peak of his career. The effect this would have had on American, and world, culture, would have been enormous, as he was the epitome of the masculine ideal in the Hollywood dream factory. But Hudson balked at taking the step because his lover couldn't bear the prospect of breaking his mother's heart. And so, instead of a life-affirming example of hype-busting honesty, we were treated to the sad and shame-filled deathbed disclosure that he had AIDS. He chose to let his lover's fear of standing up for himself in his family take precedence over his own conscience. Perhaps that's the mark of the respect he had for his lover – but I hate to see shame win, even if it is in the name of love. Perhaps for many of us, shame and love are too tightly entwined.

This smalltown boy fled to the big city long after most of his other gay friends had left Dublin. More accurately, I didn't flee – I crawled reluctantly away, for, unlike my friends, I had stayed around long enough to witness that Ireland could change, and cease to be a theocracy. My friends know that they're better off in London or New York, whereas I have no such certainty. In this, like so many other things, I hanker after a life that could have been, routes I might have taken.

And so, to grandfathers. I don't have them in my life; my own died many years ago. I'm not going to provide grandchildren for my folks to dote on either.

The tribal culture of queerdom has no place for elderly men, coping with the uncomfortable decay of old bones, with warm smiles and time to listen and laugh and tell stories again and again. Sexual misfits, finding home in the urban anonymity of world cities, steeped in the materialism of the body beautiful, the life lived fast, young, and to excess, lose out on so much natural wisdom. What happens to old queers? The place for us is not yet imagined. Unlike grandfathers, old age for us can bring a narrowing of our lives, a closing in of the walls of one's home, a house full of ghosts and gifts.

Unlike Lionel, I won't have a house full of young life at the weekends, with children clambering on my knee and spilling ice cream on my shoes. I will have achieved many other things, but that, alas, is not on my cards.

LAST WEEK, ONE OF MY CLIENTS DIED
12TH JANUARY 2002

Began the new year in an eccentric way; a dear friend rang me out of the blue on New Year's Eve afternoon from Stansted saying she was on her way to Edinburgh, did I want to come? Checked the Net for seats on her flight, decided not to balk at the price (my inner bargaining went along the lines of: so much for the CD player I was promising myself); entered my card details, got my reservation number, told her I'd see her there, and off I went, a toothbrush in my pocket. Within a few hours we were wandering the streets of a festive capital city in good company, saw amazing fireworks at midnight, received the sincere good wishes of many a strange Scot in a kilt, went to a club and drank till the wee small hours, walked home and crashed out on the living room floor of her kind-hearted friends' apartment. After a few hours' sleep I staggered out of bed, having set three alarms to wake me, slithered into a taxi, and was back in a sleepy London by noon, and a friend's New Year's Day do at 1.30pm. I think I spoke some sense.

In some ways I still haven't recovered from the shock to my system. But I'm glad I made the gesture, for spontaneity is something I've been lacking in recently.

I was aware, as I was making my way to the airport, that I had the freedom to do something as ridiculously extravagant, as gloriously frivolous as that, only because I was single and solvent, with no responsibilities except to pile up my cats' dish with plenty of food, and drop an extra pellet in the fish tank.

The single life is the envy of many a soul, and although Sondheim's wonderful line on marriage – "You're always sorry, you're always grateful" – speaks to the complexity of interdependence in a relationship, for many a year I've been blind to the joys of being single, carrying the burden of yearning for a merged coupledom like a lead weight, feeling incomplete and somehow alien. The sorry/grateful experience of life itself was not available to me; I was only capable of feeling sorry for myself. In my own particular situation, financial stress had added a sense of feeling trapped in my life, thereby cancelling out any potential benefits of not having to take an Other into account.

Much to my surprise and relief, at the end of last year I sold a small loss-making internet business for a respectable sum. The chains have fallen away. Though not rich by any stretch of the imagination, I am no longer on the struggling student-poverty line, under which I've been labouring ever since I moved to London nine years ago. I feel empowered now to be fully responsible for myself and my life, in a way that I couldn't have appreciated before. And the best part is that I feel I fully deserve every goddam penny.

Money and relationships are so intertwined symbolically that it's hard to separate them. Money can't buy you love, it's true; but its lack corrodes self-love and self-respect in this materialistic society, without which true relationship is impossible. The imbalance of power, when two people have different financial clout – which of course is most people, and to this day is mostly gender-related, with women the losers in most cases – is something that cannot be underestimated.

The insights I gain from my work as a counsellor into people's lives are many and profound, and my clients' stories would make a powerful book. But of course writing about them is not possible. But, just before Christmas, I got a phonecall to say one of my clients had died of a heart attack, and I found myself crying like a baby, much to the consternation of the receptionist who called me. Mostly I was sad that someone should know such despair and pain in the last week of his life, should feel so imprisoned. He was in the middle of a messy divorce, waiting for snail-like lawyers to resolve a complicated settlement; depression had prevented him from working; his sick leave had run out; and he was sleeping on the sofa in his home, with his wife not talking to him, and his children withdrawn because they could not bear to take sides. A prescription list as long as his arm did not provide him with the inner peace he craved. Sitting with him, the last time we met, I saw the look of a drowning man, the absolute wide-eyed terror of someone believing he had nowhere to go. His gentleness prohibited him from making any demands to ease his situation; his inclination was to disappear emotionally, with alcohol, rather than tell anyone – least of all his wife or children – how much he was hurting. My only comfort is that he told another human being how he really felt, before he died; I have no idea of course whether or not he felt unburdened or terrified after he left me. Maybe it was both – but maybe his heart could not bear the thought of upsetting another human being, and faced with the prospect of breaking the habit of a lifetime, it gave up the ghost.

Money, or more accurately his capacity to feel that he was worth something by being paid, was crucial to his identity. Without it, he felt impotent, a pricked balloon. Men in particular are driven by a need to prove themselves financially, for we attribute so little value to other qualities. It's a societal bias. Financial poverty is a symbol of failure in the West, whereas spiritual wealth is unrecognised. I'm not saying that poverty is a picnic in the mythical East – that's nonsense. But there are other values, other ways of judging success. My client's capacity to move me was not based on his earning power; the devotion that his friends showed to him through his troubled last few months was a testament to his other qualities. Although he recognised their loyalty, he could not untie the knot he had deep inside, which was that as a non-earning man, he was worth nothing.

I may wonder about the price one pays when one chooses to avoid hurting other people; I may surmise that his compliance was at the root of his marriage failure, for there was no one there for his wife to relate to, to bounce off, to engage with; but still I'm left with a doubt that it's as simple as that. However flawed his desire to please others was, I for one want to honour his passing with these words, and the wish that our society may change to allow men to feel valuable for qualities other than that desired by the marketplace. Soul is priceless, and his touched me in a way that few have.

LISTEN TO THE BOY SING
20TH SEPTEMBER 2002

I was standing outside a shop waiting for my friends one Saturday morning – the girl beside me in my "first day at school" photo, now 40, and her two beautiful daughters – when I heard singing. I looked up, and a handsome lad of 18 or 19 was sticking his head out of a window two storeys up, surveying his world. Perhaps it was just because it was another sunny day, perhaps because he had a date that evening, perhaps because his football team won the night before – but he was letting rip with a ballad of sorts. I couldn't hear the words but his voice had a cracked, soulful quality. Perhaps he had just woken up. He wasn't a "good" singer by any means, too slight a range, but he put his heart into it. He didn't see me looking at him, or didn't care. It was self-expression at its simplest. I was transfixed, as if I were under a tree listening to a blackbird bursting with natural joy. A communion. He finished his song and disappeared. No one else seemed to have noticed him. My friends came out of the shop, and we went for a cappuccino down the road. We were in Italy, in southern Tuscany, in a small town. It was market day. The sun was shining. All was well.

One of the first books I ever read as a child was about an Italian ice-cream maker, who had a secret recipe for the most beautiful *gelati* in the world. It made him famous – and, I forget the plot, it was so long ago, but the secret to the exquisite taste was that he sang while he was making it. I understand that now. I get to Italy as often as I can, courtesy of the ever-frustrating but essential Ryanair, and stay with my Irish family friends, Dubliners all, who have woven themselves into Italian rural life with apparent ease – not that it wasn't without working themselves to the bone. They miss the craic, but the riches around them compensate, in an eternally beautiful countryside. Ferociously guarded by strict planning laws, there are no hacienda-style bungalows ulcerating the Tuscan landscape the way they do in Ireland. The food is sublime and cheap (euros making the difference appallingly obvious), the pace gentle, the attitude to life, and to eccentricity, is warm and engaged. Like country life the world over, everyone knows everyone else's business, and the politics of a small village are often intricate and pressurised. But what one loses in privacy, one gains in a sense of belonging. Big City anonymity offers the opportunity for re-invention like no other. But, once you have reinvented yourself, then you need to put roots down again somewhere, or something fundamental about life is lost.

Coming to England nine years ago to study has done me a lot of good in many ways; hopefully next year will see me completing my student days, once and for all, with a Master's degree. With it comes the prospect of being able to afford to move back to an increasingly unfamiliar Dublin. I've learned a lot about myself and the world while I've been away. But there is something about living in England that has worn me down in a subtle fashion – and I only notice it when I get to experience the effortless swagger of the Italians, or the chutzpah of New Yorkers. Englanders are repressed, there's no two ways about it. There's a look that I get from some people in England that I only *ever* encounter here. It's a look of slight alarm, as I launch into one about politics or philosophy, or anything that matters to me. The unease is often fleeting, and is covered up very efficiently, but, each time I see it, I wish I was back in an Irish pub putting the world to rights without anyone thinking my passion was (even slightly) odd. I don't feel judged in that way in Ireland (I bring that around me wherever I go). But the English don't really understand the passions of foreigners, especially the fiery Latin or Celtic cultures, and, for themselves, they mistake passion for sex. They're not really the same, and I'm only just beginning to figure that out.

The Latin storyteller, Pedro Almodóvar, has come up with a stunning example of what I mean in his latest movie, *Talk To Her*. It is a sensuous and moving film about emotional, passionate men, like no other I've seen. One of the men, an Argentinean journalist, shamelessly weeps, and it's one of the main motifs of the film. I left the film cheerfully wet-faced. But for the weather, I think the Irish are Mediterranean at heart.

Perhaps, being an arousal junkie, I use travel, or anything that gives me the illusion of novelty, as a key to escape the sameness of being me. But the mind-broadening qualities of travelling are about perspective and perception, the opportunity to see for yourself the endless ways human beings have invented to fill each day, and the spirit in which they do so. In my puzzlings over this often oxymoronic business of being a gay Irishman, I have found that a good dose of Latin *joie de vivre* blows away the clammy Celtic fog of shame, original (sex) sin, like no other. Listening to that young man singing shows me the way I can sing in my life. It's that simple. There is no knack to it, no mystery. You just need to hear it to know it.

AM I HUSBAND MATERIAL?
16TH JULY 2003

I don't know whether I want a husband or a wife. I think that's my fundamental problem. (Well, this week's fundamental problem, anyway). I don't mean whether or not I want a man or a woman as my partner – that choice is not mine to make. It's just that things would be so much easier if I had an idea as to what role I'd like to play in a partnership. And full partnership is what I have a right to expect, it seems, as the Western world is finally shifting in our favour, with the US Supreme Court decriminalising homosexuality in all states (ten years behind Ireland), and the Canadian government announcing it won't contest recent court decisions allowing gay marriage, both in the same week.

The argument for gay marriage is so persuasive that I doubt it will be long before it reaches these islands. Mainly because the institution of marriage is strengthened, not weakened, by including same-sex unions. To introduce a second-tier "cohabitation agreement" or "declaration of partnership" legal framework – marriage lite – to accommodate queer relationships would only lead to heterosexuals wanting it too, as in everything else. When change comes, it will be total. And then, finally, sexuality will have to be talked about properly in schools, which is when queer misery in adolescence will really begin to lessen, and as a result, in generations to come, there'll be less of us walking around hurt and damaged and treating our capacity to love like a cancer. It's a bright future. We're not there yet, but it's on its way.

Not that fulfilment springs from rights alone, of course. The heart is a curious beast, and when released from bondage it may mourn the safety of the prison bars. But it should never have been put there in the first place.

Anyway. That's the bigger picture. What about me? Giving myself permission to dream of walking up the aisle (which, funnily enough, I never have before) I ask myself: do I want a husband? Am I husband material? Or, given the success of feminism, are we all, man and woman alike, lamenting that we don't have wives anymore? Personal assistants and cooks and cleaners and personal shoppers and chauffeurs and childminders and hostesses and nurses – and sexually available too? Can I have one? Oh, they don't make them like that anymore. What's the point of marriage, then? Exactly. It's confusing for everyone, really.

It's all negotiable now. It's unhelpful to have a preconceived paragon of divine perfection as the ideal spouse, because we're all flawed and human, and no one can match up to it. I know queer theory is supposed to herald a Saturnalian revolution in everything remotely traditional and biologically determined, but chaos can't be tolerated for long. It's not about whether I put my fleshy bit in your moist orifices or you put yours in mine, or both or neither. One cannot live life without some guidelines, some general rules of engagement – when driving, we need traffic lights and white markings and a general agreement to drive on a particular side of the road, otherwise there'd be a bloodbath. (Although, sometimes, at the end of a night out, I imagine if some psychic camera could detect the vibrations from broken hearts, the stragglers would be wading through gore across the dancefloor.)

It's a question of attitude, of the stance I take in life when meeting or hoping to meet new guys. In other words, this summer, I want to date, and I want to entertain, and I want to get out there and acknowledge that I've no excuse anymore – I'm no longer a student with a shitload of work to do and no money. Well, I'm no longer a student, anyway. Faint heart never won fair maid, and that goes for the fair guys too. But just because I've been that fair youth, and I've known what it's like to be on the receiving end of attention from bravehearts, doesn't mean I know how to become one. But become one I must, it's the only option.

Christ it's terrifying. The real thing is fucking terrifying. To meet people properly, good-humouredly, naturally, without chemical assistance, without falling over or stammering or sweating like a terrorist, and without looking like a practised Lothario. The last time I went out, I didn't check the label properly on the deodorant I'd picked hurriedly off the shelf. (It gets very hot and clammy in London). It said "powderfresh" which I thought was innocuous enough. But it didn't specify which powder. As the evening wore on, and I had not managed to catch anyone's eye, let alone chat anyone up, I realised that I was powerfully exuding the aroma of a woman's compact, circa 1977. I was standing there, sweating like a pig, painfully aware of being forty and fourteen stone, and smelling like my mother. I didn't manage to make a success of that evening. Didn't quite get into my stride.

To go up to someone at a bar or in a café on my own and come up with a line that is amusing, unthreatening, not desperate, not too earnest, not too postmodern, that successfully manages the tightrope between self-deprecation and overconfidence, and that has a subliminal subtext woven into the words that says, let's have some fun, let's be kind: that's what I'd like to do. And when I'm met with a stony glare or an awkward silence or the mutual anxiety levels reach hysteria, I'd like to be able to smoothly and painlessly move on and let my self-loathing scar remain firmly unpicked. True confidence is not about being sure you'll get what you want every time – it's about knowing that you will survive it when you don't.

The easier choice, the quick-fix answer to all that messy vulnerability, is to play the sport of sex and score without putting your heart anywhere on display at all. We guys can do that all the time with each other, it's instinctive and it's arousing and it's addictive and it's insubstantial. And, ultimately, immature. It's not what makes a good husband. A man, as opposed to the *puer aeternus* – the eternal playful boy of the contemporary gay scene. Marriage requires people to grow up – and gay men need marriage, as other men do, if not more so. It's not to get a wife: it's to aspire to being the best we can be, as men.

MAN, CALLING ME LIKE A SIREN
18TH MARCH 2003

I was walking through a train station when I saw him. I was changing trains, from one line to another, going home after work. My mood was good – over the previous couple of days I had felt the clouds lift inside, a lightbulb back on, one that had flickered out in December. I was wondering whether I had Seasonal Affective Disorder or not, for the sunshine I had enjoyed a few days previously was the first I'd had in months, and I felt at the time as if my batteries were literally being recharged, as if every pore in my skin was lapping up energy. A couple of days later, I woke up and it was like a Prozac spring – everything colourful and manageable. I was thinking I must google SAD. Then I tripped over him.

I didn't physically trip over him. He was sitting on a bench ahead of me, long legs stretched out in front of him, jeans and boots. It felt as if he had psychically tripped me up. I looked at him, and he was gazing at me like a lazy lion, unflinching, piercing, direct. He was tall and in his twenties and thick set. Handsome, in an army kind of way. And he was cruising like a vampire. And, as if I were bitten, I could instantly see through his eyes, feel what he felt, know what he knew.

There was only one explanation for his presence there, and I looked around to confirm it – sure enough, the Gents was across the way, one I hadn't noticed before.

I hadn't noticed a cruising area? How many times had I walked down that corridor? I must be getting old. Or at least growing out of it. Or something.

Time was when I would be acutely attuned to the pheromonal nexus of cottaging. As if wearing X-ray specs, I'd be able to see the dark currents of energy whirling around the men hovering around the cottage, like bees around a hive. My guts would be racing with adrenaline, tugging me there, taking my breath away. I'd be hyperaware of the subtle signals being emitted like batsqueaks by the other players. On the surface I'd be cool, but inside I'd be a jumble of intensely conflicting feelings: a hollowness, a void, screaming to be filled. A strength, a power, from being able to command such sexual energy and play with it. A thrill from breaking all the rules, defying the "no loitering" signs, the taboo of public sex. The stench of ammonia, pine disinfectant, and tobacco. The buzz of secrecy, of playing a game that only afficionados could play. The mirror play, the lingering by the relentlessly droning hand driers. The high of turning each other on, in exquisite exhibitionistic flashes: visual stimulation sometimes being trumped by physical contact.

The language of discreet coughing and foot tapping and sighs. Lewd notes scrawled on toilet paper. Shadows telling tales. Door squeaks our alarm system. Shoes. Aftershave. Trackies. Rucksacks. Cigarettes. Poppers. Stony faces, large pricks. Eyes averted. Risk, danger, shock. Fear. Lust. Panic. Watch me coming, the rush, the fiery pleasure. Over. Tissues. Guilt. Flee. Fuck it. Fuck it, fuck it, fuck it. What a waste of time.

It's all there, in this man's stare. He is completely in and of the underworld, and he's calling me like a siren, with everything he's got. But there's no corresponding tug in my gut, no ache of emptiness to be filled. Today. My dick doesn't go hard. And that's not out of willpower. It doesn't work like that. If only it did. But today, I'm not finding that game horny, and I'm relieved. I meet his cold stare; I let him know I know the game. But I'm not playing. I walk past, go to the train platform. I look back every now and again, and he's still there, eyes locked on me. Still in his sexy pose. He's frozen, stuck, can't think of anything else but the sickening horniness of it all. There's no reaching someone like that. Not in the moment of it. It's too visceral, too entangled, too hormonal, too irrational. Too greedy, too needy, too selfish. Too child-like.

I don't know how I got from there to here. From dark to – well, not dark. A kind of grey. I think it's something to do with finding ways of soothing myself. Something to do with growing up.

I don't know at what stage I left the underworld and stopped being sensitised to the fix of cruising. No, correction: I'll always be sensitised. But instead of it taking me over now, it's just something I notice. It's like being addicted to emotional broken glass, the jaggedness of it, the crack-cocaine-ness of it, the blood-throbbing fucked-up-ness of it. The rollercoaster of it. The emptiness of it. The shame and disgust of it. Above all, the lovelessness of it. And, like the period after any addiction has been left behind, things do seem a bit flat for a while, in comparison to high drama, until subtleties reclaim their fascination.

Sometimes, I miss it. The adventure of it. I fell into it once or twice after I was beaten up last year, which more or less confirmed, as if I needed confirmation, that at its root is a lot of distress and pain. Shame.

And, sometimes, I think there are worse ways of reacting to pain and loneliness. It's only sex, men giving each other pleasure. It's all consensual, private dramas that harm no one else.

I catch my train, and see him through the window, still following me with his vacuum eyes. What he really needs is a hug. I went home to see that war had started.

A TERRORIST IS SOMEONE DOWN THE ROAD
15TH MARCH 2004

I deliberately infected myself last Monday. I was in a sort of daze, but also curiously aware of the daze, like when you're dreaming you're awake. Reality and fantasy weren't separate enough. I had a hangover, I was a bit ropey and at a loose end, unable or unwilling to focus, to get a grip. I knew it was dangerous, I knew I could lose everything, and I watched myself do it. As if overtaken by a mysterious force, with a dull, pleasurable horror, I could feel my jaw clench as I put myself at risk to a new strain of virus.

I clicked on the attachment. All my experience told me not to do it. Part of me knew my outdated anti-virus software couldn't have caught up with it yet, I hadn't seen anything like it before. Another part of me just wanted to see what was going to happen, like lighting a fuse and standing back; wanted the excitement of placing my fate in the hand of a mysterious other, to allow myself to be invaded, corrupted, probed, exposed, damaged, as he wished. The anonymity of it, the thrill of inspection and destruction. Beyond safety and common sense. Everything I've ever known about email, in all my years of being a webmaster and running mailing lists, went drifting out the window. Something was making me stop playing safe. I had to be reckless. I had to live a little. Correction: I had to go to the edge to feel stimulated and alive, which is not the same thing. The edge of what is known. The edge of what is proper.

My hard-drive started straining at the leash. But the screen didn't disappear. No obvious destruction. The virus started replicating itself, infecting other files; it tried to go online, and began raiding my address book. I knew enough about computers to be able to pause it, to stop it in its tracks – then I did the research to find out what type it was, to ascertain the precise level of my stupidity. It had only been discovered the day before, and the anti-virus people had only uploaded their report on it a few hours earlier. A "medium risk worm". It took me three hours to extirpate it from my system. And another hour to buy and install the latest anti-virus software.

So now I'm safe again.

That's alright then.

Isn't it?

I sometimes think the urge to destroy is as prevalent in our psyches as the urge to survive. Freud certainly thought so, with the concept of *thanatos*, the death wish, which he posited worked in dynamic opposition to *eros*, the creative life force. He was writing in the dark inter-war years in the middle of last century, and as the beginning of this century seems to be matching it in foreboding, with Madrid licking its wounds and London actively preparing for the worst, I wonder, not for the first time, whether Freud was right.

The solutions, then and now, lie in psychology, in understanding, especially, the minds of young men: to understand rage, pride, hurt, vengeance. There is a shocking lack of awareness in our political leaders of the circumstances and motives that propel a young man into a life of destruction, be it an obsessive virus-writer causing havoc in the word's communication systems, a man sleeping around refusing to use condoms, or a suicide bomber, devoted to a cause, filling his need for the certainty of a belief, a faith, the promise of glory and redemption. A fair amount of the world's ills are caused by these men, and yet I have yet to hear a politician seriously attempt to understand or alleviate the conditions that created them. This is not to excuse anyone – I do not believe people should escape justice if they've chosen to destroy – but unless we start creating a world in which such states of mind are less likely to ferment and spread, it's going to continue. By remaining deliberately ignorant, we are unconsciously ensuring that evil remains. Do we like having enemies, scapegoats? Does it make us feel better to name the monster outside, to remain whiter than white ourselves?

As we in Ireland know, a terrorist is someone down the road, someone's son, brother, cousin, uncle. Someone who is probably grieving for someone they cared for, who was attacked/imprisoned/killed by the other side. But the grief has been twisted into something powerful, menacing. Men can do that, in a particular way, if we are left to our own devices. It is no coincidence that the current wave of terrorism is inspired by the segregated, misogynist Saudi Arabian/Taliban culture. Nazism too, with its homosexual-influenced stormtroopers, depended on keeping women at bay, to enable the language and practice of violence to become commonplace. The absence of women in the body politic has disastrous results. Leave women out (either by hiding their eros behind a veil or transferring the erotic to the male) and you invite thanatos at its most extreme. This is not to say that women cannot be fascists or suicide bombers or bugchasers, but a culture that supports extreme terror is always male-dominated.

We need to understand men more. It seems self-evident to me, obvious. Common sense. But who speaks like that in politics these days? Why is politics so adversarial, so thought-less, so manipulative, so simplistic?

6: AIDS: THE BIG DISEASE
WITH THE LITTLE NAME

THAT PECULIAR THREAT OF EXTINCTION
9TH MARCH 1995

I know that I want to write about AIDS, but I am having a problem addressing it. It feels a bit like deciding to go for a stroll around the neighbourhood, having forgotten that I live in the middle of the Himalayas, and that there's a blizzard raging outside.

News of Thom McGinty's death reached me quickly from Dublin, thanks to a good friend's phonecall, and my sister arrived in London the day after his funeral, bringing newspapers with pictures of the cortege down Grafton Street, and accounts of who carried his coffin and the silence of the crowd and the spontaneous round of applause outside Bewley's.

When my friend rang, she was concerned that I was alright. I assured her that I was fine. He had died in his sleep. That's all I wanted to hear. It could have been worse.

I belong to a group that is dying off. More and more people I know are HIV positive. More and more people I know have died or are at death's door. It is deeply frightening. There is a taut sinew of panic running through every gay man I know. It's similar to finding a hard knot of tension in someone's shoulders as you massage them, except that this panic, this terror, is collective. But each person reacts to it, copes with it, lives with it, in their own way.

One way that I reacted to it was to believe, for a short while, that HIV does not cause AIDS. I became involved in a discussion group on the Internet organised by people whose working hypothesis is that other factors, most notably recreational drugs, and the supposedly beneficial AZT, cause people's immune system to collapse. They are supported by quite a few eminent scientists, biologists and statisticians, armed with plenty of persuasive evidence to support their view. I do not propose to go into that evidence here, for it appears to be genuinely contradictory and confusing. It all goes a long way towards proving that Truth is not an absolute, but is the lowest common denominator of the perspective of each member of the majority.

The theory that AIDS is the result of self-destructive behaviour such as drug-abuse is quite seductive, for the prevalence of drugs on the gay scene, from poppers to Ecstasy, is undeniable. Such a theory empowers HIV-positive people to believe that they are not doomed to die of AIDS, that by changing their lifestyle and avoiding immune-suppressants that they can dismiss their status as an irrelevance. But the fact is that these theories are unsupported by those who actually work with people with AIDS. Healthcare workers and epidemiologists believe that HIV is necessary for the onset of AIDS. But they acknowledge that it does not follow that HIV causes AIDS in all that are infected.

Even the most conservative estimate is that at least 8% of people who have tested HIV-positive will die of natural causes at a ripe old age rather than of AIDS. Those who have read *Love, Medicine and Miracles* by Dr Bernie Siegel, a cancer surgeon, will be aware of the power of the human will to survive, and of the importance of hope in healing. If you believe that you are going to die, then you will. If you believe that you are going to be one of the 8%, then that belief in itself can contribute to its coming true. That is not to say that we can cheat death; sadly, we are mortal. At some stage, we have to work out what on Earth it's all about;

what the purpose of our own life is. Most people only have to face that in old age. For some of us, that must come earlier.

I believe that there are many gay men who have internalised society's deathwish, and unconsciously engineer their own destruction through alcohol or drug abuse or unsafe sex. Perhaps controversially, I believe that it is possible to talk of unsafe sex even prior to the 1980's. Excessive penetrative sex with multiple partners has always been unsafe, in any era. The fact that doctors and clinics kept on supplying gay men with antibiotics to cure the latest dose of gonorrhea or urethritis lulled us into a false sense of security. There was a collective lack of respect for our own bodies, disguised as a hedonistic ideology of liberation.

Society's deathwish towards gay people is powerful; all the more so because it is invisible. In this year of commemoration of the liberation of the deathcamps in Nazi Germany and Poland fifty years ago, not one official statement that I am aware of has been made to acknowledge the hundreds of thousands of lesbians and gay men who died there. Some suffered unbelievable torture by being the subject of scientific "experiments". I have visited Dachau, seen the original pink triangles, and gazed in horror at the photographs of the mutilated human rats in a cage. Their deaths are not officially commemorated. They might as well not have lived.

It is for us to remember them, and to grieve for them. Then the healing can begin.

I don't claim to have known Thom McGinty much more than any other Dubliner, or visitor to Dublin, knows him, as The Diceman. We spent a day together working on an agitprop demonstration outside the Dáil a few years back; he was calm, funny and sweet. And with a great generosity of spirit. On the *Late Late Show* in which he talked of being HIV positive, I believe he did more to remove the stigma from others in his situation than any amount of health education leaflets could possibly do.

But what was wonderful about that show was listening to one anonymous caller, a young Dublin woman, who spoke for me and our generation, the Dandelion market teenagers, in a moving tribute to his capacity to make people smile. As he was wiping away the tears I felt jubilant that he heard it, and utterly proud to be a Dubliner; that we should show such love to someone in our midst when he most needed to hear it.

While he was still alive.

WHAT WOULD YOUR MAJOR CONCERN BE IF YOU WERE DIAGNOSED HIV POSITIVE?
30TH MAY 1996

Tuesday 12:10am. If you are reading this, then I'm HIV negative. I've been unable to think about anything else for this week; later this morning I take a test, with results in the evening. Out of superstition, I had decided that I wasn't going to write about it in advance, and I would choose some other topic to entertain you; but at the eleventh hour, everything else seemed inane in comparison. And whatever else I do, I don't do inane. If the news is bad, this article will be trashed, and Bootboy will go on holiday. And I'll have a lot of grieving to do. And you won't know. I may write about personal things, but there are some things that cannot be disclosed in this way. I am reminded of when I went on TV and talked about being gay, when I was still at school. A lot of people said that I'd regret it; that my personal life was my own business, and no one else's, that I would come to harm for being so public. I never regretted it for one instant, to this day. But HIV is beyond the pale, still.

9:15am Woke up to a stab of pain; I had snapped my teeth together and bitten hard on my lip. On the next-door radio I heard something vague about RTE not wanting to do the Eurovision again. I fell back asleep, and then woke up late, anxious, annoyed with myself.

11:30am When I arrived at the clinic, the receptionist was one of those unthinking cheerful people, who, nine times out of ten, do manage to cheer you up because the intention is kind. A sort of "if you smile, the whole world will be just that little bit brighter" attitude. A Dawn French special. Trouble was, I wasn't in a nine-in-ten mood.

They were late. She kept on offering me coffee; but my heart was pounding enough, thank you very much. She was answering the phone to queries. She gaily told a caller: the second appointment of the day, to hear the results, would take ten minutes, or half an hour if the result was positive. My blood went cold. Half an hour. It's such a ridiculously arbitrary period of time. In twelve half hours I will be at the receiving end of either a ten minute counselling session, or a half-hour one. Which is it to be? It's one or the other. Risk factors and percentages go out the window. It's one or the other. It's black or white. Life or death.

I picked up a brochure from the table about something called the B.I.G. project. It's a research study "which aims to try and improve the sexual health of gay and bisexual men. B.I.G. stands for Behavioural Interventions in Gay Men." Basically, they'll split a group of volunteers, those who come for testing in that clinic, into two groups, one of which will get twelve hours of an additional "skills course" run by trained facilitators. The idea is to find out how useful 12 hours devoted to "improving their sexual relationships and their lifestyle balance skills" will be.

Academics never fail to disappoint me. They come up with a good idea, and then instead of trying it out to see what the reaction is, they have to insist that an equal number of people are denied access to the good idea for the duration of the test. I know, I know, I can hear all the rationalists say, how else can you objectively evaluate something? The answer seems to me to be that if a procedure is harmless, and involves giving people the opportunity to share their experiences about sex and sexuality, then on a human level it can only be priceless. But that, of course, is the point. The price. The real exercise is to raise increasingly scarce funds.

My disappointment was especially keen because of the name of the project, and the leaflet's cover image of five men with their arms around each other and their backs to us, sitting on a beach watching the sun rise. Or, probably, set. The really big project for gay men is to look at sexual and emotional health in a holistic way; to try and see the big picture. To explore whether the fact that we divorce our emotional and sexual lives is something that is healthy for us – physically, mentally, emotionally and spiritually. But that doesn't fit into the behaviouralist view of the world. And it definitely can't be evaluated in research studies.

The only other thing to read was a 1994 copy of *Tatler*. I read all about Albert of Monaco and his yacht. And his women. In the meantime, the receptionist was nattering to her friend about how busy it was, and how, if it got quiet, then she'd hate to be made redundant. She'd have to go downstairs and do filing.

Imagine that. A quiet HIV clinic. What a tragedy. I was having murderously dark thoughts towards this creature of light when I was called in to see Mike, the counsellor.

Bless me Mike, for I have sinned. It's been three years since my last confession.

"What would be your major concern if you were diagnosed as being HIV positive?" says he, after I had filled him in on the nitty-gritty. Oh shit. I actually have to imagine myself with the virus to answer that correctly, which is his intention. So I think back to the moment a couple of years ago when I witnessed my lover being given the bad news, and I am speechless. I stare out the window, and there is nothing I can usefully say. Concern? I ponder. Worry, care about, consider. Concern. I would be concerned about... I said to myself, waiting for the words to pop up. Nothing. If I were diagnosed as being HIV positive, I would be... enraged. I would be gutted. I would be terrified. I would be shouting, screaming and roaring, kicking the walls down. I would not be concerned about anything.

After what seemed like ten minutes, I told him what he wanted to hear, which was that I would naturally be concerned about staying healthy for as long as possible. He seemed satisfied. He knew that I knew that he knew that I knew the counselling game.

The nurse who took the blood was jolly and efficient. "Quick and easy, just the way I like it," said she, lightly, leaving it in the air as a joke if I wished to take it. But I didn't.

"See you at ten to six," said the receptionist, as I went out. I smiled, weakly, in return.

As I walk home, I imagine crying with relief on hearing good news. Then I imagine laughing hysterically on hearing the good news. But I daren't imagine the bad news.

10:15pm. Back home, tired, immensely relieved. On the way to the clinic, having met up with my friend who was going to keep me company, we passed a traffic accident; a woman lay unconscious on the street, with her legs being strapped by paramedics, and an oxygen mask pressed to her mouth. It was horribly ominous. My friend carried on talking. I had informed her that I was incapable of making any sort of sense at all. We arrived at the clinic, I gave her a hug, and within a minute of entering the building, I was being told that my result was negative. I did burst into tears. I had been worried about it for a long, long time.

So I'm not going to die. Just yet. Useful to know.

THERE SHINES A BEAUTY THAT ISN'T ABOUT LOOKS
15TH MARCH 2000

Paradox. *n.* seemingly absurd though perhaps actually well-founded statement; self-contradictory or essentially absurd statement; person or thing conflicting with preconceived notions of what is reasonable or possible.

Oxford Concise Dictionary

"Look outside," he said. The street outside the café was crowded. "The light. It's getting darker. The wind is picking up, see? Look at the tree. There's rain coming."

We were catching up on news over five years, filling in the huge gaps in our information about each other, which had only been sketchily filled in by gossip from people who vaguely knew how close we had once been. There was something in his eyes that had changed; a wariness had gone, and his eyes were full of curiosity; about me, the people around us, and the world outside. He also seemed happier. Which was odd, because we were talking about his being HIV positive.

"I've come to realise it's harder on the people around you." He looked at me. Both I and his best friend had left him after his diagnosis; he had been through a hellish time of loneliness and grief that would have finished off many a weaker soul. And yet, here he was, five years later, full of plans for the future, free of bitterness and resentment. Something happens to the faces of those that have endured terrible hardship and come through with their dignity intact; there shines a beauty that isn't about looks, that, indeed, seems to increase the more worry lines there are, the less hair there is, and the baggier the eyes have become. It's not about survival. "Damaged people are dangerous," says Josephine Hart, in her novel *Damage*, "they know how to survive." The quality I saw in his face was not the hunted, haunted look of a mere survivor. It was deeper than that.

"It's as if you have to face death in order to start living," he said. I had a flash of how he had lived before; a pugnacious wheeler-dealer, driving himself to extreme lengths to succeed, to make money, to survive in a world that seemed forever hostile. Litigious and confrontational, he was constantly on edge, pushing limits, pushing himself, coping with demons, both internal and external.

Outside his flat, earlier that afternoon, when I had gone to meet him, there were well-tended flowers in window boxes, in February. When I saw them, it was so unlike the guy I used to know, that I double-checked to see whether I'd got the right address, before I nervously knocked on his door. He guessed my thoughts, and laughed. A laugh of recognition, seeing, in that moment, through my eyes, how he'd learned how to soothe himself, nourish himself over the years. He brought me through the back of the house, to proudly show me his patch of garden, naming each plant, and telling me its story, how he'd treated one for mildew with tea-tree oil shampoo because it was supposed to be antifungal, and it had worked, how he'd planned to transplant another, a little tree, and expressing surprise at how last year's daffodils had re-emerged so fast.

We drove to the café, found a place to sit where he could smoke his rollies, and we told each other what had happened in the intervening years; both had tales of loneliness and recovery, both of us were learning to step outside victimhood and blame, seeking a sense of living that wasn't based on the past, which was unchangeable, but on what was going on right now, and what might be possible in the future. It seemed that despite the bitterness of our parting that some room had been made, in both our lives, to cope with experiences that seemed, at the time, to be insurmountable, unforgivable, and impossible to digest, for both of us.

HIV and AIDS has always been difficult for me to write about, mostly because it's been too close to me, and I've been too close to it. But then, that could be said about any gay man who's had sex in the past twenty years; or anyone who's done smack or had sex with someone who has, or lived in Africa or taken it up the arse without a condom (and I'm not talking gay sex here.) In some ways, it's any sexual being. But in our Western culture, in my gay subculture, it's all I know; it's present every time I have sex. I learn to deal with it, and sometimes can forget it; but there's a price to pay when you numb yourself to danger, as appears to be happening all around me. A weird sort of denial consensus can emerge, when you diminish the problem in your mind and take stupid risks – because if you were to really take in the enormity of the mortal dangers inherent in your daily actions and interactions, you wouldn't stay sane for long. It's a defence mechanism, which however understandable, is not the best way to cope with the dangers of sex.

But I had a sense, talking to this wise and brave man, that somehow he's come alive in a way he wouldn't have, without his experience of facing his own mortality, alone. It's an aliveness and a vitality that isn't aggressive, but serene; a calming sense of enjoyment, of noticing the world. In the same way he'd noticed the rain approaching, he drew my attention, after our chat, to the fact that it had stopped.

"I can see a patch of blue sky," I said. He smiled.

We hugged and parted.

I WANT TO GET AIDS
6TH DECEMBER 2000

I want to get AIDS. I want to die a gory undignified death, lying Christ-like with gaunt cheeks and lolling eyes and tubes transporting juices in and out of every orifice in my skeletal frame, my mind long fragmented with dementia, leaving my grieving family and friends lost in the crazed exhausting tedium of ministering to my wasted body, my personality long having ceased to exist. No farewells, no camp ironic jokes, no gallows humour; just a few last, wheezy breaths and then silence, followed by a low, whining complaint from the machine.

Before I die, I want about ten years of living on medication; a regimen of about 15 horse-sized pills full of caustic toxins to be taken four times a day. I want my time to be segmented into quarters, enslaved by an electronic beeper that "reminds" me that I must get swallowing within minutes, no matter where I am. I want ten years of constant diarrhoea and frequent nausea and a strange, fatty transmogrification of my body shape. I want around ten years of feeling that I am a walking bag of poison, careful not to get cut or grazed, reluctant to travel away from home, to withstand the suspicious glances at customs as they rummage through my pharmacy of a suitcase. Most of all, in those ten years, I want to endure that special feeling of anxiety as I meet each potential partner – to come to know, by weary experience, that the only way to ensure some real contact without that cringe-making moment of revelation and irrevocable fear is by being immediately upfront about my HIV status.

Gradually, over time, I want HIV to become part of my identity, how I present myself to the world, and to give people an excuse to drift away, muttering that it's not right to be proud of being sick, that gay pride isn't sick pride – being gay is not a sickness, surely. Gradually my friends will become only those with HIV or AIDS, with the odd maverick mystic or caretaker thrown in, who's excited by the opportunity for vicarious suffering. I will learn to search for fuckbuddies, playmates, and avoid lovers – for involvement becomes unbearable with those who keep on dying, or with those who live so fast that no rest is possible, no calm, no peace. Every day will become a search for sexual excitement through variety, an escape from contemplating mortality. I will become a card-carrying member of the tribe of Death-Defying Warriors Against Mother Nature, and each day alive and fucking will be another blow for survival, for twisted glory. We will all be James Dean, hurtling glamorously and sexily through the firmament, dying inside.

I want the experience of being ushered into a small, carpeted room with a filing cabinet and a potted poinsettia on top and a tired but pleasant face indicating the chair for me to sit in. I want her to make a show of ruffling through a manila file until I'm ready to hear what I've already guessed. I want to hear her say that the results of my blood test have come back positive, which means that I have the antibodies to the HIV virus in my system. I want her to patiently but pointedly ask if I understand what she has just said, and I want to politely tell her that I've known about AIDS ever since I was 24, when the panic hit Dublin. When the panic hit me.

I'll give her a weary smile and shrug my shoulders. She will suggest counselling and advise considering the combination therapy as soon as possible. I will of course comply, for I have joined the ranks of the afflicted now, as I have long wanted, and all the care and attention that the State can provide will be gratefully, if ironically, accepted. My mission, Jim, as I've chosen to accept it.

I want my skin to go weird and inflamed and my tongue to go yeasty and for a strange purple blotch to emerge just behind my ear. I want strange dancing specks to distract me when my eyes get tired, and to get cold sores on my nose and left cheek and to wake up in the middle of the night wrapped in sodden sheets. I want to have everyone I meet tell me how much I've lost weight until I get tired of hearing it, and can't shrug it off any more.

I want to have sex with lots of men because I want to feel powerful and take risks in a western world that doesn't offer much meaning to my life. I want to defy convention and, instead of challenging it on the outside, risking mockery and shame, for some perverse reason I'm doing it on the inside, mocking and ridiculing the part of me that wants to be boring and have a safe and comfortable life. I want to turn the anger in on myself and not really care if someone slips his naked cock inside me without reaching for his pocket first. I want to make believe that it's more exciting that way, to get high on the fix of sex, to see how far I'll go playing this trendy game of barebacking, and ignore the hollow thud the next morning at the pit of my gut wondering what the Hell possessed me to be so stupid.

I want to ignore my feelings so much that, somewhere deep inside, I decide that I'd rather give myself a daily struggle to survive an illness with my horny fellow tribe members, rather than face my own loneliness and rage. I will catch the fire in the eyes of those I fuck without a condom, who will not ask if I'm positive – and I won't tell them. Adrenaline rush to beat the band. There's fire, there's passion, there's death.

BUG CHASERS AND THE COMPULSIONS THAT DRIVE THEM
6TH FEBRUARY 2003

There's an article in the current *Rolling Stone* about an Internet subculture of gay men who have eroticised becoming HIV positive, and seek out known HIV positive men to get fucked bareback by them, in a Sadean epiphany. The journalism is thorough and clinical, by a well-regarded mainstream investigative journalist, whose last book was on an accident in the Vietnam war that killed dozens of American soldiers. He lives with his wife in Georgia.

I mention his heterosexuality because it is pertinent to the tone of the piece, which had a subtly anthropological air of detachment and a neutral "objectivity", which I found disingenuous. The tone of the piece is understated-scandalised, and therefore salacious. I doubt if a piece written about another self-destructive phenomenon on the web – websites for anorexics who encourage each other to get thinner, for example – would have quite the same tone. To my ears, there's an icy absence of compassion. It appears that once sex is involved in self-destructive behaviour, especially in men, it cannot warrant an empathic response. If they are "enjoying" themselves, they can't be hurting inside. How dare they fuck up their lives and get pleasure from it! What's missing from the piece is the dismal inescapable truth: their lives were fucked up long before they discovered how to turn themselves on. And that's sad, in my book.

I was asked to write about this article – the first time I can remember I've been asked to write about any particular topic in these pages. Apart from a pithy rhetorical rant I produced for a World AIDS Day issue of HP a couple of years ago, I've not really tackled the issue in a personal sense. When I clicked on the link in the email from Dublin, and realised what topic I was being asked to address, I found tears coming to my eyes. I knew the time had come to tell a particular story. Unwittingly, Our Beloved Editor had asked me to write about one of the most life-changing and painful experiences of my life. When my boyfriend deliberately infected himself with HIV.

On the 3rd May 1994, in a clinic in central London, and me just a year living in the city, I was with my boyfriend of six months when he was given a HIV positive result. In the shocking aftermath of that news, looking for clues and redemption, it transpired that he had been having unsafe sex with men he knew to be HIV positive, while he had been going out with me, and long before that. I should declare now that I was not infected by him, we had safe sex, although it took me years to pluck up the courage to get tested. I stayed with him for another six months, but his compulsive desire to have unsafe sex with strangers did not abate, it increased. We tried couple counselling, but it only provided me with the forum in which I could find the courage to leave him, wracked with guilt, traumatised, with my trust in men, and faith that my life would turn out fine, gravely damaged. I had been burnt by getting too close to someone's deathwish, and such an experience takes a while to integrate.

Classical mythology comes closest to describing experiences like this: I felt like Persephone, being raped and carried off to the underworld, my innocence blasted to smithereens. I lay there for quite a while, fearful, dismayed, licking my wounds. My own self-destructive patterns, hidden in my concern for him, became apparent, and flourished for a while. It took me two years to begin to get over it, starting by getting angry, in a week-long introductory course to my counselling training – angry at him, angry at me, angry at the world, angry at fate. I was so angry I even dallied with the "HIV is not the cause of AIDS" brigade, for a while, as if by force of argument I could change the truth.

Since then, like most counsellors/therapists, my own hurt has been something that has propelled me to understand the nature of self-destructive behaviour, my own first, and then others. In particular, I've been intensely curious about the way gay men relate to each other, and how they can use each other sexually, and in other ways; how emotions are so easily suppressed. How, in some circles, anything is permissible as long as it's horny. Sex and emotions are separate by default on the gay scene. Those who go against the tide and try to bring the two together are not made welcome. It's worth saying that the gay scene is not representative of all gay men, but its excesses, especially in the large urban scene and in the shame-barrier-free Internet, are symptomatic of a deep wounding that I've yet to understand fully. I've become very interested in what triggers men to hate themselves, with particular emphasis on childhood sex abuse and bullying, and how powerfully our lives can be affected by our childhoods, consciously and unconsciously.

This is not about my ex-boyfriend, but I don't think I'd be a therapist now without the catalytic experience of knowing him. In the oddest of ways, in seeing the extent to which I could be wounded, I learned how much I could heal, too. And I'm grateful for that.

What was missing from the *Rolling Stone* piece, apart from compassion, was the obvious – the backgrounds of the two men he interviewed: one, Carlos, an unrepentant "bug chaser", the other, a young man who, in his depression after a breakup, shifted from reckless apathy about risky sex to eroticising it, flirting with the bug chasing discourse for a few months. To his eternal regret, he "succeeded" in seroconverting. Without their full stories, the article seemed to be another "look at how selfishly hedonistic and sick these queers are" exercise.

In every culture there are those whose apparent mission is to self-destruct, either dramatically through suicide, or insidiously through addictions or compulsions like anorexia. When each person's story is heard, there is usually a devastating account of abuse, or at the very least an atmosphere where emotional truth was suppressed. Suicidal or self-harming patterns almost always start by following the "lesser of two evils" rule – it is better to fix with a damaging substance/experience rather than to stay with the terror of my pain/rage/sorrow/grief/hate. That way, at least I give myself the illusion of being in control of my life. If I sexualise it, then it has the added bonus of being exciting, and pleasurable, albeit in a saccharine way. But, bizarrely, the eroticisation of suffering/self-destruction/humiliation – perversion, for want of a better word – often serves to maintain the *status quo*. It's as if the person who has endured intolerable experiences as a child has chosen not to damage anyone else with their rage, and to implode instead in private sexual fantasy. This used to be isolating and private. The internet has changed all that forever.

The internet is exposing the underbelly of the collective consciousness in a way that has never happened before. We can see our shadow through a window that is not yet ten years old, the world wide web. We have not found an adequate response to it, and won't for quite a while yet. It is disturbing, shocking, appalling to most – from child pornography to racist manifestos, Holocaust deniers, snuff movies, instructions on how to make bombs. Sites on body modifications and mutilations – the eroticisation of the grotesque and the absurd.

Americans, in a way that I don't understand, seem to take sexual fantasies slightly more literally than those on this side of the Atlantic, and they do get puzzled, when visiting here, to discover that guys don't actually match up to the bravado/threat/promise of their horny onscreen personae. But I've chatted to young guys on the net over the years, who want to get fucked "raw" – some don't want a lecture, some appreciate being talked to in a non-sexual way. Most haven't actually done it – it must be remembered that internet sex chat rooms are populated almost entirely by men masturbating – and the hunt is primarily for the words/images/sounds that will make them cum, in the privacy of their bedroom, over their keyboard. Rarely are people in the same city when they've got extreme fantasies to share. And if someone wants to get infected with HIV, they only have to go down to a cruising park and pull down their jeans, bend over, and wait to get fucked a few times. We can get distracted by the words and symbols that are used in sexual fantasy, get taken in by people who are plausible in their perverse desire to dress up their pain in sexual pleasure. The bottom line is that self-destructive behaviour has its roots, always, in a lot of pain.

Should the law intervene in such matters? Should we punish those who rot their livers with alcohol, who shrivel their lungs with tobacco? Can we intervene when a girl wants to starve herself to death? Can we prevent a man from wanting a terrible illness? I don't think we can.

But the least we can do is to try to understand the reasons why people want to do those things, and to work to prevent the next generation from repeating the same patterns.

DANCING YOUR OWN DANCE OF DEATH
12TH NOVEMBER 2004

The 69-year-old playwright, novelist and gay political activist Larry Kramer delivered an extraordinarily impassioned speech in New York recently, in the week that Bush was re-elected. Hyperbolic and not a little hysterical in style (he believes you get more done with vinegar than with honey), with a rhetorical rhythm that is theatrical and provocative, at its heart is a damning indictment of the gay (male) community, its pathology, its political impotence, its immaturity and apathy. Undoubtedly distressed by the comprehensive victory of the religious right in the presidental race, as well as in the eleven states that had voted to ban gay marriage, he was also reeling from hearing bad news about two dear friends of his, both middle-aged and intelligent: one had become HIV positive, and the other had become hooked on crystal meth, an increasing problem on the US gay scene, because it is often lethal in overdose.

Five times in the speech, in a treacly sentimental chorus, he tells his audience that he loves being gay, he loves gay people, he thinks we're better than other people, smarter, more aware, tuned into our emotions, and are better friends. But by the end, it's become a parody of celebration, for the body of his sermon is that he's downright ashamed of us, hates our state of hedonistic denial, and fearful that we even have the will to survive, let alone thrive.

He says that gay rights are dead. He sees the progress that the right wing has made in American politics as unassailable in the foreseeable future, and he predicts all the gains made in equality in the past few decades will roll back with the new Supreme Court. He believes that 60 million Americans hate gay people. American gays are "living in pigshit," and it's up to each one of them to figure out how to get out of it. "You want to kill yourself by sero-converting? Go on, kill yourself," he says. Or... "grow up. Behave responsibly. Fight for your rights. Take care of yourself and each other. These are the answers. It takes courage to live. Are you living? Not so I can see it."

Kramer was one of the first to start shouting when, on July 3, 1981, "Rare cancer seen in 41 homosexuals" was the headline in the *New York Times*. The figure is now 70 million. He despairs that it will ever be contained, never mind cured. He believes there is no political will to direct funds towards a cure, and attributes that to a motive that is akin to murder by neglect. He also believes that the myth that HIV is treatable is pernicious – he lists the side-effects of his medication, which he calls chemotherapy, which are many and unpleasant, and asks: "Is a fuck without a condom worth not being able to taste food?" He bemoans the $100 billion being spent on Iraq, and the fact that the AIDS organisations in the US are all about to collapse due to lack of funds. HIV infections, he says, are up 40%.

He acknowledges the tone of his criticism as being maternal. "Too much time on your hands, my mother would say. Hell, if you have time to get hooked on crystal and do your endless rounds of sex-seeking, you have too much time on your hands. Ah, you say, aren't we to have a little fun? Can't I get stoned and try barebacking one last time. ARE YOU OUT OF YOUR FUCKING MIND? At this moment in our history, no, you cannot."

One of the irrefutable tragic consequences of AIDS is that role models for the new generation are dead. "Many of you deny the horrors of what happened to your predecessors. Every moral code I know of requires respect for the dead." He cannot believe how easily young gay people remain ignorant about the horror that previous generations went through, and rightly challenges us to contemplate the likelihood that the virus will mutate faster than we can cope with, and a new plague could easily (and suddenly) cut a swathe through this young generation, as it did in the '80s and '90s, if our behaviour doesn't change. Indeed, in my work as a therapist, the grief that gay men of a certain age carry from that era of unspeakable loss, with whole sets of friends and lovers dying, is something that is still hard to express, still harrowing in its power, and completely missing from the awareness of younger gay men. Perhaps, like those who have ever served in a war, who have experienced similar levels of bereavement, such devastation is not easily talked about. Unfortunately this means that the lessons of war get lost. Was it ever thus, with mankind? "We do not honour our dead as we do not honour our selves," he laments. But whose dead are they, anyway? Do young people feel connected to previous generations of gay men who have fallen in the epidemic? It seems not.

He accuses young gay people: "You condemn your predecessors to non-existence and flounder into a future that you seem unable to fashion into anything you can hold onto, that gives you emotional sustenance. You refuse to be part of any community." He then says that without community, you don't have political strength. This is a particularly American position – it doesn't have as much logical force elsewhere, because special interest groups don't have as much power elsewhere as they do in the States. But the argument holds true for any metropolitan gay scene the world over: a sense of community is painfully lacking, in my opinion, especially among gay men. (Certainly compared to the palpable sense of community I belonged to in Dublin when I was young – it seemed then that oppression brought out the best in us.) "Why is there no useful creativity going on? Why is there no mental agility visible, no audible questioning discussions... almost anything of importance? Don't you long for some involvement in the humanity that you belong to, for your place in the scheme of things?"

Acknowledging that he's walking on thin ice, he then says that we brought "this plague of AIDS" upon ourselves. " I wish we could understand and take some responsibility for the fact that for some 30 years we have been murdering each other with great facility and that, down deep inside of us, we knew what we were doing." He then speculates on whom he has killed, and who tried to kill him, in the sexual encounters he remembers from the time everyone was fucking without a condom. "Not using a condom is tantamount to murder," he says. "I could never understand during all those years of AIDS why every single person facing death would not fight to save his own life. And I cannot understand now how, life having been given back to us again, again you treat your life with such contempt... You are now dancing your own dance of death, you know. And I hate you for this, too."

The rest of the speech is about domestic American politics, and is a deeply pessimistic, if not paranoid, vision of how the American right has come to dominate. He speaks of the highly effective, hard-working "cabal" of conservatives, active for over 30 years: "They took the richest and most liberal nation in the history of civilization, and turned it hard right into a classist, racist, homophobic imperial army of pirates." He says, challengingly, that they deserve their success, they fought hard for it.

He then asks the most important questions, as far as I am concerned: "How do we claim the God that they have subsumed into their own ownership? Is it inhuman to think that the only way we can get through to some safe other side is by policing each other, and in so doing, destroy whatever hope we have of getting along?" Here, he identifies the unconscious association that for so many (gay) men is our own undoing – the linking of (seemingly maternal) concern to a feeling of being controlled, policed. How can sexual outlaws make our own laws? If a sexual identity is built upon flaunting convention, how can we moderate our own behaviour in a way that isn't oppressive, but supportive and life-enhancing? How can we "sinners" develop our own sense of spirituality, negotiate a communal morality? How can little boys get over their aversion to being mothered and start taking care of each other, and grow into warm-hearted, compassionate men, who take pleasure from emotional sustenance, instead of fleeing from it in pursuit of the next shag? Is the anarchic, promiscuous sexual principle that dominates so many men's lives so untameable, that the only route it can take is destructive?

He ends with a passionate appeal: "I desperately want all my brothers and sisters to stay alive and well and on this earth as long as they want theirs to. Can we all help each other to reach this goal?"

Like an impossibly irascible prophet, crazy and proud of it, whose message is infuriating because it is so uncompromising, so demanding, so goddam intense, he alienates as much as he inspires. His cantankerous fury sounds so much like a moralistic Jewish Momma that one instinctive and understandable response is to react like a sulky adolescent and ignore the nagging admonishments. But we owe it to him, and to all other men and women of his generation who have fought for our lives and health and wellbeing, to listen. And think.

Speech in full: www.scotsgay.co.uk/kramer.txt

7: DON'T LOOK BACK IN ANGER

ON THOSE WHO NEED SECRECY TO HIDE
THEIR THEFT OF INNOCENCE
12TH JUNE 1993

I was lucky enough to have sex for the first time with another man at the age of 16, by which time I had decided that it was something I definitely wanted to try. It was my choice, and when, one sunny day, the opportunity arose I grabbed it by the scruff.

Before that encounter, "Dear Linda" in the *Sunday World* was the authority to which I looked in vain for some insight into my bewildering state of pubescent horniness, only to be told that "studies had shown" that homosexuality can only be "diagnosed for certain" at around the age of 28 or 29. I happen to agree with her that a certainty, a maturity of sorts becomes clear at that age, but for reasons vastly different to hers. I took her advice and turned it on its head. As I wasn't supposed to be definite about my sexuality so young in life, I decided to spend the next ten or twelve years experimenting. To make sure. It is advice I urge every adolescent to follow.

I had the pleasure of being in the Scouts in those few years prior to my first sexual contact. Outmoded, militaristic and naff they may seem now, but I did a lot of my growing up at those Friday evening meetings. And especially on camp in Ireland and Britain in rainy Augusts, eating greasy black chicken legs and baking bread in mud ovens, drinking shandy at night huddled around spitting embers, stinking of burnt lard and singing bawdy lyrics to old songs; waking to a bitter cold I had not believed possible and burning my tongue with scalding porridge. I have a fond memory of my outfit for a daytrip to Castlebar – a purple denim flared suit. Oh, happy days.

I have no racy stories about shady events after lights-out in the tent. In fact, having recently discovered masturbation, I found camp frustrating for the lack of opportunity for relief. The fly-infested latrines were the only possible venues, but, unaccountably, self-abuse lost its allure there. However, I was in love with a boy in my patrol. I never really thought about sex with him, but we would roll around on the damp grass in mock combat, laughing and shouting "Help! Homo! Rape!" loudly enough, supposedly, to disguise our covert desire from the others. And from each other.

I began to realise just how complex sex was, one twilit evening, when two of the lads came over to me and started talking to me of something about which they presumed I knew. Their expressions were so grave that I didn't dare stop them and ask for details. They had been caught together. They wanted to know about what it meant, whether they were always going to be queer, whether they thought the scoutmaster (who had simply warned them off repeating the event in question) would tell their folks. They needed advice and reassurance. It was the first inkling of how I was perceived to be gay by others. The fact that I'd never had sex before seemed not to be relevant. I am honoured in retrospect that they felt they could talk to me about something which could have been so ruinous to their reputations, but I cannot remember a word of what I said. There were no repercussions, and the subject was never referred to again.

When I watched that boy I loved die of a brain haemorrhage the following Autumn, outside the scout hall, I was inconsolable. I was not allowed attend the funeral, because there was to be a guard of honour of scouts at the graveside, and my mother shuddered at the idea. Or perhaps my misery was too raw for comfort, for public display. I never said goodbye.

In retrospect, I now see that the scoutmaster himself was probably gay – he was a kindly, prissy, middle-aged little man who lived with his mother. He was the butt of many jokes, but he was respected and well-liked. He once laid down the law that the word "queer" wasn't to be used, that it was offensive. It was accepted, without dissent, or even sarcasm, by the lads. It was a very healthy environment to grow in.

I feel lucky that those impressionable years of my life prior to sex were free of coercion, and that *no one* ever laid a hand on me except in affection. But I once met someone who gave me a taste of an altogether less naïve upbringing. He was in his late teens, and I in my early twenties. The masochistic fantasy he enacted with me was an exciting introduction to a power dynamic of which I was hitherto unconscious. I didn't see him again, until recently.

He was getting onto the Holyhead ferry with a group of boys steeped in the grey smell of an institution. Their cheap clothes, bad skin and haircuts spoke of little or no individual style or sense of self-worth. I looked at the pasty face of the middle-aged man surveying his charges with eyes that missed nothing, and it dawned on me with a shiver where my erstwhile slave acquired his penchant for sexual subservience. They piled on to a bus, meek and mild, in Dún Laoghaire, and I never saw any of them again.

I suspect there are more young men in that group learning prematurely about sex and power under the malevolant tutelage of their guardian; and I remember my innocent wrestling bouts on the fields of Mayo with a fierce territorial nostalgia.

My sexual inexperience became frustrating at the age of sixteen. It was my decision to do something about it. Those boys have probably no such choice. But there is no doubt in my mind that the man abusing his position is not the much-loathed "Militant Gay" that so upsets Family

Solidarity. Gay pride is anathema to those who need secrecy to hide their theft of innocence.

ALLOW ME TO DIGRESS AND INDULGE MYSELF ON THE THEME OF BATS
16TH OCTOBER 1994

When I was eleven years old, my father brought me out to a river in Meath, smooth and unruffled, one summer's evening. We had brought equipment that belonged to his father, fishing rods and an old book of river maps and angling lore, wrapped up in brown paper smeared with blood and oil stains. I remember a battered tin case, like a cigar case, and inside there was a display of colourful flies made of delicate pieces of feather tied to savage flesh-tearing hooks with fine strands of catgut, which, I was assured, did not come from the guts of cats. There was also a beguilingly heavy metal box, the size of a matchbox, with hundreds of little lead weights inside. These were not for use that day, because they poisoned the fish if they fell off the line and were swallowed by them. But they came with us, because it was a day of ritual, not of sport. He had gone fishing with his father, and so, in turn, he was bringing his boy out.

We passed a pleasant few hours, catching nothing. There was a knack involved in casting the fly to the pool near the opposite bank, which I didn't have. But then, as dusk was falling, something tugged on the line as I was whipping the fly way over my head. My father put down his pipe and came over, and we reeled in our catch.

I had caught a bat. What was most remarkable was its size; from wingtip to wingtip it was no bigger than the palm of my father's hand, and the frail mouse-like creature, with enormous ears, was panting helplessly, screaming inaudibly. It had not swallowed the fly, mercifully, but had been hooked in the membrane of its wing. Gingerly the hook was teased out of the bloodless tear, and the little thing was gone in a flash. Dad and I went home, laughing, close; father and son proud to share the same sense of humour, if not comparable angling skills.

Recently, biologists from Boston on a research trip in Malaysia have discovered that a species of bat, the Dyak bat, is unique among mammals. It is the first species of mammal known to us whose male adults suckle their infants, *i.e.* produce milk from their nipples, in exactly the same way as their sisters.

Allow me to digress and indulge myself on the theme of bats.

As we all know, bats sleep upside-down. But what is less well known is that they give birth up there too. When the youngsters are born, they are blessed with an extraordinarily tight grip. It's a long way down, and although Mum can cradle you in her wings for a short while, so you can catch your first breath, it's up to you to grab onto her fur and never let go.

Darwinian evolutionists will tell you that the infant's tight grip developed through natural selection – the stronger the grip, the more likely the bat would survive. At birth, the weaker-gripped go bunjee-jumping with a dodgy cord, and end the family line with a splat. Over a few hundred generations, they all have vice-like grips, to cope with the change to upside-down living.

But there's one thing I don't understand. You either give birth upside-down or you don't. There is no halfway house. Before bats went upside-down, little batlings didn't need to grip on, because it wasn't really a life or death situation. They would have behaved just like their cousins, the mice – huddling underneath their mother and attaching themselves to an adjacent teat. Why would they need to grip on? After a few seconds on the evolutionary clock, mummy would be flying to catch the plentiful airborne food – but she wouldn't need to bring the little things with her, any more than mice would. Or birds, for that matter. Now, let us revisit the scene: at some stage, one mother bat (there must have been a first) decided to give birth hanging from a tree or a cave-roof. She wouldn't have chosen a tree or cave-roof a few inches from the ground – the whole point, surely, of elevated birth would be to escape predators. So, she hangs upside-down way up high, goes into labour, and watches her babies fall to their doom as they emerge with mice-like optimism, unaware that their mother is a trendsetter. Nobody told them they had to hold tight. She was born in a tree-trunk or a burrow or a nest, in a gravity-friendly environment. Why should she experiment? She would have no children to survive to tell the tale, or if one did, against the odds, the lesson would not have been learnt in just one generation; her grandchildren would be equally unprepared. End of experiment. Her sisters, normal flying mice, continue giving birth on the ground or in nests. Just like birds.

But there are no such creatures as flying mice. Science does not explain how the leap was made. But it was. So the theory of evolution fails to hold true. QED.

I offer the bat as a symbol of the joyously irrational and unscientific principle in nature, to those of us who feel, sometimes, that nature has played a practical joke on us. Those of us whose nature marks us apart. Those of us who love our own sex. Our purpose, if human beings have a purpose, is an irrational one, far removed from scientific cause and effect; we do not breed, by and large. We do not obey the laws of Evolution.

The presence of the bat in human form in our mythology, as the bloodsucking Dracula of our nightmares, or as the heroic saviour of our race, Batman (with or without the Boy Wonder as his faithful companion), suggests the potency of the species in our imagination. Now, in 1994, the bat seems to have given us a symbol as radical as the revolutionary mother bat, who defied the supposed laws of nature and triumphed. A symbol that empowers men to feel that their own nurturing and caring side is natural.

That symbol is father's milk.

MY SECRET CACHE OF PORN WAS A SYMBOL THAT I WAS NO LONGER A LITTLE BOY
12TH JULY 1995

Pornography: explicit description or exhibition of sexual activity in literature, films, etc., intended to stimulate erotic rather than aesthetic feelings; literature *etc.* containing this. [from Greek pornographos (*pornē* prostitute, *graphō* write)

Oxford Concise Dictionary

The crazed sexual frenzy of adolescence is not something to which I would gladly return. The insatiable horniness of a pimply thirteen- or fourteen-year-old male has to be one of the most powerful psychic energies there is, all the more so because there is little hope of it finding expression with another human being, or leading to anything remotely resembling satisfaction. The years stretch ahead, without hope of ever finding someone else to cope with the volcanic power of freshly-brewing testosterone.

In that season of the permanent stiffy, one thing seems to be more sought-after than anything else, and that is pornography. But in adolescence, the above definition of porn changes. The intention of the person who creates the image becomes irrelevant: teenagers, hormonally provoked, can use any available image as wank fodder. National Geographic magazine specials on Borneo. Sports photographs in newspapers. Encyclopedias. Biology books. Ads for underwear. The packaging for underwear. Anything that remotely resembles the object of desire, that reveals something about the human body. On this obsessive journey of exploration and discovery, everything becomes erotic. When I went through that phase (and some may argue with some justification that I have never left it), real pornography was a revelation to me. I have to say that, as well as being very exciting, it was also very confusing and upsetting. I didn't understand it, for I was still a child in many ways. The confusion I felt over which bodies I found attractive was one source of misery; the other was the feeling of breaking serious taboos, giving myself my first real taste of what a guilty secret feels like. It was something that instinctively I knew could not be sorted out with my mother, as everything had been until then. My secret cache of porn was a symbol that I was no longer a little boy. But of course I was not yet a man.

When I was that age, all of my coveted treasure trove was on bits of paper. If I were that age now, it would all be stored on floppy disk. Gigabytes of the stuff. Probably marked, clearly, "Liam Cosgrave's Fine Gael: history project" to deter prying eyes.

The Internet is a pagan, lawless jungle. It is raw, seething humanity at its most vulgar and at its most sublime. It is a world of incendiary passions and undergraduate ignorance, mixed with an incredible generosity of spirit, for most of the wealth of the Net is offered freely by its denizens. Learning about any subject is made effortless; if you are interested in Sumerian symbology or the Ford Escort or the best way to breed budgerigars, you will find many, many people out there who will be only too glad to share their experiences and knowledge with you, and to help you with any problems you may have. I am constantly amazed at the willingness of complete strangers to jump in and offer assistance when I have posted a question, for example on how to get a particular piece of computer software to work.

Germaine Greer speaks at the beginning of Sinéad O'Connor's 'Fire In Babylon':

"I do think that women could make politics irrelevant by a kind of spontaneous cooperative action, the like of which we have never seen, which is so far from people's ideas of state structure: a viable social structure, that seems to them like total anarchy; and what it really is, is very subtle forms of interrelation, which do not follow a sort of hierarchical pattern which is fundamentally patriarchal. The opposite of patriarchy is not matriarchy, but fraternity, and I think it is women that are going to have to break the spiral of power, and find the trick of cooperation."

I believe that the Internet is precisely this anarchic social structure of which Greer spoke. But, interestingly, it was not women who created it; it was, and is, a mostly male construct. By far the majority of Netters are spotty undergraduate males, reflecting the strong sense of fraternity and cooperation of which men are capable, but for which they are rarely given credit. But the Net reflects all aspects of young male creativity, including the less socially acceptable stuff. Attempts at imposing hierarchical morals on its operation are doomed to failure, in my opinion, although many will try.

As the Trojan War was fought over the beauty of a woman, so the hottest political battle at the end of the 20th century will be over erotic images of women, being brought into the home via our telephone lines. Although there is plenty of homosexual male porn out there, it has always escaped the white heat of raging controversy, because gay men aren't protesting about being objectified or degraded by pornographers. Whether they should or not, is of course a different issue.

Everyone who signs up for the Internet should be aware that any pubescent teenager with the slightest spark of ingenuity, if they are left alone with the computer, will have downloaded images of people having sex within half an hour. Or, if they wish, not even people.

We have to be aware of this, and plan accordingly. Those who are anti-censorship of any kind, like myself, will have to arm ourselves with arguments to debate with the fundamentalists, who will demand that new laws will have to be passed to prevent the corruption of young people. We have to foster a more open attitude to discussion about such matters in young teenagers, encouraging them to talk about what disturbs or excites them, in the presence of an adult who is not full of recrimination, but of understanding. In such an atmosphere, pornography's effects can be dealt with, and placed in a healthy context. In an atmosphere of censorship and guilt, the child faced with powerful pornographic images may find it becomes an addiction, and instead of seeking emotional contact with others, withdraw into a fantasy world of sexual objectification, not knowing that there is an alternative.

It is children's natural instinct to be curious. It should be our natural instinct to protect them. Next time you talk to a young teenage kid with a computer, ask him where he hides his porn. If he goes bright red, offer a sympathetic ear, if ever he wants to talk about it. And leave it at that.

If he wants to, he'll talk. It will do him a hell of a lot of good.

OLD FRIENDS ON SPEAKING TERMS AGAIN
20TH AUGUST 1999

I'm thirty-six years old now, which feels strange to admit. I've taken to bleaching my hair, while I still have some on top, in defiance of the creeping grey that is showing itself, now that I've ceased shaving my head daily. It looks good. A bit punk retro, a tad arty, a touch of the sad '70s rebel about my eyes, but a little eight-year-old boy in my building said it was "wicked". That's alright then.

Why don't I just settle down and go with the flow and be happy with the way I look? Grow old gracefully? Bollocks. Not for me is the role of responsible thirty-something father, escaping from the baby powder and the relentless wonder, for an occasional quick pint with friends. I've *no one* to look after except myself, and that's not a task I've been doing that well to date. A policy of casual neglect has been in force for too long now. It hasn't stopped me complaining.

I've been thrown into a vivid meta-view of my life, surveying the twenty years since I was at school, comparing how I am now with how I was then, because I've had the most wonderful gift, in the shape of a bolt-from-the-blue email, and subsequent long transatlantic phone conversation, with someone I haven't seen, or heard of, in twenty years. She and I were both part of the same gang that hung out together in the Summer I Discovered Sex and Drugs, 1979.

I'm not going to tell her story here; what she and I managed to cram into a couple of hours' telephone conversation cannot do two decades justice, and, besides, people in my life aren't all fodder for my insatiable journalistic appetite. Only the select few get that special treat. I hope she does get to write about her life, if she hasn't done so already; she's travelled all over the world, and has done so many amazing things, that I know there's a book or a film there somewhere. But, here's the thing, she and I parted over a particularly explosive, and painful, clash of values. Both of us had newly-acquired exotic badges of identity at sixteen. For her it was religion, me, sexual politics; it seemed, back then, a matter of ginormous importance that those identities were defended to the death. These things do matter, at sixteen.

She says she remembers distinctly the "horrible" things she said in the telephone conversation that ended our friendship back then; I don't. I remember feeling so threatened by what she was saying that I was seething with an impossibly disproportionate rage, which I tried to disguise with a pained rationality. My confusion lasted for many, many years; it took me over fifteen years to stop wanting to disembowel other members of her religion when I came across them. I saw her as a victim, ensnared by a cultish force that offered redemption, but squashed her individuality, and demeaned her sexuality.

How different to the choice I made, then, to join the gay tribe. As a teenager, I went to hear my own gurus: American speakers visiting Dublin, enthusing about the lifestyle of endless sexual adventuring, challenging the heterosexual orthodoxy. We would be free of the oppression of the defunct nuclear family, and would stand with our feminist sisters against the horror of heterosexual man, and save the planet from annihilation in the process. I defined my "individuality" by buying my first pair of Doc Martens at the age of nineteen; I have not been without at least two pairs since. Docs, Levis, t-shirt: yes, my individuality really shines through in that uniform! My sexuality I used, and abused, as a way of combatting loneliness, and escaping feelings. I didn't know how to say no to the anarchy of deregulated gay sex, or even why I should bother; any reluctance or fear on my part was equated with a patriarchal shame-based attitude to sex.

Religion was the enemy; it said we were bad, so we thought it was bad. The fact that I felt bad on the inside, the more sex I had with men I didn't know, was irrelevant; I didn't really see the connection for years. Then, when I did, I put it down to the damage the Church did to me when I heard what the priest said at Mass, when I was a weekly attender at fifteen, about the abomination of homosexuality. And I carried on seeing myself as a victim like that for nearly two decades.

Enough. What was true twenty years ago is no longer true. My friend and I have lived lives that have arced gently in, over the decades, from the hyperbole of rigid dogma to the richness of experience. She sent me a picture of herself in outrageous costume in this year's San Francisco gay pride march, where she was visiting with friends. Although her faith is still important to her, she's not sixteen any more; she doesn't have to prove anything. And I, training as a Psychosynthesis counsellor, am attending classes that are influenced by the selfsame spiritual teachings that I found so threatening from her as an adolescent.

I'm beginning to wonder if I have ever been deeply sexual with anyone in my life; that sort of intimacy and trust that comes from really knowing someone, not just finding interchangeable partners to play games with. Perhaps that tender side of me can be allowed to grow, now that I'm no longer afraid.

I'm glad I'm not sixteen anymore.

25 YEARS AGO
14 APRIL 2004

Adolescence! Christ I wouldn't revisit my adolescence again, the shrieking furtive shame-filled existential torture of it, the hormonal explosion of acne and obsessive wanking and a lust that felt sick, lost, painful, hopeless. So far, so typical, for any pimply youth. But when the objects of your overwhelming fantasies are members of the same sex, and you didn't know that that could happen to *anyone*, let alone you, then the confusion is truly baffling, isolating, dread-full. That was my experience aged 14, in 1977.

Who knew about me then? No one. I didn't "know" about me. And I was in a middle-class, liberal Dublin family, luckier than most. Who could I tell? What, exactly, was there to tell them? That I ache inside, my loins stir confusingly, nothing makes sense – I like girls, but not in that way; or I *really* like girls, but not in *that* way. What way? The way everyone else talks about them, that low moan of yearning. But I can't say, what I need to say: it's not the same for me, it's other boys who do that for me, it's you guys. Not all of you, but him with his cocky arrogance, *him* with his latin looks, *him* with his blue eyes and gentle, smooth body. I couldn't breathe sometimes when overwhelmed by an older boy's beauty; the smell of sweat in the changing rooms rocked me to my core. It was intense and disturbing because it wasn't like anything I'd ever experienced before, and I believed that it was impossible to explain to another. To anyone.

Other boys sensed something was different about me too, before I knew. Whether by teasing or bullying, or by asking me with a respectful curiosity what it was like. But I didn't have the words. I didn't have a clue. The guilty feelings, the erections, yes – but no words. Not in 1977. I did have an image – I remember a scene from *Rock Follies*, where two men hugged, in a way that gave me goosebumps. But Ulster TV soon dropped the series, and there was no one I could ask about it.

In Ireland, then, there were only a few sources of information about sex – of any sort, never mind my particular affliction. According to the newspapers, I had one goal to look forward to: that of being "diagnosed" as homosexual, when I was 29. Until then, therefore I was undiagnosed. Undifferentiated. Unsure. Un-sick?

In Ireland, then, the Catholic church's statements on sex were, of course, *enormously* helpful and relevant to Irish young people, as is right and fitting for a pastoral organisation. In 1975, "Persona Humana – Declaration on Certain Questions Concerning Sexual Ethics" was issued by Paul VI, and in it, among many other pronouncements, masturbation was deemed a "grave moral disorder". A "mortaller", as my dear old Nana used to say. When it came to homosexuality, the "serious depravity" could in *no case* be approved of, as it was judged to be "intrinsically disordered". Our "culpability" was to be judged "with prudence", even those of us with "some innate instinct or pathological constitution judged to be incurable". I was lucky to escape the ravages of such hate-filled dogma personally, as I managed to avoid priests while growing up – but this Catholic dogma influenced every level of education and all of the media in Ireland then. And if I ever did anything with another man, then the guards would arrest me and put me in jail for life. Really.

The British Sunday papers and their colour supplements used to bring some foreign glamour into our house back then. I still have a cutting somewhere from the *Observer* magazine in the '70s about a gay teenager called Clive, in dungarees, talking about what it was like being gay. I didn't fancy him – but the clipping was exotic in its cheerful ordinariness, a prized object of endless wonder. I used to take it out and look at it, read it and reread it. He seemed to be happy. He was smiling in the photo. He didn't look sick. He looked normal.

I longed for some way of finding out what his life was like. In England, there was a species of human being called a gay teenager. It might as well have been the Moon. I searched my sister's copies of *Jackie* magazine for information, after she had cut out the pictures of David Essex and put them on her wall (and which I would stare at, lovingly). There was intelligent advice about sex there, but it wasn't aimed at me, and pickings of insight were rare.

In Ireland, the word "gay" was reserved for Gay Byrne. He was Ireland's most prominent broadcaster. He ruled the world. Public figures had private lives, and no one really passed comment – a thing I like about Irish media, in the main, but it meant in those days that no gay or lesbian people were visible. The great actor Micheál MacLiammóir was buried with a green carnation on his coffin in '78, and all the papers mentioned Hilton Edwards at the funeral, in a different way than normal. But no one made it explicit that these eminent men of the theatre were partners. There were vague references to Oscar Wilde – but there seemed to be something very English about the vice of homosexuality, the prison sentences and the theatricality of it. Not Irish at all.

Also in England was the dark species of being that was Norman Scott, a queeny little man who reached lurid tabloid notoriety by accusing the married Liberal leader Jeremy Thorpe of having "homosexual relations" with him. Scott claimed, in 1977, that people had killed his dog, and later that Thorpe and others had conspired to kill him, to silence him. This was the atmosphere of the time – homosexuality was inextricably linked with blackmail, murder, crime, conspiracy, paranoia, and a queasy feeling of unease and shame.

A university lecturer called David Norris founded something called the Irish Gay Rights Movement in the '70s – but there was scant mention of them in the press. They had a PO Box number, I remember, because I wrote to them in 1978. Trouble is, they had disbanded by then, split, the way most groups split at some time or another. My letter remained unanswered for nearly a year, until the National Gay Federation was born, and my cry for information and help went unanswered. I felt like I had shouted into a vacuum, and there was no echo, no noise at all.

But by the time they did answer me, and I began to find out how to meet other gay people, something wonderful had happened. I had begun to read the new magazine called *Hot Press*. As I write this now, I find myself with tears welling up. Tears? Don't be ridiculous. It was only a music magazine.

No, it was never only that. For me, at that time, locked in my isolation cell of ignorance, it was the first magazine, the first *anything*, that took it for granted that sexual difference was OK, that theocracy was not OK. There was no inner debate, no immature angst, no "we are being awfully rebellious here" – sexual equality was a given. It was assumed that readers would agree. It never patronised its readers – it always assumed a level of intelligence and a maturity of political views, and combined that with being funny and passionate and questioning. In '78, when Tom Robinson issued his EP with 'Glad to be Gay' on it, I read all about him and his views and the history of gay rights and how to learn about sexual politics, *all* in the pages of *Hot Press*. The editorial tone of the magazine to him was a very Irish, cool, laid-back acceptance – curiosity, sure, but always welcoming.

It seems impossible to imagine, now, how dark those days were before HP. Reading through this year's official report "Implementing Equality for Lesbians, Gays and Bisexuals," I find it saying: "Ireland is at the forefront of countries that protect LGB people against discrimination". Looking at the way Irish lesbian and gay people are so visible now – as lovable characters, like Anna Nolan and Brian Dowling from *Big Brother*, like Shirley Temple-Bar and Graham Norton, and of course the national treasure that is David Norris – it's unimaginable from the perspective of 1977. Seeing *Gates of Gold* at the Gate, being moved by Frank McGuinness' elegant tribute to Hilton and Micheál – that feels like a deep healing going on, making up for the wounds that fear and ignorance and the theocracy inflicted on Ireland for so long.

Hot Press was one of the main engines for change in Ireland – it raised the level of intellectual and political discourse among young people to one of independent-thinking maturity, based on sane, liberal values and an abhorrence of hypocrisy. Remember this, always. There were Dark

Ages in Ireland, and they began to end when *Hot Press* started, in 1977.
~ *For the 25th Anniversary issue of Hot Press* ~

I FEEL LIKE RUTGER HAUER IN BLADERUNNER
28TH NOVEMBER 2002

"I've seen things you people wouldn't believe. Attack ships on fire off the shoulder of Orion. I watched C-beams glitter in the dark near the Tannhauser gate. All those moments will be lost in time like tears in the rain... Time to die."
– Rutger Hauer, *Bladerunner*

I feel like Rutger Hauer in *Bladerunner*. It's a dark wintry night and there is a storm overhead, with great bangs of thunder, and blue flashes of lightning illuminating my damp courtyard. I'm in my little cupboard-sized study, green Venetian blinds at the Georgian window, only the limpid glow from the computer to help me type.

My time is nearly up, as a gay man. I'm nearly forty. I need to go out in the rain and find a halting place to rust gently away. Not quite with the bathos of von Aschenbach in *Death In Venice*, with hair dye trickling down his face, but you get the picture. A part of me needs to be laid to rest, and given a decent send-off. A wake for the boy in me, as my hair, no longer shaved or bleached or mohicaned, turns a subtle but unmistakable shade of grey. Women call it distinguished, find it attractive – but that's not the standard I've been plugged into for most of my life.

My head-turning power-cell is reaching the end of its natural life; the fuel of attention, which coursed giddily through my veins since I first walked into a room of gay men when I was sixteen, now runs low. My capacity to "switch on" and catch the light in a crowded room and know that people have taken me in, have admired, have fantasised, is over. Time to change to another, longer lasting fuel – perhaps one with a little less toxic side effects, kinder to the environment and to the heart. But it's also time to pay homage to that extraordinary power that I once wielded, and which all young men wield, when they realise that their youthful presence is yearned for by older men.

What I could do with that attention! I've seen and done things you wouldn't believe, with people you couldn't imagine, in places beyond your wildest dreams. The erotic power of youthful male beauty in the homosexual world is an extraordinary, anarchic phenomenon. It opens doors to all social classes and generations, it mocks all romantic/social conventions and is truly subversive in its disregard for the law.

Young men aren't supposed to know they're beautiful. We aren't prepared for it – we have never been encouraged to imagine it, for all sorts of obvious reasons. But girls are encouraged all the time to look pretty and appealing and to flirt with all and sundry, with make-up kits and toys and comics and magazines, all about attracting attention. I think for many reasons boys should be prepared for it even more than girls, for the combination of raging testosterone and plenty of attention is a heady one; for all the talk of "ladettes" and girl power, young women are still more cautious and responsible about sex than young men. Emotional literacy is not a notable feature among teenage lads.

But the prospect remains slim that any teacher could talk to 14-15 year old lads and tell them that, within a year or two, some of them may discover a route to limitless exciting sex (without commitment if preferred), the prospect of being the centre of attention in a group of admirers of all ages and incomes, and offer advice on what care they'd need to take. Gay teenagers, I suspect, are going to have to discover that for themselves for some time to come, unless the nettle of male sexuality is honestly grasped in education. The only way it's going to work is if, as part of sex education, gay men are brought in to talk about gay relationships and personal safety to classes of teenagers. There would be outcry from the media, and the orcs would come streaming out of the catacombs of the Vatican at the prospect, but it's the only sane way I can think of to warn young gay kids of the dangers out there, of the responsibilities that come with sexual power. Having been a kids' teacher, I know how a lesson could be taught with respect and humour and as little embarrassment as possible to teenage lads. I wonder will it happen in my lifetime?

I remember being overwhelmed when I first went on the gay scene. I had no way of judging what was happening to me – the attention I got was almost constant. I responded innocently and truthfully, I'm glad to say now, but I also got hurt when men seemed to lose interest once they had scored with me, and I took it far too personally. My sense of self-doubt began to increase, the more I realised that what was attracting people was not my character, but that mysterious phenomenon over which I had no control, my youth. Seeds of uncertainty were sown then that took a while to germinate and bloom later in my life, a sense of confusion as to what was valuable or attractive about me inside. The timeless me.

Christ, though, it was mad, crazy, wonderful. In my heyday, I've met with ambassadors and politicians and builders and crack addicts and sportsmen. Rentboys and accountants, judges, teachers and fathers-of-four. Fellow actors, of course. Musicians, poets, academics, writers, journalists. Crooks, prison officers, drug dealers, DJs. Faces that are familiar on national television now, are faces I've seen where they "shouldn't" have been. There is a code of ethics among us for those who haven't come out – it's a camaraderie of sorts – although I've sometimes erred on the side of secrecy at the expense of justice or truth.

I've been stopped by a policeman for cruising only to have him in my bed, trembling like a child, a few hours later. I've had sex with a priest in his dog collar in a public toilet, fucking him in intense revenge. I've read a news report of a number of soldiers being shot, with no obvious suspects or leads – and recognised the face of one of them, and remembered the smell of wintergreen on his smooth skin, and that I had his telephone number scrawled in kohl on my National Gay Federation membership card. I've heard stories of one of the founding fathers of our state regularly going cottaging, but although I believe the man who told me, he has since died. Our national heritage, not to mention his family, is safe from scandal.

Like much of gay life, the stories that come from it are transient, sensory, thrilling and insubstantial, memories that indeed vanish like tears in the rain. It's not a heart-filled world, it's crass and disturbing and isolating and commercial and, if one doesn't have a strong sense of identity, the pain of passing one's sell-by date is too much to bear. I've been lucky – very lucky – to have escaped with my good health, having been a teenager at the "wrong" time, in the celebratory, hedonistic years just before AIDS was discovered. But what's disturbing is that teenagers these days, according to research, are still not all practising safe sex – as many as one in five don't use condoms. It's not in a young person's nature, really, to worry about the future – live fast, party party party, just as I did – but it's a sad indictment against the gay "community" that our newest members aren't being taught the basics of self-respect and self-care by those of us who know the score.

Too many older guys are in the thrall of youthful erotic power, and can't think beyond their knobs – but then that's how they learned about relationships themselves. The hard way. The fun way. The intense way. The way that doesn't last.

WE ALL HAVE THE SAME CORE ISSUES OF PRIDE AND SHAME, LUST AND LOVE
14TH DECEMBER 2003

Reviews are subtle but powerful things: like when we are asked to account for ourselves, to say how life has been for us since last meeting someone, at a wedding or on those calendar events like Christmas and New Year, or personal ones like birthdays or anniversaries, and we really stop and think. In my work as a therapist, the first session with a client is really about listening to someone review their life to date. Some people have never done this before, and may even not be able to, other than to list dates and jobs and partners, like a CV; others have over-examined their lives to a crippling degree. In many ways, the work of therapy is a function of narration – if we can tell our story in such a way that we own our own part in its unfoldment, and not blame others for our misery, or endow others with sole responsibility for our happiness, then we're almost there. In some ways, therapy is a process of eliminating resentment – especially among those who drink too much, their addiction fuelled by the smouldering self-pity that their life is not as it "should have" been. But the only way to detect resentment is to listen for the whiff of victimhood when people tell their stories, review their lives.

But: physician heal thyself. I can't bear writing about how the last twelve months have been for me, so I retreat to professional musings. It's safer that way, less risky. I buggered up on getting my MA this year, and have had to face profound feelings of stupidity in the face of stinging criticism, while reworking my referred final submissions. Whether or not I can get it done by the next deadline is uncertain right now. I've got a stinking, sneezy cold and it feels like I'm all emotion, with not a brain cell to call my own. Could someone rescue me, please? Oh, no. Life's not like that.

I'm still finding it a hollow joke that I'm 40 now. It makes no sense to me whatsoever, as I remain the person I was when I was in my early twenties, behind the baggy eyes and the lined forehead and the greying, thinning hair. It is amazing how invisible I feel now when I go on the gay scene – it almost makes me consider a life of crime, as the scanning, cruisy eyes that used to ping me when I had the "look" now don't even flicker as they pass right through me. I could get away with murder and there would not be witnesses. A club I've been going to for the past couple of months every Sunday has a doorman who, despite having chatted to him regularly, asks me each time if I've been there before. I don't mind it anymore. I don't function on a visual level, that's my understanding of it now. That this should matter at all is a symptom of remaining single, for which I have no remedy except to persevere and carry on carrying on. That is beyond my control.

The only thing that has improved in my life is something that I don't underestimate, which is that I'm finally earning enough money to pay off my (student) debts and to begin to be able to save and plan long-term treats like holidays and wheels. Not having enough money to live on is a debilitating, corrosive experience, and eats to the heart of self-esteem and stability – so my hope is that this doesn't ever fade away on me again. I think part of what kept me from taking on too much work, unconsciously, was my fear of getting stressed and returning to my depression of three years ago. Fear is a bugger. In some spiritual schools of thought, fear, not hate, is the opposite of love. I can understand that.

This year has been one in which a very personal struggle from my adolescence reached world headlines, the split in the Anglican church around the appointment of an (openly) gay bishop. This cuts to the heart of the chasm in Christian teaching between sexuality and spirituality, and as it is debated and taken seriously, I feel my own split lessen in hurt. I wasn't such a freak, then – it may have taken it 25 years to get out in the open, but finally hypocrisy on matters sexual is being addressed for the deeply moral question that it is. The fact that the dying Pope still found it necessary to blast homosexuality this year, at the same time as his clergy were lobbying against gay marriage and spreading rumours about porous condoms, just confirms for me that no self-respecting gay or lesbian person could be a Catholic. Actually, scrub that – no self-respecting thinking person should be a Catholic. But there's hope yet for some Christians, and the New Hampshire Anglicans are leading the way. I'm not saying that the answer to the queer sexual dilemma is domestication and Church-blessed monogamy, but I do know that having it as a serious option is a freeing and life-affirming spiritual advance. Without it, sexual anarchy can seem to be the only self-respecting choice.

A special mention for the end of the much-loathed Section 28 in the UK – the reprehensible Thatcherite injunction against local authority schools "promoting" homosexuality, thereby perpetuating the myth that homosexuality is learned or "caught", and keeping young gay and lesbian kids in ignorance and fear. I am of the firm belief that so much suffering in queer lives is caused by the trauma in adolescence of keeping one's lovelife a dirty secret, instead of something gleefully gossiped about and shared with friends. I am certainly not saying it's easy for anyone in adolescence; I know it's not. A survey this year showed that the same percentage of gay/lesbian people were bullied at school as were the others – the only difference being that the cause was more obvious for the queers.

The more I learn about life, especially through my clients, the clearer it becomes that queer problems are everyone's problems – we just seem to have been sensitised to them earlier, and have a vocabulary to express them. I listen to more and more heterosexual men in my work and the challenge of how to tame the beast of sexual desire is the same. Different opportunities and lifestyles, perhaps, but the same core issues of pride and shame, lust and love, hate and fear. Everyone imagines that there are people out there who have sorted out their sexuality, eradicated confusion – but I know no one for whom this is true.

In telling our stories, it is, perhaps, how much we can tolerate the disappointment that our life isn't how we wanted it to be that shows us how mature we're getting.

Bah. Humbug. I'm still throwing out the toys from the pram, here.

I DON'T REMEMBER THE LAST TIME I WOKE UP WITH SOMEONE AND BROUGHT THEM COFFEE
24TH OCTOBER 2003

My dream life is haunting me at the moment. Visions of quirky isolation and flight: *A handsome, tall, blond young guy leads me by the hand to his bedroom, late at night, and we lie together. He quietly excuses himself, and then it gradually dawns on me that he's gone, he's left the house. It's a family home – and I'm in his bed, sleepless, mortified, listening to the house creak, waiting, hollow inside. My vacuum envelops the room, the house, the world. Sheepishly, in the morning, I tiptoe down, introduce myself to the family in the kitchen and apologise that they appear to have a missing son on their hands. They are blasé about it, as if it happens all the time, and start showing me proudly around the house, pointing out its architectural features and the design of their espresso cups. Your man turns up in time for breakfast, nonchalant. I feel like I'm the mad one, for being concerned. For noticing his absence, for being the only one to think it mattered. For having wanted to be with him so much.*

That's the feeling I wake up with – the empty arms syndrome, bafflement, the sight of the young face looking blankly at me, not getting me. I can't tell if he looks guilty or not. I do not know if I'm crazy or not.

In real life, continuity in sexual/romantic relationships persistently escapes me. This watched kettle is not even above lukewarm. In sex, jagged departures no longer rip me apart, my edges have become smooth, like tumbled pebbles on the shore. I'm polite, charming, humorous with the men I meet. I am most emphatically, most assuredly, most definitely the opposite of human velcro. I know what spoils the game. We are emotionally absent, in order to be present with each other. As a dear friend said to me about twenty years ago – the most yearned for is the most elusive: the conscious kiss. Frenzied, lustful, fast and furious snogging with a hot guy, who takes your breath away? Check. Knowing someone in all their complexity and absurdity and fear, and tasting his lips with your lips as testament to the affection you have for him? Cheque, please. Got to run. Is that the time?

Or is it that I have the knack of picking guys who only want to play the sport of sex? Is my unconscious pitting me repeatedly against the archetype of Teflon Man to teach me the meaning of Buddhist non-attachment? Gee, thanks.

If one has learned the rules of pleasant non-committal exchange, avoiding intimacy and maximising stimulus, can they be unlearned? If it's quiet, calm intimacy that I really want, then what am I doing in the middle of the playing field? The easy answer, one that many guys use, is: "what else am I to do while I'm waiting for Mr Right?" I know there's a more difficult, more honest answer, but I can't quite put my finger on it.

I cannot command intimacy, I cannot conjure up a friend. I know of no working recipe to bake a long-term lover – I imagine there's an algorithm sometimes, like time x opportunity / acceptance x kindness = interested party – but I've heard so many different stories of how people met their lovers, there is no right or wrong way. It's either going to happen or it's not.

I meet people in all sorts of different ways, and try to keep in touch with as many of them I like as possible. It's a shame that none seems to have had an interest in me romantically or sexually for a long time – but I value their friendship nonetheless, and we have a lot of fun. I've got used to the transition from first tentative dates, where anything is possible, to the "let's have coffee sometime" text, after the decision has been made. I can honestly say, though, that I've no regrets – I've never let someone big-hearted slip away, for want of attention or perseverance. Faint heart never won fair, erm, maid. Having got a new dinner table in my living room recently, I'm planning to do a very grown-up thing and invite people to dinner parties, with people I don't know that well. And ask them to bring friends, etc. etc. etc. I bounce back and keep on trying. It's what I do. It's what I have to do.

I don't remember the last time I woke up with someone and brought them coffee. It was last year sometime. At night, in that liminal state between wakefulness and sleep, I still hear myself mutter the name of the last man I loved, which I'm sure would surprise the hell out of him now, all these years later. It surprises me, too – for I never consciously think of him, I don't miss him at all during the day. But my body, at night, remembers that lost pleasure of his smooth chunky body, and calls out for that warmth, that comfort.

I've discovered, at 40, as if for the first time in history, the horrific truth about age – that, in essence, nothing changes on the inside, as you change on the outside. I'm still the same curious, intense, adolescent exploring the world that I ever was; still just as sexual, still just as sensitive, still just as uncertain, still just as in need of attention and physical affection.

I would have thought things would change. I am more solid, though, and more resilient, and I don't do things I don't want to do anymore, and have a greater capacity to find things funny. But I remember what I thought of older guys when I was a teenager or in my early twenties – I remember their kind, sad eyes and warm faces, bewitched by my youth. And I remember that they didn't do a thing for me. I liked them, but they didn't appear at all on my radar screen of potential partners. Now that I'm their age, and similarly astonished by the openness and warmth of youth, the wheel turns full circle.

Like all good parents of the '60s, mine told me that it didn't matter what I did in life, as long as I was happy. I've done some interesting and worthwhile things in my life, and hope to do many more – but their prime directive has eluded me in the past few years. Happiness, for them, is a loving marriage, of over 41 years now. It's a tough act to follow. But this much I know: it's out of my control.

ON BEING A STUDENT
17TH SEPTEMBER 2004

Last week, a certificate arrived in the post. It was an MA. It's my first ever degree, gained at the age of 41, and getting it was one of the hardest things I've ever done in my life. In contemplating the lessons I've learned on that journey, and attempting to distil them, I realise that I haven't really come to terms with the wildly conflicting attitudes and feelings I have towards academia. I am, as they say in psychotherapy-speak, split.

Of course, I blame my mother. She once typed out, on an index card, a paragraph of the wisest words I have ever read on the subject of formal education and, after a painful time when I was struggling with this split at school, and freaking out about doing the Leaving, pasted the card on my Swiss Cheese plant in my bedroom so I would see it when I came home. "You are in the process of being indoctrinated," it began. These were words written by Doris Lessing, in the preface to her masterwork, *The Golden Notebook*. "What you are being taught is an amalgam of current prejudice and the choices of this particular culture. The slightest look at history will show you how impermanent these must be. You are being taught by people who have been able to accommodate themselves to a regime of thought laid down by their predecessors." She goes on to encourage those who are robust enough to leave this "self-perpetuating system" and educate themselves, hone their own judgment, and offers advice to those who stay in the system to remember, always, "that they are being moulded and patterned to fit into the narrow and particular needs of this society."

Like a lightning bolt, these words hit home, and fanned the flames of my individualism, my anarchistic sensibility that (rightly) found fault with all authority. The trouble with such a fierce manifesto for individuality, is that it's tough to live by. Artists in garrets starve for a very good reason. The forces of conformity are powerful. Very few individualists manage to succeed outside the system.

The other message I received loud and clear from my parents and teachers, was the need to get a qualification, almost any qualification, in order to give myself some kind of choice later in life. But it seemed to me to be too high a price to pay. Once a scholarship boy, with a record number of As in what, at the time, was called the Intermediate Certificate, I stewed in an unhappy adolescent soup of guilt and fear in the last two years of school. The fear was around being judged – for as much as I despised the "authorities", part of me badly wanted their approval. But, for that, I needed to study, and come up with the goods that demonstrated I was compliant. I could not find the maturity to separate the goal from the fear, to see the whole endeavour as a necessary evil, a means to an end. I took things far too personally. If my words weren't good enough, then I wasn't good enough. But then, as an adolescent, everything is personal. On my last day of school, my history teacher took me aside and wished that he could have written on my report card "this pupil shows a good sense of revolt". (Happily, he was to become headmaster eventually, after the old retainers and fascists had their turn.)

The downside of this choice to flunk the Leaving and avoid University was that I've been relatively poor for most of my adult life. I trained as an actor, and in my twenties found that I could make quite a good living from it. But actors are like divine children – we give ourselves over to the gods of theatre, and if we're lucky, we find that the gods smile down on us. I'd receive a tax bill for a thousand pounds one day, and get an American ad that paid me twelve hundred pounds the next. Chaotic living. I worked in the Abbey, when there was a National Theatre to speak of, and was able to wine and dine myself most evenings of the week, travel the world and get paid for it, and through that mysterious, fateful, Bohemian mechanism of show business, I was the right face at the right time in enough auditions to make my twenties fulfilling and comfortable. In between jobs, not having a degree, I worked as a waiter – but when you're young, restaurant work, while exhausting, is highly sociable and fun. You can eat at the restaurant, live off tips, and the wage pays the bills and the taxes. I still have friends from that time, that I wouldn't be without.

But, in the end, when Hollywood wasn't beckoning, and I became tired of speaking other people's words, I reluctantly realised that I needed that which I had spent all my life resisting: a qualification.

And I've gained a few, over the years, in London. The most rewarding one was a diploma that enabled me to become a teacher myself, in a subject that is wildly, determinedly esoteric: psychological astrology. The college where I teach is world-renowned, but it resolutely avoids the pitfalls of becoming an institution, a hide-bound authority − its loose. modular structure, and its encouragement of students to excel in their own individual talent and personality, is beyond the remit of traditional education. Students there who seek validation or approval from the staff invariably drift away, and do not complete the course: those who have a sense of their own inner authority and wisdom thrive in the Platonic atmosphere, and allow themselves to be educated − from *educare*, to draw out what is already there. I am blessed to be associated with it.

But the Masters pitted me, finally, against the demon of conformity, a psychology department that prided itself in being in the "top third" in the UK league table. And it almost defeated me. It was touch and go whether I could find the words that retained my sense of the world and its chaos and confusion, and simultaneously demonstrated that I was embedded in the academic conventions, had accepted their necessity. It took a year longer than it could have, I had to rewrite everything I presented in the final year. I found some original ways of writing, employed unconventional methodologies. I had to face my fear of being fiercely criticised and come through it, and not take it personally enough to cripple me, although I was wounded for a while. The thing that sticks in my throat still is the absurd notion that academia is impartial. While most people in it attempt to maintain that illusion, all it needs is one teacher to take a dislike to your work, and you're sunk − because they'll couch their criticism in seemingly objective terms, that are nearly impossible to counter. I managed to, but the unfairness still rankles.

As a strange, final gracenote to my last days of studenthood, the director of training did a strange thing when my last piece of work's mark had arrived – he told me, with a long face, that he had bad news for me. Then he said "only joking, you've passed."

He did me a service. I have a piece of paper. It's a necessary joke. It is both worthless and highly valuable; for I have empowered myself to have real choices over the next few years, with the opportunity to get some very interesting and lucrative jobs, should I choose to. That's it. It's nothing more than that. The real stuff I've learned in spite of academia, not because of it.

Of course, my mother deserves no blame, only my most profound gratitude. She was speaking to the highest in me, challenged me on a level that, although risky, has borne a harvest of fruit later in life. I'm proud, finally, to have had a life inside and outside the self-perpetuating system that is education, to have experienced both.

Dear student, I could wish no more than this: that you should be so lucky.

8: ALL THE PEOPLE, SO MANY PEOPLE

WE CAN NEVER KNOW WHY
3RD MAY 1995

My ex rang up the other day. "Richard's killed himself," he said. "The magician," I said.

He was one of the most attractive people I knew. Not in the sense that I wanted to have sex with him. But he was instantly likeable and handsome. He was tall, lean and dark, with a dashing, almost shy, grin. He had friends from all walks of life who were devoted to him; there was a gentleness and straightforwardness about him that was irresistible. I sometimes found being with him awkward, because I felt like a neurotic mess beside him; his lightness of touch and enviable laid-back affability required nothing of you but to be yourself, and to be at ease with yourself. I, however, am nothing of the sort at times, and find it extremely hard to pretend otherwise. When in those moods, social disaster always loomed, for I could never avoid feeling self-conscious. Richard was above all, in my mind, the King of Cool; everything about his persona was effortlessly stylish and angst-free.

A few months after my ex and I started going out together, we were invited by Richard, who was a good friend of his, to a party in some woods in the North of London. It was a cool, clear night; we drove off in a convoy, following Richard on his motorbike. Unlike other gay bikers I know, Richard's relationship to bikes was unaffected and unpretentious; he drove recklessly fast, loving the speed and danger.

He led us to a clearing in the woods, and began organising us to collect firewood and build a huge bonfire. I remember the striking sight of this man striding through the forest, carrying what were practically trees on his shoulders, over to the clearing, and tossing them on to the fire.

In about an hour we had arranged ourselves on logs, around the blaze; quite a crowd had gathered. Richard then began doling out the magic mushrooms that he had harvested and dried, and ground to a powder. We queued up, as if for communion. He mixed a spoon or two of the brown dust and some Fanta into a mug, and we swilled it down. He clearly spelt out the possible side-effects to those who had not taken them before, such as dry retching, and told us that they would pass. He was charging a fiver a shot. I remember I hadn't been expecting to pay, and I didn't have any cash on me. My ex told him that he would take care of it. To this, Richard snorted, knowing full well what that meant. That jarring, odd note is a niggling undertow to the time I spent in Richard's company. I never quite did get it right.

The next forty-eight hours were the most blissful of my life. After a while, staring into the fire, I began to notice how the sparks had started to dance in unison, as if choreographed in a Disney fantasy. In my innocence, I pointed it out to others, and then caught myself on, and began to laugh. I laughed practically non-stop from then on – for it had finally dawned on me that nature has a profound and rich sense of humour.

It was an extraordinary night in many ways. It was the defining moment in my new relationship. I had avoided hallucinatory drugs all my life; now I had found someone I could trust to trip with. We held on to each other on the forest floor all night, diving and swooping on an inner rollercoaster ride of new experiences and feelings. I became aware of other people's characters in a new way, sensing their interior landscape instead of how they appeared on the outside. I realised how much I had dismissed "people on drugs" in the past, precisely because of the way they looked. Now I became aware of what goes on behind the glazed eyes, of the intensely spiritual dimension to exploring the uncharted waters of the mind. A pagan, sensual, passionate spirituality. No wonder it's against the law.

Throughout that starlit, blazing night, I was aware of the luminous, leather-clad figure of Richard, watching over us, tending the fire, or lying like a sleek black panther on the trunk of a fallen tree with his lover. He took on the mantle in my eyes of a 20th-century druid; something in him shone through like a bright, white light that night. I was so taken by him, and the shamanistic role he played, in mine and in so many other people's lives, that I became even more tongue-tied and awe-struck in his presence afterwards. I wanted to say: "You arranged a magical, safe space for me, so I could discover something precious and timeless about life. Thank you." But it would have simply embarrassed him. It would have been Uncool. To my regret, it is destined to be unsaid.

The Samaritans recently published a report saying that the number of men under 25 who commit suicide every year has increased by 71% over the past ten years. There are many theories about why so many men make that choice; the fact is we can never know. Richard left no clues; he kept his feelings to himself.

Perhaps that is the most telling clue of all.

I STILL FEEL GUILTY ABOUT MYLES
29TH NOVEMBER 1995

A well-thumbed black book with musty, yellowing pages sits on my shelf. It's an old friend. Inside the front cover I've written the date, March 1983, my name and address, and underlined in big letters the words PLEASE RETURN. It is stuffed full, with little scraps of paper and card, and on them are scrawled lots of parallel lines, along with names and dates. The book is the I Ching.

I was shown how to throw the coins for the "Ching" by my first real boyfriend. We went out for six turbulent months when I was seventeen. I still have the copy of *Double Fantasy* that he bought for me, the day John Lennon died. He had been a teenager in the '60s. He taught me how to cook brown rice and tasty vegetables, how to massage, how to roll a joint, and how to get angry. The basics, really.

For those who are unfamiliar with it, the I Ching is a repository of ancient Chinese lore, in 64 parts. It is used as an oracle by throwing three coins six times; depending on how the coins fall, a particular chapter is indicated as an answer to your question. Of all the divinatory arts, it is the gentlest; it doesn't go for the blood and guts of the Death card of the Tarot pack, or the planet Pluto in astrology. The Chinese invented subtlety. The chapters have such wonderful names as "Work on What Has Been Spoiled" and "The Corners of the Mouth (Providing Nourishment)". The answers are given in the third person, indicating what the "superior" or "wise" man would do in the given circumstances.

I reached for the I Ching the other day for the first time in two years. I was in a quandary, of the romantic sort. Should I call him, even though I've already written to him a fortnight ago and he hasn't replied yet? That was my question. For the really important decisions in life, such as those of matters of the heart, you can't rely on logic or reason. Asking the Universe seems a much more sensible thing to do. And this is how the Universe responded:

"Often it seems to a man as though everything were conspiring against him. He sees himself checked and hindered in his progress, insulted and dishonoured. However, he must not let himself be misled; despite this opposition, he must cleave to the man with whom he knows he belongs. Thus, notwithstanding the bad beginning, the matter will end well."

As I was pondering that encouraging answer, I looked through the scraps of paper with the different answers that I, and others, have divined over the years. Some are old lovers, the answers a testament to a shared magic. Some are friends who have gone their own way; happily, most of them I'm still in contact with. But one name chilled me, a name I haven't thought of in a while. Myles. Beside him is a date, in June, 1983.

We spent that Summer together. Or at least, as together as it was possible to be with Myles. He was a free spirit, someone who looked genuinely pained if you suggested anything as ordinary as commitment. He had classic Roman features, with long dark curly hair, a wicked half-grin and deep chuckle, and beautiful brown eyes. He would occasionally turn up on my doorstep, and I would gladly take him into my bed, no questions asked. Then I wouldn't see him for a while. Until the next time we'd bump into each other, and then we'd begin our dance again. I was never quite clear what Myles actually did. I knew he had gone to art school; the time I was close to him, he was signing on, like most everyone I knew. He was wonderful to sleep with; he was always gentle and soft. When faced with a difficult situation, he would get embarrassed, flash a bashful grin, and look away. It was impossible to imagine Myles angry. Or, indeed, to be angry with him.

At Summer's end, I met someone else and fell in love. Myles had drifted away by then, but he called around a month or so later. He wanted to stay, but I wasn't into it. And so, we drifted apart. We'd see each other around town, but he never opened up to me again. I'd meet him drunk, and he'd be sarcastic to me – a tone I'd never known before from him. I can't quite escape a feeling of guilt, even though I know it's not my fault. He started to get involved with shadowy-sounding groups of people; going to Thailand or Amsterdam and returning with heavy scars on his neck, refusing to talk about them. The last time I saw him was three years ago, one lunchtime. He looked terrible, he was drunk, and he was utterly lost. I bought him a drink, he slipped away. He died a few months later, accidentally choking on his own vomit in his sleep. He couldn't have been older than 32 or 33.

What shocks me about his memory is that there is so little of him left. He was such a private person. He was an only child; his parents were divorced. That much I know. But not a lot more. Yet I can't help but feel that if I don't remember him, then he might as well have never existed. I know this is unfair to his parents, and his grandmother, with whom he sometimes lived; of course they miss him. And I know he was greatly mourned by at least one good friend, who had kept up with his meanderings.

But I don't have even a photograph of him. All I have is his name, written beside a chapter number of the I Ching. The chapter is The Cauldron. Fire over Wood. The commentary is: "The fate of the fire depends on wood; as long as there is wood below, the fire burns above. It is the same in human life; there is in man likewise a fate that lends power to his life. If he succeeds in assigning the right place to life and to fate, thus bringing the two into harmony, he puts his fate on a firm footing."

I HAVE A CURIOUS RESPONSIBILITY LIVING THROUGH THESE TIMES TO RECORD HOW MUCH IT ACHES
2ND OCTOBER 1996

I saw him arrive. It was hard not to. He strode through the crowded gallery, wearing a red baseball cap and black combat-like trousers, the tallest man in the room. He wasn't looking at the exhibits, nor apparently was he looking for anyone in the crowd. He walked through each room, not pausing for a second. He passed me coming down the stairs, on his way out, his tour of the exhibition having taken all of two minutes. But on his way down, I eyeballed him and held his gaze for at least half a second.

The only conclusion I can come to as to why he went to the event, the opening of the Robert Mapplethorpe show in London, was to ensure that he was seen. I realised, although it should have come as no surprise to me, just how awful it must be to be Morrissey.

It didn't stop me wondering how I could have spent my fifteen minutes with him. "Footballers" is how his sexual tastes were described to me once by someone who knew someone who knew someone who hung out with him a few times. True or not, it sounds oddly right; the working-class soccer hero, lean and arrogant, having his wicked way with the last great English dandy. Ageing maybe, but still magnificent.

As his eyes met mine, I pondered the impossibility of passing myself off as a footballer. I continued up those stairs, certain that I, alone, could handle him. But one has to leave those certainties behind to stay sane.

And so, reluctantly, on to Mapplethorpe, who brought us together. I am familiar with practically everything he's done; no self-respecting middle-class queen's coffee table is complete without his collected works. For those who are not, he was an American photographer who became infamous for his images of men having sex, shot with a cold elegance and formality. This was not his only subject matter; he photographed other nudes, as well as a smattering of actors and some striking flowers.

Through Mapplethorpe's icy gaze, a handsome black man with a very large cock seems statuesque, the antithesis of passion. A picture of a forearm delving into a shapely pair of buttocks right up to the wrist has the same formality and appeal as that of a curiously antiseptic white lily, displayed in this exhibition right next to it. These are the aesthetics of anaesthesia, sensing nothing but light and form. Two leather-clad figures: one, standing, pisses into the mouth of the other, who kneels. It is a photographic record of an intense sexual activity; but, bizarrely, it is not a photograph of ardour or intensity. These are still lives.

And none more still than a large study of a human skull, which perversely has more life in it than anything else. I spent some time gawping at it, hung in an awkwardly high position. It seemed to be strangely totemic of this culture in which I find myself, this gay life. Mapplethorpe died of AIDS seven years ago.

It occurred to me recently that I have a curious responsibility, living through these times, to record how much it aches, despite the danger of repeating myself. Indeed the repetition of death and illness is the main cause of the ache, the wound that cannot heal. But I am one of the lucky ones; I do not have the virus in my system. I will probably die another way. And, currently, my close friends are all healthy too. In London, this is unusual, and is probably due to the fact that we're all Irish, and in the early '80s before we heard of safe sex, the virus hadn't taken a grip in Dublin the way it had in other cities.

What shakes me in my restless search for community – or perhaps I should say communion – with others is the presence of death in the lives of so many I meet. It looms, like Mapplethorpe's Skull, over our culture. What I and so many others try to do, is to condense the denial and the grief and the rage and the other stages of bereavement into manageable chunks. But of course this goes against human nature. The alternative is to lament the falling of the most sensitive, the most special in our midst. But lamentation is not a pretty sight; and endless lamentation is one dimension of madness.

Andrew Sullivan, author of *Virtually Normal*, an inspiring book, recently came out as being HIV positive. And this month saw the demise of one of my heroes, writer Oscar Moore, whom some of you may have read over the past three years in the weekend supplement to *The Guardian*. He wrote a monthly column called PWA, in which, with blistering honesty and elegant, heartbreaking simplicity, he chronicled his life and his struggle with the illness. Now, his struggle is over.

PWA: Looking AIDS in the Face by Oscar Moore

WHAT QUEEN WOULDN'T GET A BIT MELODRAMATIC AFTER ALL THAT TRAUMA?
11TH AUGUST 1999

The recently bereaved Andy Sipowicz comforted a distressed John with a hug in the last of the series of *NYPD Blue*, and I bawled my eyes out. If you don't know the series, then I'm sorry, I can't help you. Might as well stop reading now.

John, the receptionist in this top-notch cop series, from the makers of *Hill Street Blues*, is one of the most exquisitely truthful characterisations of a camp gay man on television to date. Played wonderfully by Bill Brochtrup, his neurotic self-dramatisation is not unknown to me; his narcissistic obsession about how he might upset others, merely by existing, rings a bell too. He is the epitome of highly-strung. The triumph of his character lies in the fact that, finally, political correctness about representing gay men in mainstream television drama has been overtaken by emotional truth. It's not to say that all gay men are like him, of course not; but his tissue-thin hypersensitivity, that is recognisably part of a gay sensibility to anyone with eyes, has only been the stuff of comedy or tragedy before.

The major step forward, of course, is that it wasn't John who was killed off in the shooting spree that resulted in Mrs Sipowicz's death. Traditional values would have him leaping in to take the bullet to prevent her from dying. As he's lying in his, possibly tainted, queer martyr's blood, Sipowicz is urged by his injured wife to comfort him; magnanimously, the hypermasculine tough guy rises to the challenge, tiptoes through the gore, and pats John on the head. John, pathetically grateful that his life might mean something at last, naturally pushes it just that bit too far, and tries to hold the burly detective's hand; but then, just at that moment, he croaks. Sipowicz is spared the humiliation of overcoming his "thing" about queers, but is eternally grateful to the freak that spares the mother of his child.

But that's not what happened. The fate of the modern homosexual seems to be changing, in the minds of those who create our mainstream fiction. Instead, John does get shot, but only superficially, in his valiant attempt to prevent a murder; he manages to alert others, while dramatically propping up a wall, bleeding – he does that as only a drama queen can, with panache. But it's too late; the gunman is too determined. That's America for you. Another day, another massacre.

Shock! Horror! The token gay character didn't die gothicly, in his prime, his pathetic waste of masculinity demonstrably intolerable, yet again. Admittedly, he did get a bit melodramatic in the last episode – what queen wouldn't, after all that trauma? – but he was put in his place by that sensible Kirkendall woman, and told not to assume that everything revolved around him. You can tell she's a working mum. Bit hard to take, that; but then Sipowicz turns up, tells him he's a hero, that he's not angry with him for his wife's death. Collapse of John into tears, and Sipowicz gives him a great big bearhug. Boo hoo hoo. It's a gay thing, believe me. Probably unresolved father stuff. Don't mind me.

John Inman, Kenneth Williams and Larry Grayson were the camp figures of my childhood television; they sent up their delicate temperaments and neuroses, for comedic effect. In film, Murray Melvyn as the tragic Jeffrey in *A Taste of Honey* would send any effeminate man hurtling off a cliff in despair. To those who argue that I'm making the mistake of confusing effeminacy for homosexuality, I can only say that I'm not buying the ideology any more that says gay men are exactly the same as heterosexual men, except for whom they share their bed with. This ideology underestimates the importance of the emotional impact of bedsharing. It's not true to say that men and women are the same, when it comes to sex and relationships. I don't know why I ever thought so in the first place.

Why does it matter about how sensitive, camp, gay men are portrayed on television? Because, like it or not, our culture is influenced by the way it is mirrored in its media. The fact that, for a while, gay characters on television had to be guy- or girl-next-door types so as not to offend gay activists was understandable, but in the end unsustainable. Stereotypes, like cliches, are there because there is a grain of truth in them; but for the truth to emerge, we must engage our brains and see who's behind the caricature. It is through serious, intelligent dramas such as *NYPD Blue* that the complex variety of human sexualities and personalities can be portrayed, and the archetypally doomed queer can evolve into someone far more subtle and interesting. He's going to live, after all.

MR RIGHT IS JUST AROUND THE CORNER
24TH AUGUST 2002

Here's the premise: three "experts" (style, assertiveness, and body language, respectively) coach a willing sacrificial lamb, who hasn't dated in years, in the arts of flirting and meeting people. *Would Like To Meet* is sadistic TV, but the pay-off is that we get to see a more confident, less cobweb-ridden soul at the end of the hour. Richard, a school teacher, was the first gay man in the series – a sweet, slight, apologetic, self-loathing soul living in splendid isolation in the country, with tweedy clothes and "body issues".

It began to get surreal for me when one of the (female) experts was showing the hapless chap how to cruise, down in Soho. They had kitted him out in trendy gear – "gay men are so much more aware of clothes, you've got to send out a signal that you're a single gay man" – and instructed him in the fine art of objectification. "Lock eyes – break eye contact – count to three – turn back, see if he's looking back". It was like watching someone being given their first taste of cocaine – a queasy mixture of envy and guilt and pleasure. "Don't do it!"

But of course he did. And, what's more, he become more playful, more energised in the world, less bashful. Cynics might say that he had just been given the tools to his self-destruction – the keys to a kingdom of surfaces, projections, the ecstatic drug of constant arousal by strangers, the absence of warmth and continuity. Give him a few years, and we will watch how he's taken up residence in the hell and damnation of the gay scene, lonely automatons fucking each other's pneumatic brains out. A "community" whose publications are funded by the sex industry – phone lines and prostitution – its writers and opinion-makers, in the main, blind to the way the community exploits its younger members, celebrates their objectification.

If I have to dance, I don't want to be part of your revolution.

But Richard himself didn't see it like that, and in many ways he rose above the standards that the programme makers were setting for him. Thank God he didn't crop his hair.

One of the more interesting strands to his progress in the show was his assertiveness-training. In common with practically all of the previous subjects in this series, he had no idea how to be assertive. But there was a flavour of his subjugation which was very familiar to those of us born under the sign of Narcissus – the interpretation of verbal challenges as punishing personal attacks, receiving them with puppy-dog-eyed compliance, to be followed, eventually, when the wind changes, by a desperate, pained retaliation. "Victimy" is how his behaviour was termed by the "expert". Mmm, know that one.

So, he was brought along to a martial arts studio, and we watched in amazement as he started letting his frustration out – with more power than his stature would suggest. But, having spent a year in a dojo myself, I know just how much force there lies simmering beneath a sweet-looking poofter.

He was also brought to a "Talkaoke" bar, a weird, talking-shop karaoke setup, with a round table and microphones and a host to keep the debate going – a 21st century version of the Restoration salon. There, one of the most common traits of "victimy" folk was exposed: the capitulation/ attack paradigm of conflict resolution. He had no capacity to stand his ground confidently or humorously, didn't know how not get panicked into sarcasm or hysteria, or forced to fade into the background in smouldering, resentful, bitter compliance.

The debate, interestingly enough, turned to the gay scene – and it was roundly denounced by someone at the table for being shallow, sex-centred, promiscuous and hateful. To which Richard could only retaliate, with sad '70s-style fervour, that the speaker was homophobic, before murmuring something arcane about the percentage of masters' students who were gay. But the scene critic turned out to be gay himself. Pity, I didn't get a look at him.

Anyway, Richard learned the lesson: he has a right to his own opinions, to stand his own ground. It doesn't make him a bad person to disagree. This, more than anything, seemed to liberate him from the prison he had created for himself – or, perhaps, said the shrink, the prison he grew up in – and, in the last part of the programme, we saw him mischievously flirting and having a lovely time with a sweet, straight-laced American boy.

It makes sense that he ended up with an American, for the concept of self-worth and pride in oneself as a gay man has American roots. The English don't do pride very well – it flips into arrogance too easily, and sexual embarrassment seems almost to be woven into the tweed of Englishness – but an American pride and dignity in one's essential nature is basically what these three "experts" were teaching Richard. At times, I cringed, worried that what they were trying to do was change a polite, self-effacing young man into a bolshie cocksure shit. But then I remembered my own discomfort with conflict, and that something was obviously well planned in the experts' strategy for him, emphasising the importance for gay men of standing their ground with other men. On the BBC website, he writes that things didn't work out with the American, but that he's enjoying being single and being confident. OUT, the internet community that he's part of, that featured on the programme, is buzzing with excitement and pride in him, with comments that the programme "normalized" gay relationships in a way that is rare on TV. Hmm. Single, plenty of dates, full of hope, Mr Right just around the corner... yes, that's my kind of normal.

So many of us gay men fear conflict in relationship, so much so that we allow ourselves to feel smothered rather than disagree, and then we stay single rather than experience smothering. But it's really an inability to realise that we have grown up, and that we have the capacity to say "no" to those who are close to us, nourishing us – or attempting to at least. Not with murderous rage, not in a childish tantrum or with a sarcastic sting, but a simple, clear, confident "no, thanks, I don't feel like that". And not to fear recrimination or guilt.

We may have had early experiences in which saying "no" was met with all sorts of subtle, or not-so-subtle, disconcerting reactions – but that was then. This is now. It's about separation from Mother, a process which can – and does – happen at any time of life. The more we are merged inside with Her, the more we hate ourselves for being different, and hate everyone else for not being Her. The more we separate, the more we love and respect, ourselves and others. Gay, straight, man, woman. Finis.

THE BLACK AND WHITE WORLD OF ROGER CASEMENT
12TH MAY 2003

I've been thinking about Roger Casement a lot recently. The complexity of human personality is no more evident than in his colourful life, and the exercise of piecing it all together, nearly ninety years after his death, is fascinating and compelling. Like all posthumous biography, it can only ever achieve the status of educated speculation, and, as with all controversial figures, biographers have their own agendas and identifications and points to get across. But if, by some miracle, he were around today to tell us what his life was really like, I'm not so sure whether or not he'd know how to articulate his truth. I suspect the reason there is so much animosity around his legacy, so much suspicion and vitriol, is that he was a fantasist, and his inner psychological split, between sexual predation and celibate piety, was worked out in his diaries, in "Black" and "White".

The inconsistencies in content and style between the two – the fluent, engaging white and the stuttering, innuendo-laden, lascivious black – have led some people to believe that the latter are British forgeries, which suits a particular mystic Irish nationalist sensibility down to the ground: the devils are external, and both sins of perversion and dastardly deception are laid at the door of the perfidious Brit. Once the British confess to the forgery, then we can get back to the business of celebrating his martyred whiter-than-white life with his reputation intact.

But someone who has no such Celtic axe to grind, whose passion is Latin American history, Angus Mitchell, in his celebratory reproduction of Casement's "White" 1910 Amazon journal, writes in the preface that he simply does not recognise the writer's voice in the Black Diaries. Convinced that they were not written by the Casement he had come to know so intimately, he says: "Whoever wrote the diaries had a desire to portray Casement and homosexuality as a sickness, perversion and crime for which a person should suffer guilt, repression, fantasy, hatred and, most of all, alienation and loneliness. These are not the confessions of a Jean Genet or Tennessee Williams, W.H. Auden or Oscar Moore. Rather than sympathising with the struggle of the homosexual conscience, they are clearly homophobic documents."

That statement alone suggests to me that there is only one person who could have written them: Casement himself. Homosexuality and self-reflective creative talent are not synonymous, and it is disingenuously "liberal" to suggest it. The clumsy, furtive, pornographic aides-memoire that he churned out in the Black Diaries were meant to make sense only to himself, as wank-fodder, whereas his White Diaries were his job – he was a report writer, a civil servant, writing and recording daily, his diaries intended for publication, with no pretensions to creativity. Whatever evidence there is to speak of a gay consciousness or sensibility in the 21st century, there is none to suggest any such beast at the dawn of the 20th, for Freud was only just beginning then to lift the lid on sexuality, and Wilde's ignominy and death in 1900 cannot have done anything but to dismay anyone with a similar predilection. The word "homosexual" itself only began to gain currency in English after Wilde died. Back then, things were black and white – the concept of the rainbow, the symbol for human diversity and inclusivity that can be found hanging as a flag somewhere in every gay bar nowadays, would have been alien to Casement.

The "struggle of the homosexual conscience" is not a generic thing, it is always individual, and has more in common with any man's struggle with his desire-nature than anything specifically to do with finding men or women horny. The fascinating thing about Casement is not that he had struggles with his sexuality, but that he wrote about them, in quite a dull-witted way. He was no Wilde. Why should he have been? There is no doubt that many public figures of that era had seedy private lives, but none of them was daft enough to record them. It is this unthinking folly that is Casement's signature, it's his leitmotif, his *hamartia*. It is in keeping with his idiotic quest to go to Germany to persuade shell-shocked Irish P.O.W.s to switch allegiance and betray their fallen comrades on the battlefields of France, and matches the poignancy of his arrest, preventing him from carrying out his intention to stop the Easter Rising. He was a bear of little brain, but a great big bleeding heart. I know someone just like him today – passionate, intense, driven, easily wounded, highly political. He bumbles through life following one campaign after another, is adored by his many friends, but he's impossible to argue with because he wears his heart on his sleeve – it's a matter of faith, not reason. To look at him is to want to catch some of his warmth, like there's a fissure in his defences, letting you warm your hands on his unprotected heart. It's not the cleverest of ways to get through life, but his ambitions aren't thought-through, they're heartfelt and mercurial.

T.E. Lawrence described Casement as having "the appeal of a broken archangel." Joseph Conrad thought that "...he was a man, properly speaking, of no mind at all. I don't mean stupid. I mean that he was all emotion. By emotional force... he made his way, and sheer temperament."

The self-hating voice that Mitchell identifies has a familiar, bitter twang to it. We can have no more powerful nemesis than that which our own unconscious can provide; there can be no more severe critic than that voice in our own head. As with anyone struggling with an addiction, our own psyche creates the perfect tool to drag us down. It's as if our own trajectory through the firmament above is mirrored by a corresponding tunnelling through unconscious murk below — the madonna/whore, priest/pervert dyads. The brighter the light, the darker the shadow, and the further we travel away from a holistic, messy, complexity into the light, the more dangerous the dark becomes. For some people the split can drive us to the edge of madness. This split, this struggle, can leave us raw and open. And it can also drive us to do extraordinary things.

The heart of darkness of the Congolese and Amazonian jungles — this is where Casement was drawn, as soon as he could leave home, spending 20 years in Africa. His role as conscience for the western world, with high-minded aspirations for humanity, may have been spurred by his struggle against what he perceived to be his own, primitive, base nature. In other words, the very split that he tried to come to terms with, between his ideals and his desires, might very well have been the engine for his extraordinary missionary zeal, that led to such wonderful improvements in the lot of the Congolese and Amazonian natives, suffering at the hands of Europeans. I am trying to think of the impact he had on the world's media, a hundred years ago, with his reports from Africa detailing the barbarity of the Belgian King's rule there. The only equivalent I can think of today is Michael Buerk's reporting of the Ethiopian famine of 1984, which spurred another humanitarian Irishman to get political, change world opinion, and to get a knighthood for his trouble.

Owen Dudley Edwards has puzzled over how such a fine humanitarian could also be sexually predatory, holding views of other people that are sexually exploitative. If one can hold that paradox to be true, then we are on the way to grasping the complexity of Casement, and indeed of masculinity itself. If he were alive today, he might be a public figure, but he'd have a Gaydar profile, and he'd be wanking over the profiles with the biggest cocks he could find on the internet. Would he have had the balls to actually meet men for sex? Or would it all be cyberchat, staccato thrusts into the dark corners of his psyche? And if we were to find his hard drive ninety years from now, would we know, reading it, if he actually had sex with men or not?

Would it matter?

A FEATURE OF BEING A CREATURE WHO LOVES MEN
24TH NOVEMBER 2003

Dear Jason,

I asked you the question as I went to the kitchen to make two cups of herbal tea. It was late at night, you had just arrived, and been shown straight to the cat-hair-free bedroom because you were allergic to my feline companions, my usually reliable secret weapons of hospitality. I said "fuck it" to myself, and invited the lie. "What's your name?" I asked, lightly, even though I knew you had pointedly not told me during our online chat. Don't ask for credit, as refusal often offends. I had your internet nick, handle, ID, loginname, username. That's the easy one. That's the name that offers access to your computer screen, to your private isolated self, where anything is true if you want it to be.

I heard you say "Jason". I knew it wasn't the name that your friends or your family called you. It was a different name. The name you use for sex. That truth. A slight hesitation, a little catch in the throat, a semi-tone off. But I let it go, like a spark falling on newspaper. I didn't fan it to flame, with moral outrage – I felt the slight sting, an angel sigh, and we carried on with the night of talking. Despite your hidden identity, you were not closed, but open to thought and feeling and curiosity. You weren't like other men I've met before, who were married, or fearful, those other men who have called themselves "Jason" or "Steve". I believed that you were single and gay. I believed you had been hurt after your last relationship. I believed you are searching for monogamy. So why, I wondered, were you lying? Was it another "all men are bastards" scenario being enacted before my eyes? If so, it was breathtaking.

Some things are true on whatever scale, Beaufort or Richter. We relaxed with each other easily. Our agenda was to talk and see, to explore. And that we did. And, despite the flurried heat of our initial exchange on the Net, we ended up just talking and cuddling and sleeping, avoiding the suffocating firetrap of the little death, too soon. Intact, safe. Warm.

And so you became, effortlessly, the first man who took up space in my bed at night, that wasn't a friend crashing, this year.

You told me that you were emigrating in a couple of days, leaving for a brave new world and a new life of creativity and openness. I smiled when you said that. Rueful. I've become better at avoiding bitterness. That came later, for a short while. Then rage. Then resolution. And now? Wonder.

So, this is the supreme test, I thought, of living in the moment. Can I enjoy being with a big, beautiful, inspirational man for the briefest of nights and not go crazy with regret that it's my only chance? In a city with too many brief encounters and no continuity, what am I to make of the first interesting man to come along, who also happens to have a cast-iron reason for brevity? Enjoy it. Life's too short.

And I did.

Breakfast in bed. The bread wasn't the best. I left you, stranger with the false name, in my flat while I went to get you milk. Of course I did. There are other ways of knowing about people. What's in a name? And then we parted, a bright warm smile from you and a wave. A happy day for me.

And then, the next day, the email I'd written to you at the address you gave me bounced. And that's when the rage came, a storm that battered me inside for days. I did what I usually do with such turmoil – sexualise it. It worked, in its unsatisfactory way. I calmed down. I wondered whether everything was a lie, whether I had imagined it all. I began to wonder about the citadel that so many men build around their hearts, with diamond-strong battlements of falsehoods and charm and bravado: no way in. The glossy persona that cannot be stuck to, the free spirit that will not be trapped or grounded. Men that look as if they're warm and open, but who have insulated themselves from emotional connection, and have mastered the sport of seductive no-strings sex to compensate. It's safer that way.

I knew that wasn't you. But, still, you left in exactly the same way.

I saw Will Young sing his beautiful single 'Leave Right Now' on *Pop Idol*, my date having blown me out, and found myself in tears. Here's a gorgeous young man who's taken the time out this year to produce new, personal material – one of the first ever pop artists openly gay from the start of their career, and obviously bringing that consciousness to his work. "*My racing heart is just the same/Why make it strong to break it once again.... Somebody better show me out/before I fall any deeper/I think I'd better leave right now.*"

But you said hello online today from your new life abroad – and that was sweet. You were still sticking to "Jason" but my rage had gone. What use is it being angry when there are so many more Jasons out there? It can't be just that I attract them. It's a feature of being a creature who loves men. They will open their hearts only when they want to, and won't be told. And some, bless 'em, never do.

You told me enough for me to google you, and find out your real name and something of how creative you've been. I've ordered the book you wrote, and I'm looking forward to reading it. The problem with creating brave new lives in new continents is that the internet is already there waiting for us, reminding us of who we were. It's not a bad thing. But only if you need to keep your truths separate.

Someone told me this week about a Hindu saying that, paraphrased, speaks of how someone who loves always, knows freedom – whereas someone who seeks only to receive love is always enslaved. I've certainly been a slave, rattled my chains with the best of them. Poetically enough, I'm now a therapist – the word comes from *therapos*, a freed slave. But am I truly free? Can I love the Jasons of this world, and not want anything back?

I can. And do. Were I to live life over again, I'd probably do the same. I'm a bit like a moth banging its head against a light bulb, seeking the sun.

I know no other way.

With love and best wishes for your new life,

"Bootboy"

THE FIRST DEFINING CRUSH
10TH JANUARY 2004

Like ducklings emerging from our shells, instinctively fixating on the first creature we clap our eyes on, to follow until we're old enough to know what's good for us – the first time a teenager falls in love with a pop star is a seminal moment, from which some never recover. Our doom is sealed, our souls are imprinted with the exquisitely tortuous realisation that our untouchable "happy-sad" secret Self, that hitherto no one had known anything about, especially our parents, could, possibly, be understood by another human being. We are not alone! Someone out there gets us – or could get us, if only they knew us. We become alive to the possibility of relating. We start dreaming of a time when we are not held hostage by the tyrannical hormones morphing our pimply body into something scarily alien, a time when we can lose our self-consciousness and red-faced embarrassment for existing, a time when we cease writhing with overwhelming, incomprehensible desires in the dark, and are ugly ducklings no more.

We know, deep down, that we're never going to meet our idol. We may worship them from in front of the stage and send them reams of fan letters; if we're lucky, our god may smile at our prayers and reward us with a wave or a signed photo. It's the passion of courtly love – we can obsess as much as we like in the refuge of our bedroom shrines, our walls papered with icons, go to every gig and scream until we're hoarse, get every version of every record they've ever released and play them until we know every nuance, can sing every word, can answer any catechism – but this marriage made in heaven is never going to be consummated. It is, therefore, perfect.

We don't choose our gods – they choose us. For me, it happened to be Tom Robinson, who I first saw on *Top of the Pops* in November 1977, at the age of thirteen. I remember being mesmerised, and not knowing why. The explanation came when I heard his song 'Glad to be Gay', released the following year, and a strong strand of my life's pattern was set then – sexual politics and social change. Not one of the most gifted musicians in the world, with only a couple of tracks that stand the test of time, he proved himself to be a worthy, kind man with integrity – especially when he came out later as bisexual, displaying a dignified refusal to let his desire be confined by the labels he helped create. His influence on me was ultimately benign. He changed tack, he lost his magic and became mortal. He let me go.

Mark Simpson was not so lucky. His calling came not from a decent spokesman for a cause, but from an indecent artist, a crowing Pied Piper, who took children and made them old. When he was eighteen, in 1983, The Smiths appeared on *The Tube*, the television rock show of the hour in Britain, and Simpson's soul was taken there and then. In bittersweet revenge for a lifetime in thrall to the god that is Steven Patrick, he has written *Saint Morrissey*, a delightful, insightful, playful, seductive, smoulderingly intelligent and very funny book. It's a "Dear Mr Gable" love letter for our time, a gospel for the cult of Morrissey devotees, the most passionate on the planet. (I declare my late conversion: I've travelled hundreds of miles twice in the past ten years, solely to see Morrissey perform, and his handsome-devilish face still adorns my walls).

In this increasingly single society, in which we try and fill the "love-shaped hole" (that once was "God-shaped") with pop stars, film stars, celebrity and fashion, Simpson offers us a hagiographic paean that is unashamedly, defiantly, devotional in quality. The word "fan" comes from the word for temple, a place of worship. To be a fan is to be in the grip of a divine frenzy. Among the modern pantheon of pop stars, though, none is as challenging, as literate, as Morrissey, whom NME named as the "most influential artist ever". And this is a fitting, dazzling, handsome tribute.

Simpson takes as his source material only that which Morrissey has written in his lyrics or spoken in interview, and thus claims no special privilege to know him, any more than any other fan does – (*i.e.* intimately). As such, it may or may not bear any relationship to the truth as Morrissey himself sees it, for Simpson acknowledges the self-defeating nature of trying to interpret those enigmatic lyrics. But that's irrelevant. I have never read a book before like this: every page or two, I wanted to stop and talk about what Simpson had written with someone else – I wanted to discuss, argue, complain, gasp, share the experience. Mostly, I wanted to laugh. Considering that this is a book about a man whose isolation, morbidity and alienation are legendary, it is remarkable that it made me want to be sociable.

This is the Morrissey paradox. For all that he is a dark creature of the night, for all that his art is neurotic and perverse and hateful and borne out of a deep and probably obnoxious malaise, his willingness to share it with us is a relief, a joyous experience, for we can then look at our own shadow and go: thank God for that, I'm not the only freak. Our fear lessens, we can laugh; our faith in life is restored. Fear is the opposite of faith, not hate.

Morrissey "was always attracted to people with the same problems" as he had, lamenting that most of them were dead. Mark's problems are close enough to Steven's to help us understand them; he describes his work as a "psycho-bio", which, along the way, reveals Mark's own struggles, but casts a persuasively illuminating light on Steven's. At times his eagerness to make psychoanalytic interpretations is a tad earnest, but the longer I practise as a therapist the more I appreciate that Freud got it right with his Oedipal stuff, especially for a certain type of sensitive man who loves his mother and shrinks from giving his aggression and desire-nature full expression. (Which just about covers everyone, really.)

Simpson's own track record of cheerfully eschewing labels of sexual identity serves him well here, for he has no fear in tackling Morrissey's sexual and emotional complexity, from "the ordinary, prosaic, universal language" of same-sex attraction, to sex in lonely public places – the undomesticable truth of desire – to a brave and compelling chapter on the unmentionable love between Mother and Son. "By saving her sensitive child from life, the overprotective mother runs the risk of making him fall half in love with easeful death and the tomb-womb." *Oh mother, I can feel the soil falling over my head...*

All the literary, environmental and personal influences on the singer are explored with wit and respect: his hellish schooldays, his absent father, Shelagh Delaney's play *A Taste of Honey*, The Moors murders, Oscar Wilde, the '70s, Bolan, Bowie, the "Beautiful Bastard" James Dean, and a hysterical passage on how Johnny Marr came into Morrissey's life. The "scandalous virtue" of his celibacy. An uncompromising homage to the Ruffian, Morrissey's (and Simpson's) masculine muse. Violence. Rent boys. Feminism. Racism. America. Thatcher. Ecstasy. All are discussed, with Simpson's unique take on masculinity and popular culture, half-celebration, half-lament, informing everything he writes.

"For a man who is a collection of celebrated, creative pathologies and dysfunctions, normality/cure would be a kind of erasure," writes Simpson. I disagree. Firstly, that there is a "cure" for life, especially a life of such intensity and creativity, that has brought so much joy to the world. Secondly, that normality is something that anyone would – or could – choose. In the same way that Morrissey had no choice when he saw Marc Bolan play at the age of 12, his fate was sealed. Our only choice is to do gladly that which we must do.

ALL THE LONELY PEOPLE, WHERE DO THEY ALL BELONG?
21TH JANUARY 2004

I was woken the other morning by the insistent electronic warbling of my phone. It was just after 8am, and I found myself instinctively preparing for bad news. The last time the phone rang before 9am it was a "come home son, your father's in hospital" sort of call, years ago. As I stumbled in the dark towards the phone in the living room, I fuzzily went through a checklist of whether my Visa had enough credit to get to Dublin, what clients I had that day, and who could feed the cats.

"Hello?"

"I want to talk to my husband, I want to know if it's right that I should kill myself, and join him in heaven, will God punish me? I want to die. But I'm afraid if I do it myself I won't see him ever again." Her voice was slurred, indistinct. Not young. She was crying, singing the boozy poor-me song.

There are some times when I wish that life could have a pause button. Time out, gather your wits, think what's best, and then press "Start" when you're ready. This was one of those moments. The little boy in me was whimpering: "Daddy, that wave's too big, I'll drown!!!" I needed coffee, badly. I needed to pee. (I needed a cigarette and then I made myself not-think that need, the way I've been doing for twenty emancipated, empty months. And counting.) My cats were under my feet, semi-annoyed, miaowing, urging me to finish the journey to their food bowl. I needed to wake up.

I quelled the desire to be brutally rude.

The psychic punch of the suicidal − rage and hate and manipulation − is one I've been hit by before, in more ways than one. I want to hit back. The affront of it − when someone decides that you are going to be the one to deal with their despair, the one to parent them through their panic, to think, to reason, to challenge. You must pass their vicious, crucial test: they pummel you repeatedly with unarguable evidence that life is cruel, and you must still disagree and argue for life. And if you don't play the role of Persuader-for-Life on demand, will their blood be on your hands? Your free will is kidnapped − you cannot say what you really feel because they may hang up and die on you. But you can't bullshit either − someone on the edge like that has had enough fakery and hypocrisy. You negotiate with the kidnapper, appease the bully, rescue the victim. This is what you must do, if you believe in anything that connects human beings, if you believe that we are more than individuals in isolation, groping for contact and meaning in a pitiless, soulless world.

She rang me by mistake, she got the wrong person, which is why I feel free to write about her here, and normal rules of client confidentiality don't apply. She was looking for someone who was mentioned in a tabloid article that also included my details, and she got me confused with a guy who described himself as a "medium", who had "high-level guides" that speak to him in voices through his ear. I was being given a crash-course in the sort of lament that those who claim to be familiar with the spirit world must deal with all the time – the yearning to make contact with the dead, to ease the grief and loss that is the shadow of love and attachment.

She was nearly sixty, lived on her own in a village in the middle of nowhere with her 22-year-old cat, who was dying. She described herself as a recluse. Her beloved husband had died 8 years ago, and her best friend had died only six weeks previously. He was someone who had brought her out of herself as a widow, had cheered her up, got her out to do things. He wanted more than friendship, and she felt appallingly guilty that she had been "mean" to him and not gone further. She didn't want to betray her husband. Now he was gone, unexpectedly, and her cat had looked at her in farewell the night before. She had taken to the bottle, and drunk all night, terrified at losing the last living connection to her husband, to when she had a role, to when she last loved.

It took me half an hour to feel safe enough to extract myself from the phone call. I told her instead of a medium she'd found a cranky counsellor, who had to go to work. She kept on apologising for ringing me, for existing, really – and I wondered what sort of a bully her late husband was, to leave his wife so mouse-like. Or had his loss shaken her faith in life so much that her confidence was shattered?

When someone is at that level of despair, depression has taken a firm grip, and "normal" rationality is replaced by a darker, narrower version, where lateral thinking all but disappears, and it feels like there is no way out. What is longed for is certainty, an end to the heartache, and the thousand natural shocks that flesh is heir to. Reality is too painful. The appeal of spiritualism lies in the comfort of a different reality, on the "other side".

What concerns me about those who are professional mediums is not that they are fraudulent – they may have stunning insights and they may indeed have a real gift – it's whether in the long run what they offer helps or hinders the person in distress. It may be incredibly soothing to believe you are hearing from a dead lover. But what's being avoided is the reality principle – and for even a moderately healthy life, we need to grasp what's real and deal with it. The whips and scorns of time, the oppressor's wrong, the proud man's contemptuous treatment, the pangs of despised love, the law's delay, and the insolence of office. That old shit. When we're depressed we flee from it. When we're not, we're coping with it. It's not very glamorous. It's not very transcendent or hopeful. But there isn't a way out of sidestepping it, if we want to choose life.

Before filing this, I gave her a quick ring, a week afer her call. She sounds better, trying to avoid drinking, and she's admitting she's depressed, which to my ears is always a good start. She's looking forward to bending the ear of the nice woman who's on the Samaritans duty roster for Friday evenings. Her cat hasn't died yet. But the builders are in next door building an extension and she has to keep the curtains drawn to stop them peering in her window. She misses her friend. She's Eleanor Rigby.

All the lonely people. Where do they all belong?

DIARY
OF A
MAN
INDEX

ALSO FROM HOTPRESS BOOKS

THE STORY OF O by Olaf Tyaransen
Described as Ireland's *Catcher In The Rye*, this tale of teenage sex, drugs, rock'n'roll – and of course music – is hysterically funny and poignantly moving in equal measure. **Price: €12.99**

"It's like The Secret Diary Of Adrian Mole, only with cannabis-induced hazes." – *Sunday Times*.

"Very funny and searingly honest" – *Irish Times*

SEX LINES by Olaf Tyaransen
Delving into the wonderful world of sex, Olaf attempts to find a Russian bride, is asked to be an extra on a porn movie shoot, attends a fetish spanking club and much more. **Price: €12.99**

"Hysterically funny" – *Sunday Independent*

PALACE OF WISDOM by Olaf Tyaransen
The "enfant terrible" of Irish journalism is back, with a remarkable book that explores the dark and dangerous currents in which artists, celebrities, musicians, writers and politicos alike – including the author himself – are wont to swim. And sometimes drown... **Price: €13.99**

"Olaf Tyaransen is the genuine article" – Robert Sabbag, author of *Snowblind*

U2: THREE CHORDS AND THE TRUTH
The International Bestseller Edited by Niall Stokes
Critical, entertaining, comprehensive and revealing, *U2: Three Chords And The Truth* never misses a beat as it brings you, in words and pictures, a complete portrait of U2 in the process of becoming a legend. **Price: €11.49**

THEY ARE OF IRELAND by Declan Lynch
They Are Of Ireland is a hilarious who's who of famous Irish characters – and chancers – from the worlds of politics, sport, religion, the Arts, entertainment and the media. Written by Declan Lynch, one of Ireland's wittiest writers, this is a book of comic writing that actually makes you laugh out loud. **Price: €9.99**

ALSO FROM HOTPRESS BOOKS

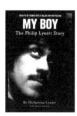

MY BOY: THE PHILIP LYNOTT STORY
No.1 Bestseller in Ireland
by Philomena Lynott (with Jackie Hayden)
The remarkable story of Philip Lynott, the black Irish street poet and rock legend, *My Boy* is not only an intimate and revealing portrait of an Irish icon, but an immensely moving account of a mother's devotion to her beloved son through the good times and the bad.
Price: €12.95

BEYOND BELIEF
No.2 Bestseller in Ireland by Liam Fay
Liam Fay has won a national journalism award for his brilliant and hilarious investigation into the wild side of faith in Ireland. Uproarious, revealing and thought-provoking, *Beyond Belief* is a triumph.
Price:€12.50

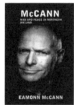

MCCANN: WAR AND PEACE IN NORTHERN IRELAND
by Eamonn McCann
Published to coincide with the 30th anniversary of the Civil Rights movement, in which the author played a prominent part, *McCann: War And Peace* In Northern Ireland is essential reading for anyone interested in one of the major stories of our time. **Price: €12.50**

THE ROOMS
By Declan Lynch
The Rooms is an electrifying new novel by one of the brightest stars of Irish fiction, Declan Lynch, that brings you inside the biggest secret organisation in the world. A love story that beguiles and challenges, it is at once powerful, moving and deeply revealing in its depiction of the world inside and outside of AA. In the doomy, wise-cracking Neil, it introduces a new kind of anti-hero to the pantheon of Irish fiction. One that you will never forget... **Price: €14.99**

"It will dazzle you and break your heart. A truly great Irish novel." - Liam Fay, *The Sunday Times*

ORDERING INFO

All of the above titles are available online from www.hotpress.com/books
Or write to Hot Press Books, 13 Trinity St., Dublin 2.
Mail order, send cheques/POs or credit card details for the price noted, incl. p&p (Irl/UK: €2.54;
Europe: Surface €2.54, Airmail €6.35; Rest of world: Surface €5.08, Airmail €10.16) , to the above address.

TRADE ENQUIRIES Tel: + 353 (1) 2411 500 or Fax: + 353 (1) 2411 538 or email hotpressbooks@hotpress.ie.